WAY COOL WEB SITES

YAHOOLIGANS!

by Richard Raucci
&
Elizabeth Crane
with
Yahoo! co-founders
David Filo and Jerry Yang

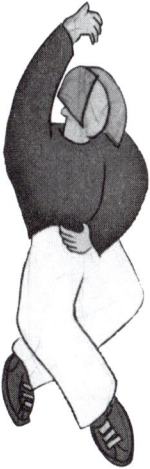

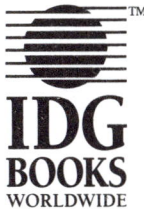

IDG
BOOKS
WORLDWIDE

IDG Books Worldwide, Inc.
An International Data Group Company

Foster City, CA Chicago, IL Indianapolis, IN Dallas, TX

Way Cool Web Sites

Published by
IDG Books Worldwide, Inc.
An International Data Group Company
919 E. Hillsdale Blvd.
Suite 400
Foster City, CA 94404

Library of Congress Catalog Card No.: 96-76834

ISBN: 0-7645-7002-1

Printed in the United States of America

10 9 8 7 6 5 4 3 2 1

1B/RY/QX/ZW/FC

Distributed in the United States by IDG Books Worldwide, Inc.
Distributed by Macmillan Canada for Canada; by Contemporanea de Ediciones for Venezuela; by Distribuidora Cuspide for Argentina; by CITEC for Brazil; by Ediciones ZETA S.C.R. Ltda. for Peru; by Editorial Limusa SA for Mexico; by Transworld Publishers Limited in the United Kingdom and Europe; by Academic Bookshop for Egypt; by Levant Distributors S.A.R.L. for Lebanon; by Al Jassim for Saudi Arabia; by Simron Pty. Ltd. for South Africa; by Pustak Mahal for India; by The Computer Bookshop for India; by Toppan Company Ltd. for Japan; by Addison Wesley Publishing Company for Korea; by Longman Singapore Publishers Ltd. for Singapore, Malaysia, Thailand, and Indonesia; by Unalis Corporation for Taiwan; by WS Computer Publishing Company, Inc. for the Philippines; by WoodsLane Pty. Ltd. for Australia; by WoodsLane Enterprises Ltd. for New Zealand. Authorized Sales Agent: Anthony Rudkin Associates for the Middle East and North Africa.

For general information on IDG Books Worldwide's books in the U.S., contact our Consumer Customer Service department at 800-762-2974. For reseller information, including discounts and premium sales, contact our Reseller Customer Service department at 800-434-3422.
For information on where to purchase IDG Books Worldwide's books outside the U.S., contact our International Sales department at 415-655-3078 or fax 415-655-3281.
For information on foreign language translations, contact our Foreign & Subsidiary Rights department at 415-655-3018 or fax 415-655-3281.
For sales inquiries and special prices for bulk quantities, contact our Sales department at 415-655-3200 or write to the address above.
For information on using IDG Books Worldwide's books in the classroom or for ordering examination copies, contact our Educational Sales department at 800-434-2086 or fax 817-251-8174.
For authorization to photocopy items for corporate, personal, or educational use, contact the Copyright Clearance Center, 222 Rosewood Drive, Danvers, MA 01923, or fax 508-750-4470.

™ is a trademark under exclusive license to IDG Books Worldwide, Inc., from International Data Group, Inc.

6/7/96

IDG BOOKS WORLDWIDE

YAHOO!™

Welcome to IDG Books Online!

Thank you very much for s̶ ... the success ...
of books, a unique blend ... paper and online publishing ...
you'll not only enjoy the contents of the book that you ...
your hands but also take advantage of the wealth of ...
related to this title that we'll be publishing on our Web site in the
months to come.

At the back of this book we've enclosed a CD-ROM containing everything you need to access the IDG Books Web site. If you've never connected to the Web, simply follow the easy sign-on procedures to obtain
an Internet account. If you're already online and connected to the Web,
you can go directly to the IDG Books Online area of our Web site:
http://www.idgbooks.com/idgbooksonline/

The online medium is an evolving one, and one that we believe
will allow us to deliver the highest quality information to you in the
fastest way possible. In order to help us improve our future products,
we encourage you to send your suggestions and comments to
online@www.idgbooks.com.

We hope that you'll enjoy and benefit from this and future titles that
we will be publishing. We look forward to hearing from you and we'll
strive to make each and every title in our line a quality, information-
rich reading experience both online and in print.

David Ushijima
Vice President and Publisher
IDG Books Online

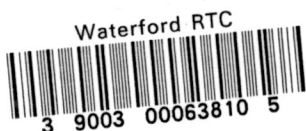

WAY **COOL** WEB SITES

YAHOOLIGANS!

Welcome to the world of IDG Books Worldwide.

IDG Books Worldwide, Inc., is a subsidiary of International Data Group, the world's largest publisher of computer-related information and the leading global provider of information services on information technology. IDG was founded more than 25 years ago and now employs more than 7,700 people worldwide. IDG publishes more than 250 computer publications in 67 countries (see listing below). More than 70 million people read one or more IDG publications each month.

Launched in 1990, IDG Books Worldwide is today the #1 publisher of best-selling computer books in the United States. We are proud to have received 8 awards from the Computer Press Association in recognition of editorial excellence and three from Computer Currents' First Annual Readers' Choice Awards, and our best-selling ...*For Dummies*® series has more than 19 million copies in print with translations in 28 languages. IDG Books Worldwide, through a joint venture with IDG's Hi-Tech Beijing, became the first U.S. publisher to publish a computer book in the People's Republic of China. In record time, IDG Books Worldwide has become the first choice for millions of readers around the world who want to learn how to better manage their businesses.

Our mission is simple: Every one of our books is designed to bring extra value and skill-building instructions to the reader. Our books are written by experts who understand and care about our readers. The knowledge base of our editorial staff comes from years of experience in publishing, education, and journalism — experience which we use to produce books for the '90s. In short, we care about books, so we attract the best people. We devote special attention to details such as audience, interior design, use of icons, and illustrations. And because we use an efficient process of authoring, editing, and desktop publishing our books electronically, we can spend more time ensuring superior content and spend less time on the technicalities of making books.

You can count on our commitment to deliver high-quality books at competitive prices on topics you want to read about. At IDG Books Worldwide, we continue in the IDG tradition of delivering quality for more than 25 years. You'll find no better book on a subject than one from IDG Books Worldwide.

John J. Kilcullen

John Kilcullen
President and CEO
IDG Books Worldwide, Inc.

For Philip (and the next one)

Foreword

Before you turn another page, we've got to warn you about what might happen when you sit down at your computer and start surfing the Web looking for cool sites. Well, at least here's what happened to us.

You're in school, right? So were we. You've got homework, right? So did we—a dissertation on computer-aided design, to be exact. So you get online because, well, you heard there was a lot of cool stuff out there, and besides, there's nothing better to do. You start looking around, and before you've had a chance to really get started, your parents (or girlfriends, in our case) want to know where you've been for the last five hours and why you missed dinner.

The Web is huge, and it's filled with some pretty amazing stuff. In fact, it's so huge and so amazing you better be careful or it'll swallow you up!

One of the reasons we ended up spending all day every day exploring the Internet instead of finishing our homework was that when we got there it was pretty hard to find stuff. One day we'd wander onto a very useful and informative site on, say, Sumo wrestling, and the next day we'd have no ideas where to find it. So we took it upon ourselves to do a little organizing.

We know, it's hard to believe: Two guys who can't even keep their rooms clean decide to tidy up the Internet, but hey, somebody had to do it. Before we knew it, word about Yahoo!, the little tool we created for keeping our favorite sites at arm's reach, started spreading across the Internet.

Now hopefully all those hours we spent on the Web will make things a little easier for you. You don't have to waste your time hunting for the coolest stuff on the Web; you've got Yahooligans! Yahooligans! is a catalogue of the best sites for kids on the Internet that can guide you through your online journey. This should mean that you'll have a little time left over to finish your homework and get some sleep (unlike us).

Actually, you'll soon discover that just because you're surfing the Web doesn't mean you're not also doing your homework. (We suggest that you point this out to your parents as soon as possible.) In spite of what some people say, we first got on the Internet because it was a great way for us to keep up with the latest discoveries in computer science. See, Mom and Dad? We were working after all.

The Web is like a giant set of encyclopedias. You can find information about everything from A (for Abwenzi, Africa) to Z (for ZooNet). And unlike the dusty sets of encyclopedias in homes around the world, the Internet is changing everyday. Information constantly is added to and updated. Every day thousands of new sites appear, and you can access them with the click of a mouse (no more bugging Mom and Dad for rides to the library). So if you want to find information on the presidential election, or the Olympics, or the latest archeological dig to uncover dinosaur bones—then get online.

But don't say we didn't warn you: it will change your life forever!

David Filo and Jerry Yang

Preface

Hey! What are you doing reading this? You're not supposed to read this part of the book! You're supposed to go straight to your favorite stuff and find the coolest Web sites. Go on, scoot!

Well, since you're still here, we might as well get on with it. This book, in case you haven't noticed, is called *Way Cool Web Sites.* Yahooligans! is a Web site: it's *the* directory for kids on the Internet. You'll find it at **http://www.yahooligans.com**. That funny-looking thing in the last sentence is the address on the Web. It's called a URL. Confused? Since you're reading the Preface, maybe you haven't found out yet that this book will help you become an expert Web surfer. Look in the chapter called "Code Words: Your Yahooligans! Dictionary" to find out what all those funny abbreviations and words mean that you'll see all over the Net. We have sprinkled tips throughout the book on how to get around online, and best of all we give you hundreds of reviewed sites (with pictures!) so you can see what's in store for you when you venture out into cyberspace.

What's in this book

We've done our best to include as much cool stuff in this book as we could, but of course we had to leave out a whole lot. No book could cover the whole Internet! We've tried to cover as many areas of interest as possible and to include all the totally cool, slightly weird, really rad sites that we could. Some of the stuff here will help you with your homework. Some of it will make you laugh. Some of it won't interest you at all (but hey, there's something here for everybody!). So be prepared to use this book as a guide, and then you'll be ready to explore and find your own favorite sites.

What you need to surf the net

Hold it. You have to have a few things lined up before you can get on-line. You need a computer with a modem, an Internet access provider, and the software to connect to and read from the Internet. If you don't already have an Internet service provider and the software to connect, you're in luck. The CD-ROM in the back of this book contains everything you need to set up an account with a provider called Earthlink. You can install Netscape—the coolest Web software, a copy of which is on the CD-ROM in the back of the book—and pretty soon you'll be surfing the Net.

More stuff about this book

This book also has a Web site of its own. Point your Web browser at **http://www.idgbooks.com/idgbooksonline/** to check out updates to this book and lots more fun stuff. Also, you'll find some really cool games and puzzles and stuff on the CD-ROM in the back of the book. Feel free to explore the CD-ROM and install anything you like from it.

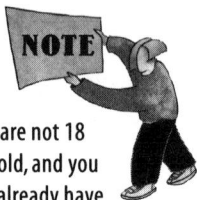

NOTE

If you are not 18 years old, and you don't already have an Internet account, you *must* have your parent or guardian set up an Internet account for you. It requires a credit card, so you will need help from an adult. Once you're up and running, then you can check out all the fabulous sites reviewed in this book.

What do you want?

Take a minute to think about what you want to get out of the Internet. Do you want the hottest new games and software? Need some help with your science homework? What about your favorite local sports teams? What are they up to right this minute? The answers to these questions—and the answers to thousands of questions you haven't thought of yet—are out there on the World Wide Web, waiting for you to find them. This book can help you go right to the places with the best information, the coolest attitudes, and the greatest stuff to do. So what are you waiting for? Read on!

Acknowledgments

We would like to thank all the people who had to deal with us while we were on deadline. You were all very patient.

Thanks to the Cyborganic people (at www.cyborganic.com) for providing us with a cool community to hang out with, and to the Cybernauts gang for interesting conversation, hints, tips, and sushi.

A special thank you goes to David Myers and Erica Myers, for answering what must have seemed to them strange questions about their friends' computer habits.

We would also like to extend our appreciation to all the Web site designers and authors who put together the cool sites we reviewed. You made our job a pleasure!

And thank you, especially, to our families, for their unfailing support and unflagging enthusiasm for our projects.

CONTENTS

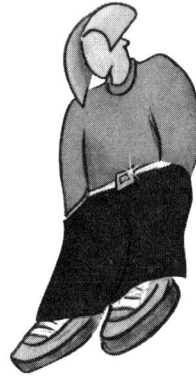

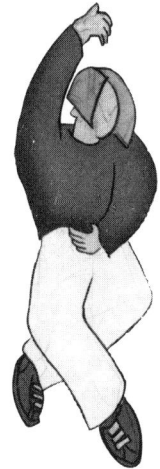

CHAPTER 1

Arts

Gather your creative energies and dive into the Arts! You'll find spaces here for everything: places to create your own artwork, places to display your offline art or your photographs, and space for your opinions about other people's art. If you have a flair for the dramatic, the theatre arts sites are for you. Gotta dance? Check out the ballet and the musicals sites. Visit museums all across the world or learn more about art history, art galleries, and artists.

Art

Focus on Photography

http://www.goldcanyon.com/photo/index.html

If you'd rather take your own pictures than look at other people's, you need to visit Focus on Photography. Learn the basics of camera use, how to set up a picture, and how to take good care of your camera. Check the History of Photography for ideas and tips on taking good pictures. You may also want to **browse** through the Reference page for information on photo classes and other online photo help. Take the quiz to see how much you already know or how much you've learned!

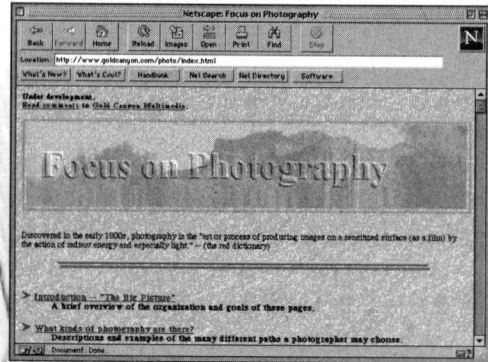

Gargoyles and Grotesques

http://www.mcs.net/~sculptor/GARGOYLE.HTML

Ever notice how some buildings seem to stare at you? That's because some buildings have gargoyles. Gargoyles are little carved figures with **spooky faces** that decorate the building and stare out at people as they walk by. Find out all about **gargoyles** (and their cousins, grotesques), how they're carved out of solid rock, and how they're used in ancient and modern buildings. These pictures are really **weird**! Check out the work in progress to see how the sculptor seems to pull the figure out of a block of stone, or just flip through the gallery for more strange **critters**.

Global Show-n-Tell Museum

http://www.manymedia.com/show-n-tell

This museum is by kids, about kids, and for kids. Global **Show-n-Tell** posts artwork by kids. The galleries are organized by age, and each "wing" has an endangered bird as its theme, so you'll also find links to information about that bird at the end of each gallery. Crayon drawings, oil paintings, computer graphics, and pencil sketches are just some of the stuff you'll see posted. To get your picture on the site, all you have to do is tell Show-n-Tell where the picture is on the Internet and a few details about who drew the picture (age, home town, stuff like that — just follow the guide). It's easy, and it's really neat to **see your own artwork** on the Web!

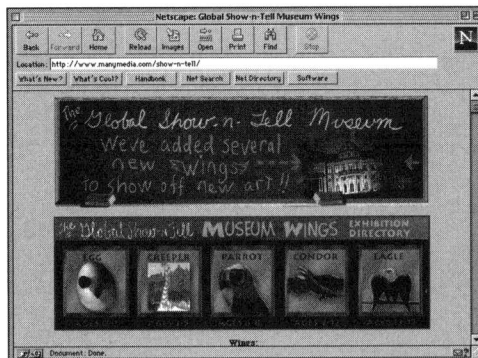

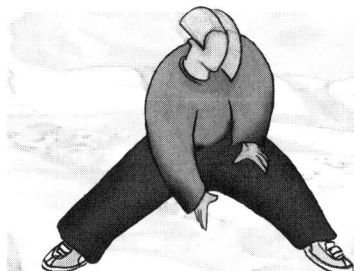

wAY CoOL

Hey, dude, it's classified info!

Giving out a lot of information about yourself online is not a good idea. Don't tell anyone how old you are, and never give out your phone number or real address on the Internet.

Kids' Space

http://plaza.interport.net/kids_space/

VERu CoOL

Do you have your own home page? Do you want someplace to show your **artwork**, publish your stories, or just talk to other kids online? Kids' Space wants to do all these things for you and with you. Draw a picture and have someone halfway across the world post a story to go with it. Write a story about someone else's picture or **visit a Village** to find other kids who have the same interests you do. Music has a place on this site as well, and of course there are plenty of links to other pages on the Net for kids that you'll definitely want to investigate.

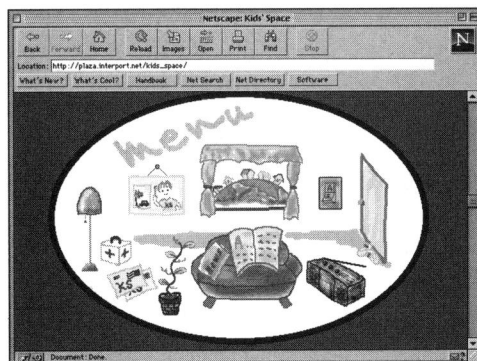

Web-a-Sketch!

http://www.digitalstuff.com/web-a-sketch/

Everyone knows how an Etch-a-Sketch works: you make a whole drawing using a single line. Well, Web-a-Sketch is a Web version of that idea. Take a look in the Gallery to see what other people have drawn (see example figure here), then **go ahead and draw** your own design right on the screen! Be sure to follow the instructions (you can't erase unless you erase the *whole* drawing) and when you've finished it, your drawing will be posted in the gallery. It might sound easy to do, but wait till you try it! Your picture may even be chosen to become the Best, Worst, or Most Realistic drawing in the monthly Best of Web-a-Sketch Awards.

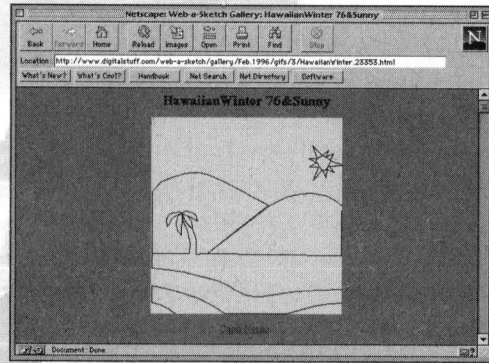

Art resources

Auricular Media Design

http://www.nanothinc.com:80/Auricular/

For sights, sounds, and beyond, check out the Auricular site. For sights, check out all the computer art that will jump out at you from your screen. For sounds, choose from the catalogs, the **Yummy Noizes** page, and other strange electronic and voice sound files. To venture far into the beyond, browse through the links to other sound pages and more art sites. Auricular wants you to buy its stuff, but there's all kinds of great information (and **it's free**) and good times here, so you never have to dig into your pockets.

FineartForum Online Art Resources Directory

http://www.msstate.edu/Fineart_Online/art-resources/museums.html

The FineArt Forum lists a lot of museums online and online research sites. Links with short descriptions (kind of like the ones in this book!) of what is on the site make this list really useful. It's easy to find what you're looking for. To make it simpler to go right to what you want, some of the larger museums have direct links to different areas within their sites. (Follow the link at the beginning of the page back to the parent site for a wide variety of arts links.)

Graphion's Online Type Museum

http://www.slip.net/~graphion/museum.html

If it weren't for typography, you wouldn't be reading this right now. Typography is how letters and words are printed in books, magazines, and even on your computer. Type (and types of type) has grown and changed over the centuries into lots of different shapes and sizes. The Online Type Museum explains the history of type and gives biographies of famous type designers with examples of their work. Best of all is a dictionary of cool typographical words with illustrations.

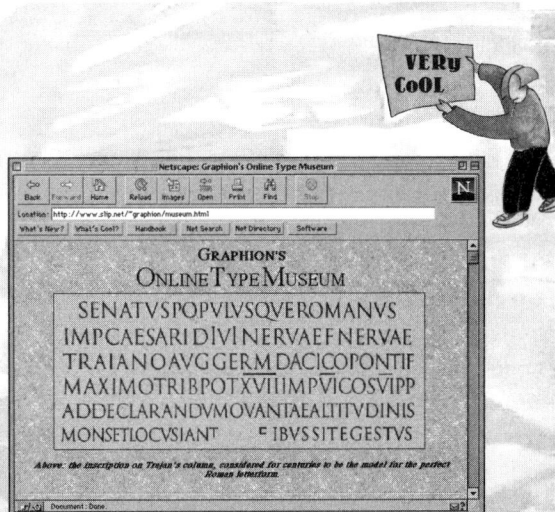

World Wide Arts Resources

http://www.concourse.com/wwar/default.html

The World Wide Arts Resources Index is a **huge** list of visual arts information. You can search for art-related stuff from among more than 7,000 resource links. The top-level page is broken down into categories (kind of like Yahooligans!) except it's all about the arts. Looking for a good art school? Go to Academic Institutions. Want to find out **what's new** in your part of the country? Click on your state on the U.S. map for a list of online galleries and linked events in that state. Art publications, art resources, museums, artists, galleries, exhibits — if you can't find it here, it may not exist online!

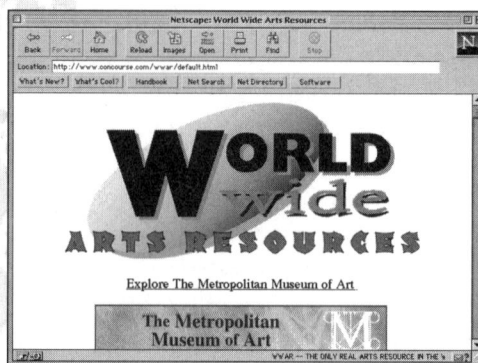

Computer arts

EZTV

http://www.leonardo.net/eztv/

The EZTV Video Center is a non-profit gallery/theatre located in both Los Angeles and on the Web. It gives computer artists the chance to **experiment with video** and computer editing and to display their work. Read up on the history of EZTV to learn more about how artists use computers and video in their work. The recent exhibits feature some really **weird and distorted** photos! The list of links to other art sites may be short, but each site listed is sure to be pretty cool.

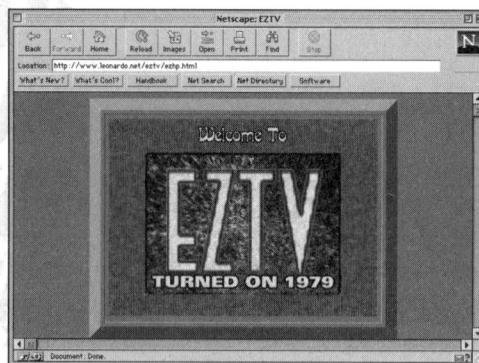

Holos Gallery Online Hologram Exhibition

http://www.holo.com/gaz/

Whether you're already fascinated by **holograms** or you've never heard of them, you have to visit the Holos Gallery. These are cool pictures, even if they are only photos of holograms and don't show all the neat effects possible in a real hologram. A history of the Holos Gallery (the one in real space, not Cyberspace) also has more info on holograms in general, but the place you want to be is the Gallery, where you can view every hologram on the site. New pictures are going up all the time, so be sure to **come back for a look**.

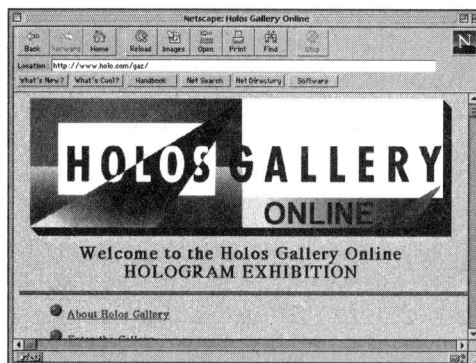

VERy CooL

There's no such thing as a perfect Web site!

Always check the information you get off a Web site. Some sites may not have accurate information.

Kondo's Stereogram Workshop

http://www.webcom.com/~kondo/stereo/

Be careful to avoid getting a headache staring at these images. Stereograms can be hard to look at, but they're also **great fun** to figure out and to make. Read the Theory of Stereograms first and learn how to focus your eyes so you can see the 3-D image. Then go to the gallery to try your luck at seeing the hidden **3-D images**. For more information on stereograms, a Theory page fills you in on the whats, whys, and hows of stereo vision. (Note: you can see this page in Japanese, too!)

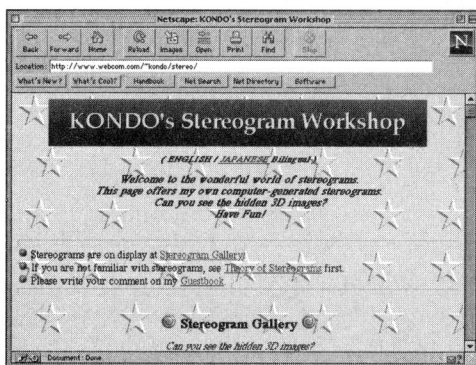

VERy CooL

Morphs For All!

http://www.physics.oberlin.edu/students/mgiles/morph/Morph.html

The word "morph" means **change**: computer morphing is the process of changing one image into another. At Morphs for All, learn more about this popular process, view lots of things morphing (people, cars, whatever), and submit your own picture to **get morphed**. Really! You can get your own stuff morphed for free! Just follow carefully the instructions for submitting pictures, and then visit the site to see a morph of your baby brother and you, or your worst enemy morphed with a baboon. **Cool!**

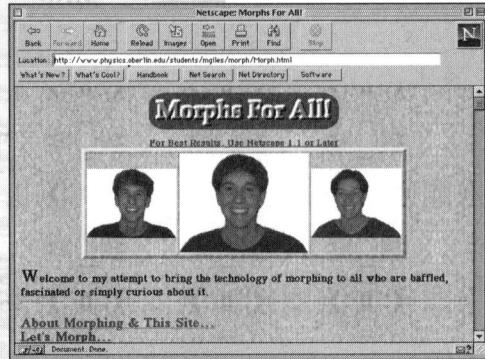

Online Gallery of Synthetic Images (Fractals)

http://www.seas.gwu.edu/faculty/musgrave/art_gallery.html

Ken Musgrave is the "first true fractal-based artist" in the world, and his artwork is available for all to see. A fractal is a curve or shape that repeats itself no matter how much you **zoom in** or out. Fractal art is produced entirely on a computer. These online galleries feature fractal landscapes, planets that never were, and various **abstract** and unclassifiable images. Some of the pictures look so real, you'd swear they were photographs! Some are so **awesome** you'll want to keep browsing for hours.

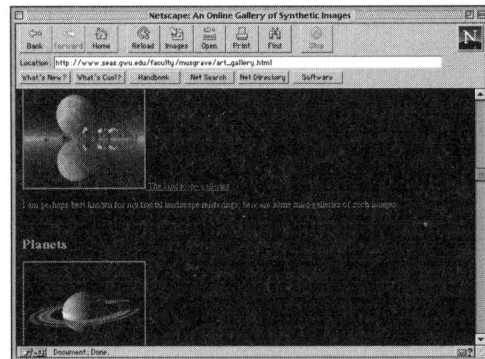

Virtual Study Tour

http://archpropplan.auckland.ac.nz/misc/virtual_tour.html

Have you ever been **curious** to know what ancient or very old buildings looked like on the inside? This site will take you on a cool architectural trip down memory lane as well as show you some exciting **new stuff**. Using computer-generated drawings, the Virtual Study Tour puts you inside buildings that fell down centuries ago, or never got built. The **drawings** on this site are by students at the School of Architecture Property and Planning (in Auckland, New Zealand). You'll find experimental artwork, plans for buildings that haven't been built, and a whole gallery of architectural artwork. For a guided tour, go to the Top Ten list and follow the links.

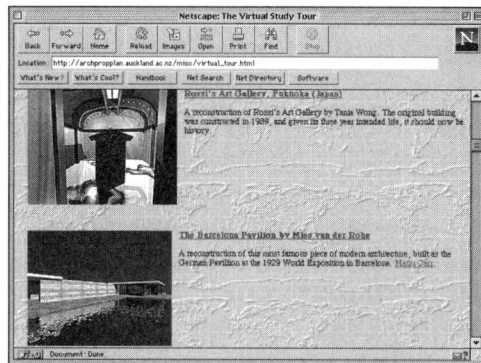

Weird Three-Dimensional Page!

http://neoteny.eccosys.com/cyrus/rds.html

This gallery of stereograms has some neat 3-D pictures for you to try to see. It also has links to other stereogram sites and really helpful information about stereograms and computer-generated graphics. You'll also find links to software that will let you make your own stereograms. So go ahead. **Drive yourself nuts** trying to see the images. These things can be frustrating, but once you get the hang of it, you'll see what all the excitement is about.

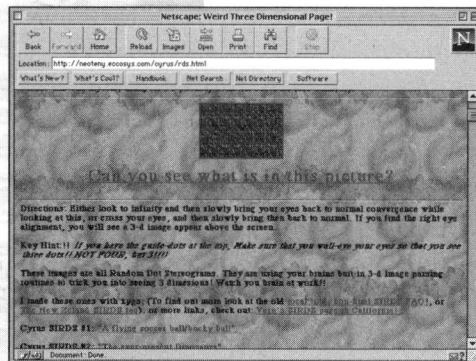

Museums & galleries

Le Grand Louvre

http://www.atlcom.net/~psmith/Louvre/

The Louvre is probably the most famous museum on earth, and since you might not get to Paris this week to see it in person, you can experience this truly **awesome** place by visiting Le Grand Louvre Web page. First, read the history of the Louvre, then see pictures of some of the most famous paintings and sculptures ever produced. This site lists other Louvre links, as well as links to places where you can **find more art** on the Web. The pictures in the gallery include descriptions and information (so you know what you're looking at) and the picture files are really small so that you can download more easily.

Nightmare Gallery

http://thomas.balliol.ox.ac.uk/gallery2/

As you might expect from a site called the Nightmare Gallery, pictures of scary, strange, and **forbidding things** are everywhere. This gallery is laid out like a real gallery; you go through it by moving forward, left, or right, as though you were walking through a room. **Watch out!** You'll bump into a wall or get stuck in a corner if you're not careful! You can spend hours in here enjoying the artwork, but with over 400 images on display, you can expect to spend some of that time waiting for pages to load.

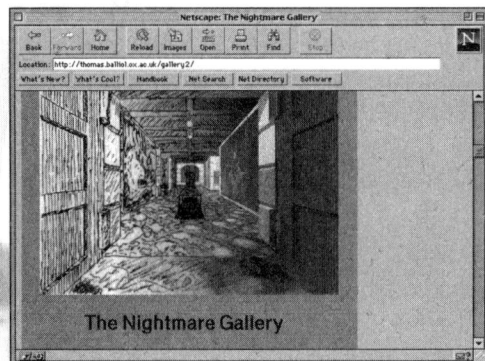

WebMuseum: Famous Paintings Exhibition

http://watt.emf.net/wm//paint/

For a brief history of European art, drop in to the WebMuseum's Famous Paintings Exhibition. The pages on this site span the Middle Ages, through the Renaissance, the Restoration, Impressionism, and into the 20th Century. **Choose your time period** and your country and you'll find a list of painters. Choose a painter and get a biography and a painting. Or, choose a style or movement (like Pop Art) to find out more about what Pop artists did and thought.

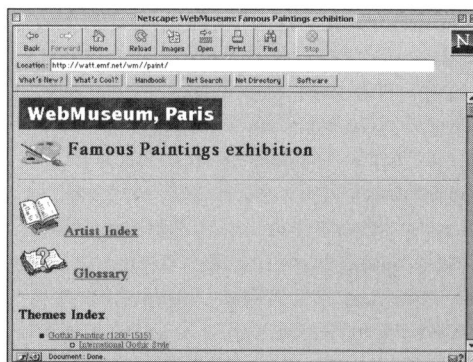

Never shoot from the hip — think before you send an e-mail message!

Remember that e-mail messages can be read again and again. Choose your words carefully because you're not going to be there to explain exactly what you mean. Don't send e-mail when you're mad, or you might end up flaming someone you like!

Theatre arts

Body and Grace

http://www.i3tele.com/photo_perspectives_museum/faces/abt.html

Body and Grace is a photo exhibit of the dancers of the American Ballet Theater and a history of the ABT. Pictures, pictures, pictures! Beautiful dancers in **beautiful poses!** The photos are small for easier loading, and if you want to talk about what you like about the site (or don't like), write your views on the Comments page and read what other visitors thought about the site. If you can't get enough of these photos, follow the photographer's link for more pictures on her page.

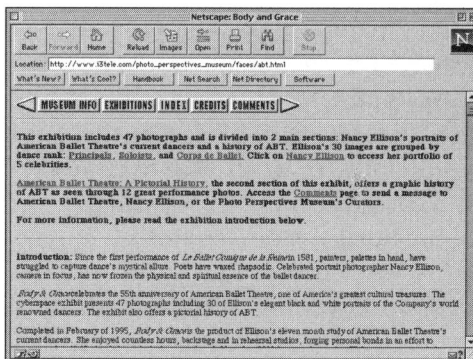

Dance Directory

http://www.cyberspace.com/vandehey/dance.html

The Dance Directory is a *huge* list of links to dance and dance-related sites. Because the links are organized by type of dance, everything is easy to find. You'll find sites for all kinds of things, from classical ballet to **belly dancing**. Different dance societies do-si-do with dance events; folk dances bow to the tango. There's even a list of other directories! If you can't find what you need to get your feet moving, you haven't looked here yet.

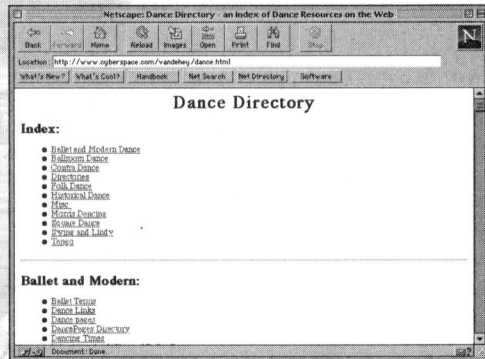

Gilbert and Sullivan Archive

http://math.idbsu.edu/gas/GaS.html

Some of the funniest light opera ever was written around the turn of the twentieth century by William S. Gilbert and Arthur S. Sullivan. Anything that has to do with their work is on the Gilbert and Sullivan site. You can download files to **hear the music** or read every libretto (the story behind the opera) in the library, from *Pirates of Penzance* to the *Mikado*. Find out where the next G&S festival will be, or where they've shown up in recent news. Or just spend some time in the photo gallery for a look at the **costumes and settings** of these famous works.

The Improv Page

http://sunee.uwaterloo.ca/~broehl/improv/index.html

Improvisational theatre, which is performed without a script, is a great introduction to more traditional theatre. Anyone can perform improv! If you can make something up on the **spur of the moment**, you can do improv. The Improv Page provides tips on how to start an improv group and what to you can do with it once you've started it. Find out when an improv group is coming to perform in your town. Links take you to improv performers' pages, to a history of improvisational theatre, and to more places for improv fans to visit.

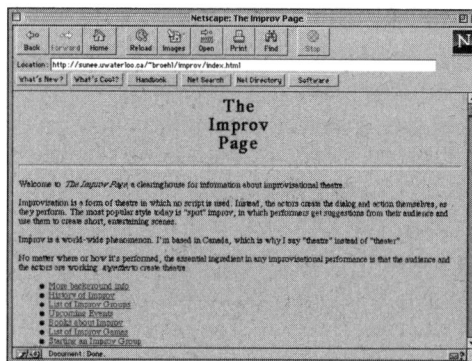

Opera and Musical Theatre

http://pubweb.acns.nwu.edu/~pib/opera.html

A real opera fan has put together a page of links for fellow opera fans. The Opera and Musical Theatre site lists opera singers' links, opera groups' links, and a really huge list of links to opera and music information sites. An opera dictionary, a site called La Stupida, and an experimental opera page are just a few of the interesting sites linked here. If you know nothing about opera, or even if you think you hate opera, go ahead and browse these links anyway. **You won't be bored!**

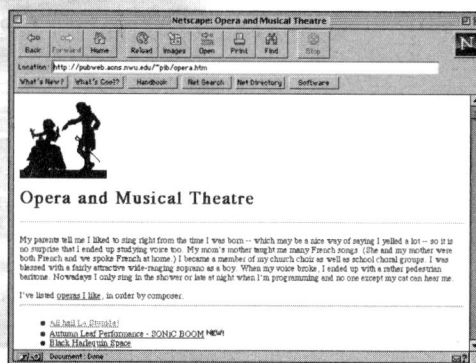

Theatre Central

http://www.theatre-central.com/

Theatre Central tries to list every bit of theatre information on the Internet, from current popular shows to theatre history, amateur to professional dramatics, and experimental to traditional theatre. People in the theatre business and fans alike will want to follow the links to **stage personalities**, playwrights' pages, Shakespeare festivals across the country and links to theatre history. This site is updated weekly, so you're sure to find the latest and most complete information available.

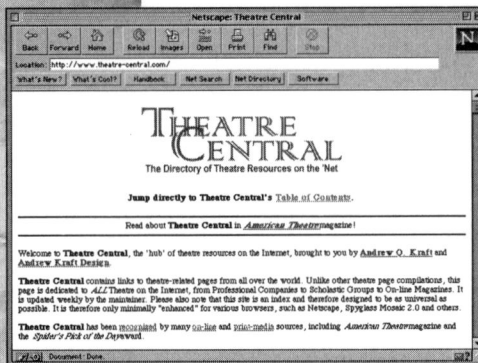

VERY CooL

THEATRE CENTRAL
The Directory of Theatre Resources on the 'Net

Jump directly to Theatre Central's Table of Contents.

Read about Theatre Central in *American Theatre* magazine!

Welcome to **Theatre Central**, the 'hub' of theatre resources on the Internet, brought to you by **Andrew Q. Kraft** and **Andrew Kraft Design**.

Theatre Central contains links to theatre-related pages from all over the world. Unlike other theatre page compilations, this page is dedicated to *ALL* Theatre on the Internet, from Professional Companies to Scholastic Groups to On-line Magazines. It is updated weekly by the maintainer. Please also note that this site is an index and therefore designed to be as universal as possible. It is therefore only minimally "enhanced" for various browsers, such as Netscape, Spyglass Mosaic 2.0 and others.

Theatre Central has been recognized by many on-line and print-media sources, including *American Theatre* magazine and the *Spider's Pick of the Day* award.

CHAPTER 2

Books & Literature

Do you like to read? The world of literature has a good place on the Internet. You can find a lot of books available right on the Web to read and enjoy. This stuff includes fairy tales, folk tales, classic literature, and even original stories written for kids. There are also sites for your favorite authors and places where you can publish your own stories online. See the storytelling pages for interesting ways you can perform by reading!

Children's literature

The Book Nook

http://i-site.on.ca/Isite/Education/Bk_report/BookNook/default.html#Nook

Book Nook has book reviews by kids, for kids. Find out what other kids think about **your favorite books,** and you might also find some other interesting books you didn't know about. The site is arranged by grade, so you can go directly to the stuff that's right for you. The categories include folktales, **science fiction**, animal stories, and **adventure** tales. There's also information on how you can submit your own reviews to the site. Get your book report on the Internet!

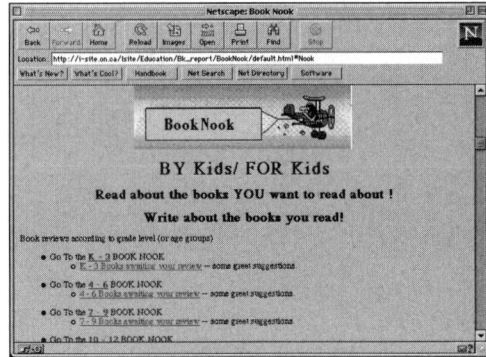

East Coast Internet Companion's Children's Literature Finder

http://www.isisnet.com/voodoo/childlit.html

This site is a great gateway to children's literature on the Net. You can look up information on book-related sites from all over the Internet by using an easy search feature. Categories linked here include **Reading and Storytelling**, Online Children's Literature (books, tales, fables and myths), Book Reviews, and Educational Entertainment. You can browse each category directly and find a nice set of well-described links to sites with good stuff. **Add your own favorite book site here,** and it'll go right into the online database.

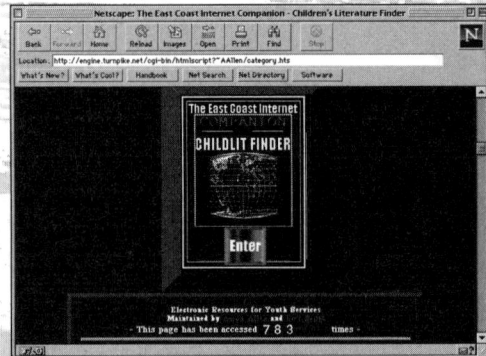

YAHOOLIGANS!

Guide to Reading Children's Books

http://funnelweb.utcc.utk.edu/~epling/readaloud.html

Here's where you can find out about the benefits of reading aloud. This site lists books you can find in your local library that are good for reading aloud, either by your parents or by yourself. Ham it up in front of a mirror! It's a good way to build reading and speaking skills, and the site also has good tips on how to make it enjoyable. Read-aloud books are listed by age group, and there are also links to related sites with more information and a section on parent's resources.

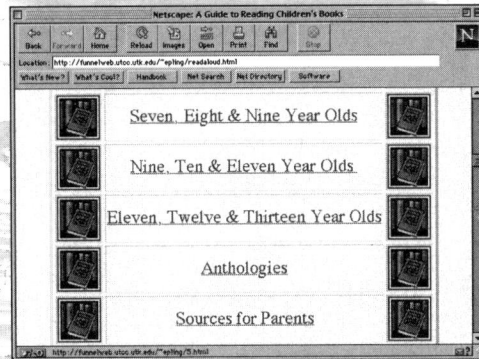

KidLit

http://mgfx.com/kidlit/

Kids, **achieve instant fame!** (At least, that's what the site's maintainers claim!) Just send your stories and artwork to KidLit, which features Art and Literature galleries with original work from kids in the junior high school range. It's all available online, and you can find a good selection of kid's artwork and stories here. There are also reviews of children's books located here and information for parents and teachers. Check out the comments section to see what other people think about the site, and post your own feedback.

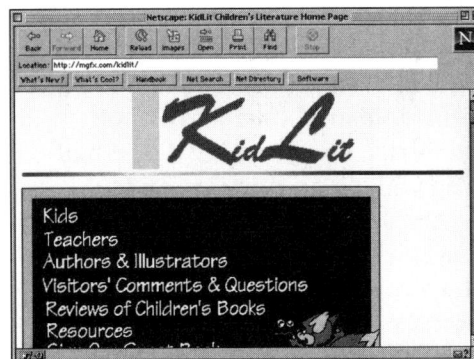

Children's Literature Web Guide

http://www.ucalgary.ca/~dkbrown/index.html

This is a big, big set of links to **cool** sites for kids' literature on the Web. Scope out the great sections with links to online book sites, lists of recommended books and children's book award winners, and author information pages. The site also has resource lists for parents and teachers, conferences and book events information, movie and TV links, and lists of sites for children's writings and drawings across the Net. The site has a special flower icon at the links that have **really good stuff** for you, too.

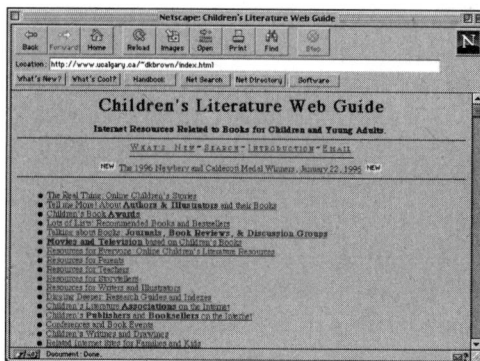

You can use the Authors section to find alphabetical links to sites for **children's authors and their books**, including biographical information, lists of books, and fan material. The links are described well, giving you a **good idea** of what's available. Also, check out the **sections for series books** (for series with more than one author, like the **Oz books**) and links to folklore, myths, and **legends** information. If you're writing a book report, this is a terrific place to start.

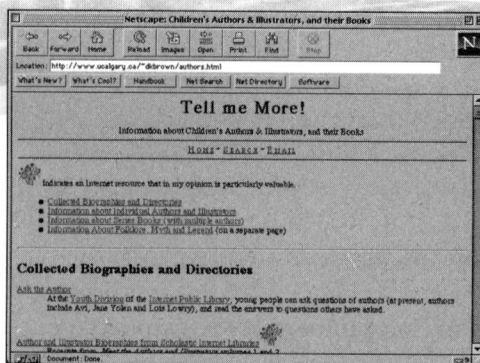

You might be surprised at how many stories for kids are already online. Go look in the Online Children's Stories section for links to story collections, poetry, classic books, and modern stuff. The site has good information on the sites linked here, and it can help you get to stories quickly. You'll not only find books from familiar and **fun** writers like **Dr. Seuss,** but also from original kids' authors whose work is found only on the World Wide Web.

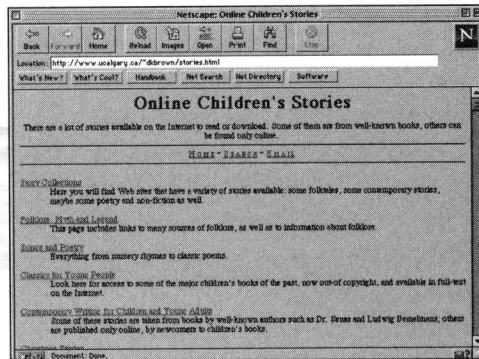

Kids also have places where they can **read stories from other kids,** and post their own. See the **Children's Writings** section for links to lists of children's stories, writing pages, and online magazines. These places are also helpful for getting started with writing. The Children's Literature Web Guide also has a lot of resource guides for more information to help you with writing, research, and storytelling. Use the search page to look for specific topics by name. There's a lot of good reading out there!

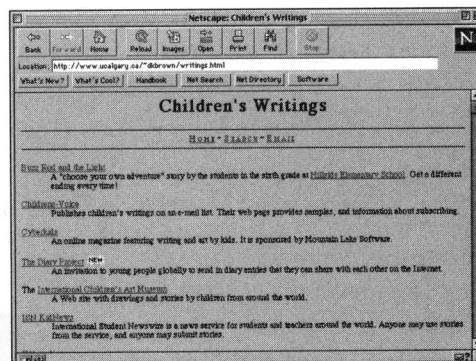

Authors

Great Writers and Poets

http://www.xs4all.nl/~pwessel/writers.html

In this site modern and classic authors' home pages are arranged in a big alphabetical index. You can go directly to linked pages that have short, **useful descriptions.** The sites linked are picked because they usually have good information on the authors and their works, including biographical material, special reports and exhibits, and links to online books. Check out the section with links to **literary prize information,** including lists of **Nobel** and **Pulitzer** prizewinners and other literary award sites.

Jane Austen Information Page

http://uts.cc.utexas.edu/~churchh/janeinfo.html

Jane Austen wrote **classic stories of** Victorian society and manners, including *Pride and Prejudice* and *Sense and Sensibility.* Those books are still popular today and are even being made into new movies. (Did you know *Clueless* was based on Austen's *Emma*?) This site has a great collection of links to online versions of Austen books, plus other reference materials, including **special exhibits and background material** on Austen and the world she lived and worked in. It's all laid out in an easy-to-use format, with **lots of useful links.**

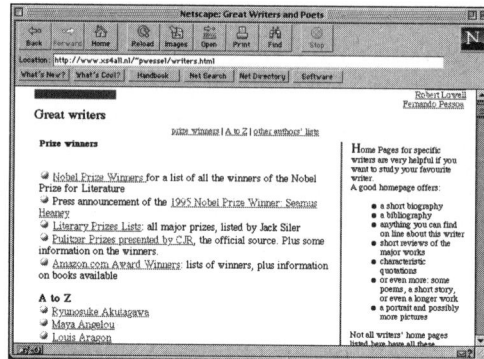

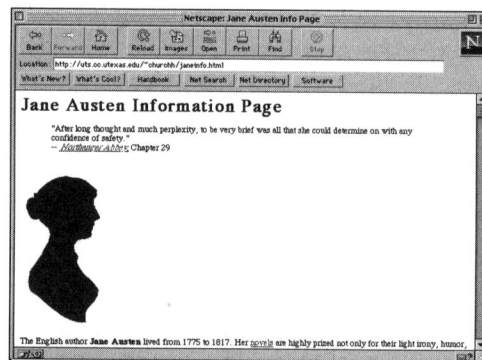

L. Frank Baum: An OZ Home Page

http://seamonkey.ed.asu.edu/oz/

Find out more about L. Frank Baum's *Land of Oz* here. The **adventures** of Dorothy, the Scarecrow, the Tin Woodsman, the Cowardly Lion, and the Wizard were just the beginning of the many books he wrote about Oz. This site lets you send e-mail to your favorite character (even **Billina the Hen**, Dorothy's **talking chicken** friend from the Oz books). Click on the interactive map to see where the Winkies, Quadlings, Munchkins, and Gillikins live, and browse the links to more information about Oz and its history. See the Interesting Links section for a good list of online Oz books and related information.

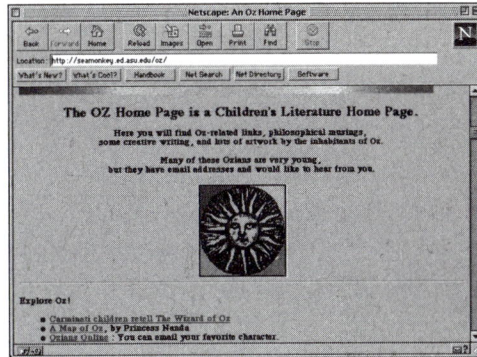

Play it safe!

Credit card numbers can be stolen online. Be safe and don't give out your parents' credit card numbers! Always ask a parent for help when it comes to credit cards.

John Bellairs: The Compleat Bellairs

http://www.pitt.edu/~jjast2/bellairs/cb.html

Wow! This is an amazing site for fans of this excellent **mystery/horror** writer. His books include *Eyes of the Killer Robot, The Curse of the Blue Figurine,* and *The House With a Clock in its Walls.* These are all great stories for young audiences with plenty of spooky action. The site has fantastic-looking **Edward Gorey graphics,** and it's a lot of fun to use. See the relevant sections for an introduction to his books and descriptions of the main series. Don't be afraid to try the **Spooky Links!**

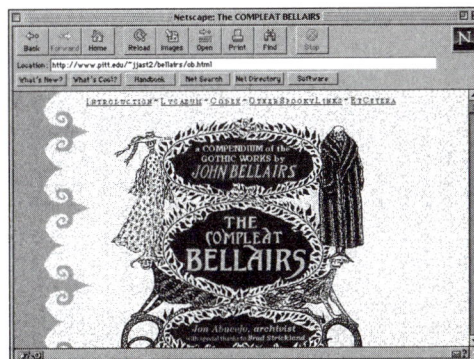

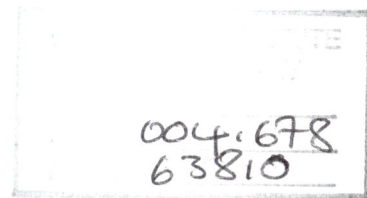

Edgar Rice Burroughs: Creator of Tarzan

http://www.tarzan.com/

Want to fight **ten-feet-tall green Martians** with giant fangs and four sword-swinging arms? Burroughs didn't just write about Tarzan! He also wrote *John Carter of Mars*, a cool series about the greatest swordsman on two planets. You can find out more about John Carter (Warlord of Mars!), *Tarzan of the Apes, Carson of Venus*, and other amazing creations right here. This site gives you a good introduction to Burroughs' life and work and includes book descriptions and artwork. There are also links to Burroughs' books you can get directly over the Internet.

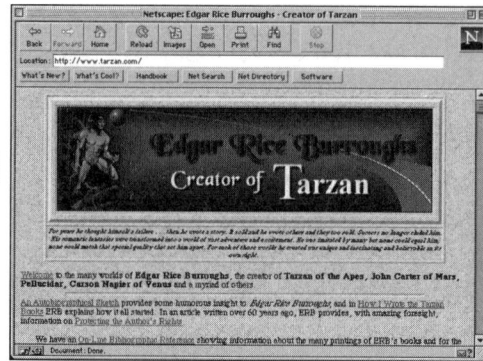

Charles Dickens Information Page

http://lang.nagoya-u.ac.jp/~matsuoka/Dickens.html

Charles Dickens was an amazing author, and you can find a lot of great information on him and his works right here. This site has a good set of links to Dickens societies, selected online books (*A Tale of Two Cities* and *Great Expectations*, for example), and related material. There's also a list of his most popular books, important events in Dickens' life, and great pictures and illustrations. Check out the links to other Dickens home pages for more information.

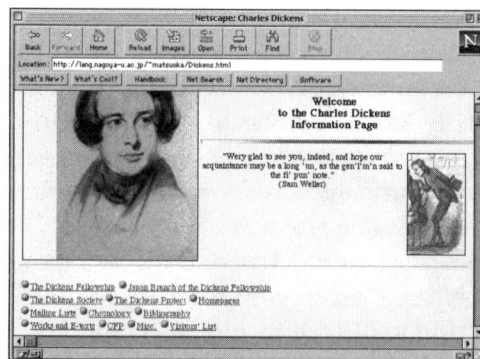

YAHOOLIGANS!

James Herriot Home Page

http://www.wpi.edu/~mazz/herriot.html

Fans of the Yorkshire vet series "All Creatures Great and Small" should flock to this page. It's a great tribute to Herriot and his books and includes articles and reviews on the series (and the TV shows that developed from it), biographical information (with pictures), and links to other Herriot information on the Web. Check out the **cool** graphics (**dog paw wallpaper!**) and go to the Tribute Wall to read how other people were affected by Herriot and his works (you can also leave your own comments). Experience the world of a country vet without getting your hands dirty!

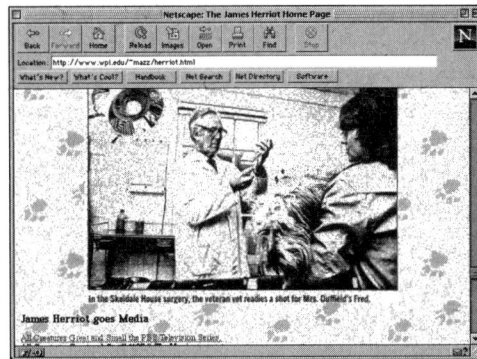

Edward Lear: *There Was An Old Derry Down Derry*

http://www.agora.stm.it/M.Graziosi/home.html

There Was An Old Derry Down Derry is a great collection of poems and illustrations by the master of **nonsense** Edward Lear. You'll find fun poems, limericks, and nonsense alphabets linked here, with pictures. Read about the "**Courtship of the Yongy Bongy-Bo,**" and "The Scroobious Pip" (a mixed-up beast). A chronology of Lear's life and a bibliography of books about him and his works are also available here. See the links to more nonsense on the Web if there isn't enough here, and don't forget your Runcible Spoon!

Madeleine L'Engle Fan Page

http://www.vms.utexas.edu/~eithlan/lengle.html

This is a **fan site** with information on the author of many good science fiction novels for children, including *A Wrinkle in Time*, *A Wind in the Door*, *A Swiftly Tilting Planet*, *The Young Unicorns*, and many more. The site includes information on **new books** coming soon, a brief list of most L'Engle books for children and adults, and a good guide to links between the several continuing series. There's also a link to a **gopher server** at Wheaton College with more information, including a biographical sketch and links to other Internet resources with information on L'Engle and her works.

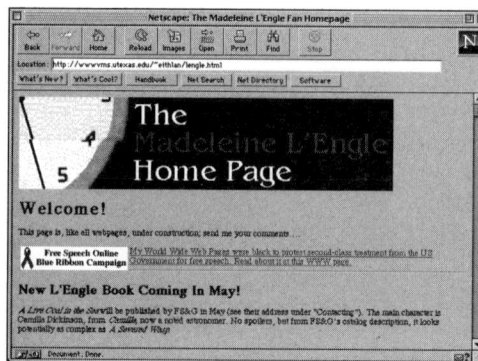

Don't give suckers and weirdos the time of day!

If you're in a chatroom and the conversation gets too weird for you, just leave and don't go back. Creepy people are online, too, but you don't have to deal with them.

C. S. Lewis: *Into the Wardrobe*

http://www.cache.net/~john/cslewis/index.htm

This is a page about the author of the Narnia series, the enchanted land where Aslan the Lion rules and **magic happens.** You can find out more about Lewis' life and works, including Narnia book descriptions, maps, and fan pages. The site is laid out very well, and it has interesting sections for poetry, fiction, **nonfiction,** and other sites with more information. You can also find out about C. S. Lewis electronic mailing lists and Chat sites (**discuss Narnia over the Internet with other readers!**).

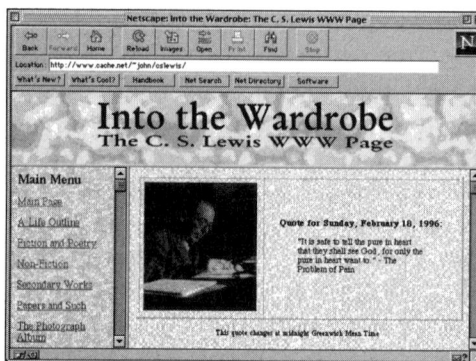

YAHOOLIGANS!

L. M. Montgomery: Kindred Spirits

http://www.upei.ca/~lmmi/cover.html

Fans of *Anne of Green Gables* and *Anne of Avonlea* should check out this site. It's got a lot of good information on Lucy Maud Montgomery and her works, including a **FAQ list** (find out more about the books and TV shows) and links to pages for Prince Edward Island and Ontario, Canada (areas she wrote about in the Avonlea books). There's also a Lucy Maud Montgomery **art gallery** (maps and pictures from the books) and information on Internet discussion groups about Avonlea.

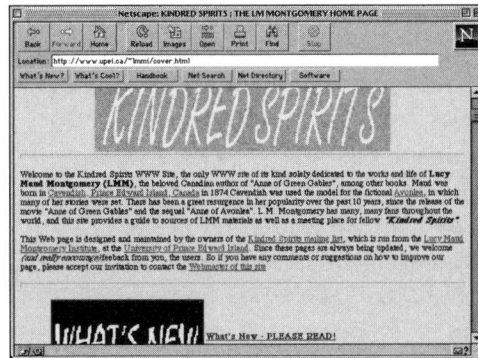

Edgar Allan Poe: *The Fall of the House of Usher*

http://infoweb.magi.com/~forrest/index.html

Go to this truly **awesome** Web site to discover the **original master of horror** Edgar Allan Poe. His stories have been chilling the world for over 150 years. This site is an author's dream—**it's got everything,** and it's set up nicely. There are neat backgrounds and plenty of artwork to look at, all in the **spooky** Poe style. Visit here if you dare, and see what you can find!

CONTINUED →

http://infoweb.magi.com/~forrest/index.html

To start your **journey into terror**, check out the Poe Virtual Library, with a complete set of links to **Poe's** short stories and poems, articles and special exhibits, and film/**TV** adaptations. It's set up like a real library: just click on the books to go to the sections. There's also information on Poe-related artwork, historical information, **humor,** and quotations. This is an excellent collection of links, and it's presented in an easy-to-use format.

The House of Usher also has its **own** collection of Poe's work, presented in a neat format with pictures. This includes the famous poem "The Raven," shown here against a background picture of a **real raven**, with links to explanations of some of the more difficult words. There are also some **sounds to download,** an art gallery, and links to biographical information, special exhibits, museums, and official historical sites. **It's creepy, but fun!**

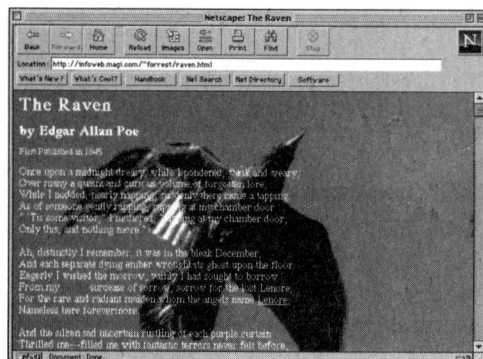

YAHOOLIGANS!

You can also read a short Poe biography here, with links to more information on the places and subjects mentioned. It's a good way to dig up more on the subject. The Poe Virtual Library also has links to serious research sites, **people related to Poe**, clothing of the times, and more Poe biographies on the Net. *The Fall of the House of Usher* Web page has it all, and **we only wish every author could have a site like this one!**

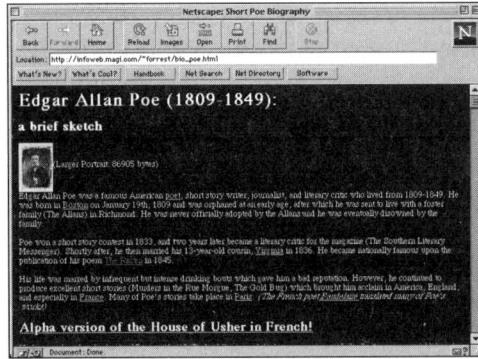

Mark Twain: Resources on the WWW

http://web.syr.edu/~fjzwick/twainwww.html

Twain was a brilliant writer, and his classic books include *Tom Sawyer, Huckleberry Finn, The Prince and the Pauper, A Connecticut Yankee in King Arthur's Court,* and more. This is a great site if you want to go deeper into Twain's writings. It includes sections with links to online versions of Twain's most popular novels and other works **(quotations, nonfiction, and poetry).** There are also links to special museum exhibits on the Web, picture files, and a reference to Twain appearances in popular culture and science fiction (he shows up in Star Trek!). This site has a lot of good information, so check it out.

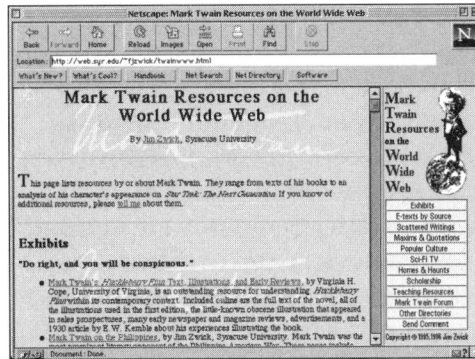

Jules Verne

http://gauss.technion.ac.il/~rl/JulesVerne/

Jules Verne is considered the father of science fiction, and it's easy to see why at this site. You'll find that his ideas can be found behind many popular sci-fi books and current movies. Some of Verne's ideas even predicted a lot of the scientific achievements of the twentieth century before they happened! The author of classic works like *Around the World in Eighty Days*, *Journey to the Center of the Earth*, *From the Earth to the Moon*, *Twenty Thousand Leagues Under the Sea*, **and** *Master of the World* shows an incredible imagination in his books, and links to these works and more are available online, direct from this site. There's also a Potpourri of Verne exhibits from around the world and links to artwork, movies, and science sites related to Verne and his works.

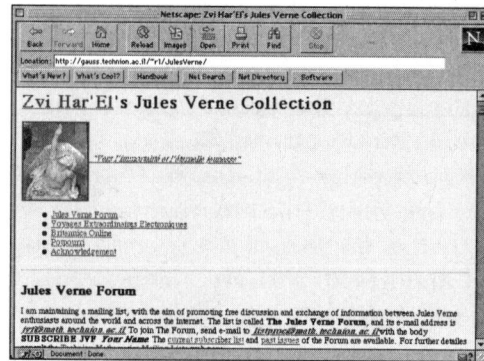

Electronic literature

Public Domain Electronic Children's Books

gopher://lib.nmsu.edu/11/.subjects/Education/.childlit/.childbooks

Want to find out where kids' books are located on the Internet? For the days when you can't make it to the library, this **gopher** site has links to popular children's books you can read directly in your Web browser. You'll find stuff from authors like J. M. Barrie, L. Frank Baum, Daniel Defoe, Joseph Conrad, Arthur Conan Doyle, Edgar Allan Poe, Robert Louis Stevenson, and Mark Twain. The full texts of the books are available here, and you can save them to use for book reports or to read later (when you're not connected to the Internet).

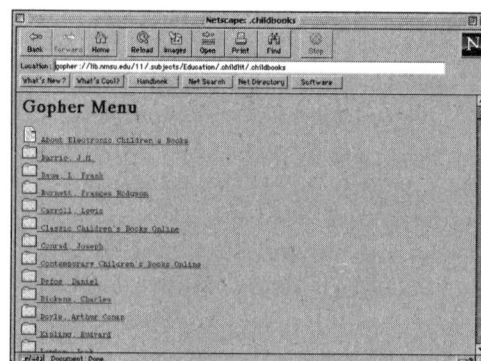

KidPub WWW Publishing

http://www.en-garde.com/kidpub/

Read stories from kids all over the world here. Each issue is a long list of stories, with the author's name and age clearly identified. You can also go to the back issues for more reading. **Learn how to submit your own story—you may end up in print!** Each story also has a short section where kids can talk about themselves and an e-mail link so you can send them mail. It's all **original stuff**, so go see what other kids can write and try coming up with stories yourself!

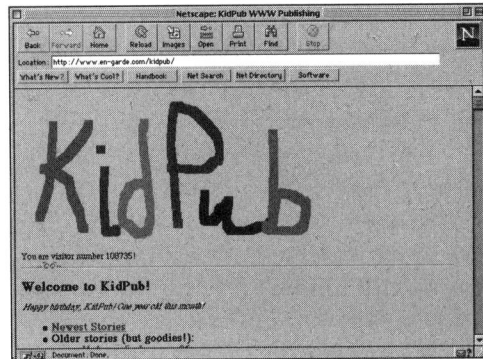

The On-line Books Page

http://www.cs.cmu.edu/Web/books.html

You can get to over **1,200 online books** from here — novels and short stories, nonfiction, poetry, essays, and picture books. You can read them **online or download** them for free. It's easy to search for a book by title or to get a list of books by a particular author. You can also browse the **new book section** or the entire list (by subject). A **huge** amount of literature exists on the Internet, and this place shows you just where to find it.

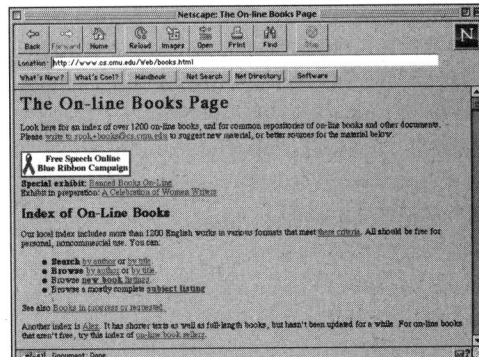

Classics Gopher

gopher://wiretap.spies.com/11/Library/Classic

Need something good to read? Get a fast list of cool classic books available online right here. This gopher server has fiction in a **wide range of categories,** ranging from Aesop's Fables to stories from Washington Irving, Edgar Allan Poe, Ambrose Bierce, and Robert Louis Stevenson, as well as novels from Edgar Rice Burroughs, H. G. Wells, Rudyard Kipling, L. Frank Baum, and many others. There are also essays from Benjamin Franklin, Booker T. Washington, Charles Darwin, and Frederick Douglass. It's not a fancy Web site, but it **delivers.** Give it a chance!

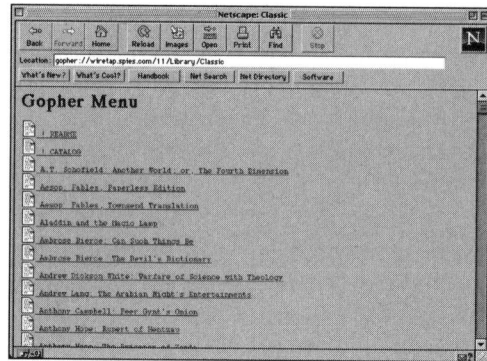

An ounce of Mom and Dad is worth a pound of comfort!

When something online scares you, back off. Talk to your parents. You don't have to put up with anyone making you feel uncomfortable online.

Fairy tales & fables

Fairy Tales and Fables

gopher://ftp.std.com/11/obi/book/Fairy.Tales/Grimm

You can get the **full versions** of a lot of great fairy tales right here, courtesy of the Online Book Initiative. (The Internet community is trying to put **more books on the Web.**) This is a link to a gopher server with popular fairy tales you can read with your Web browser and save offline. Check out the "Adventures of Aladdin," "Ali Baba and the Forty Thieves," "Beauty and the Beast," "Cinderella," "Pinocchio," and **much more.**

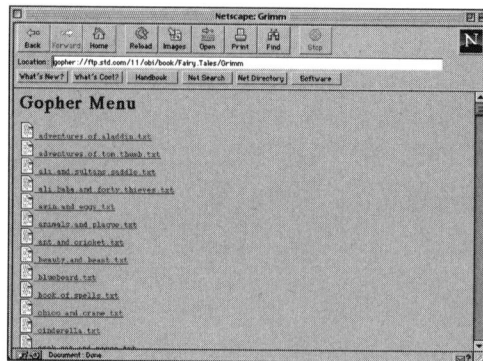

Tales of Wonder

http://www.ece.ucdavis.edu/~darsie/tales.html

This site has a great selection of folk and fairy tales from around the world, and they're all available online. Tales include "The Frog Princess" (Russia), "Ankakumikaityn the Nomad Wolf" (Siberia), "The Four Dragons" (China), "The Princess and the Mouse" (the Middle East), "The Mermaid of Zennor" (England), and "Trickster Rabbit" (Africa). These are **neat stories** you **may not have read yet.** The site also includes many stories from Japan, Scandinavia, and Scotland, and a good selection of Native American folk tales.

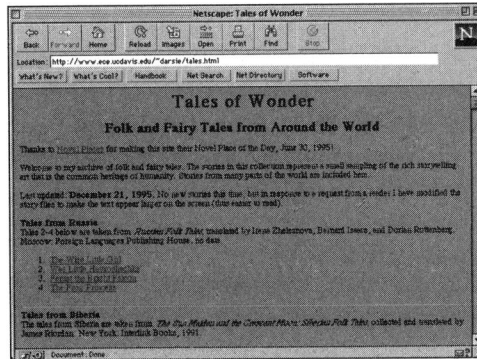

Poetry

KidzPage

http://web.aimnet.com/~veeceet/kids/kidzpage.html

This is a fun little page for all you **poetry fans. Younger kids** will enjoy a neat rhyming alphabet section. You'll find poems from Lewis Carroll and Hillaire Belloc here as well as some cool animal limericks, such as "The Octopus" by Ogden Nash: "Tell me, O Octopus, I begs / Is those things arms, or is they legs? / I marvel at thee, Octopus; / If I were thou, I'd call me Us." Also, be sure to visit the Homegrown Verse section for poems from kids across the country. You may even **be inspired** to come up with a poem or two of your own!

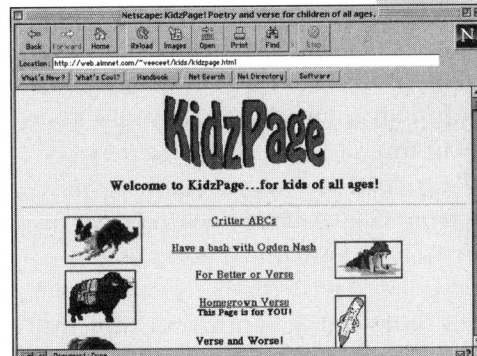

Poems for and about the Young

http://www.ece.ucdavis.edu/~darsie/kid_poems.html

Go to this Web site to find a good selection of **children's poetry**, from **famous poets** like Walter de la Mare, Robert Louis Stevenson, William Wordsworth, Algernon Charles Swinburne, and James Whitcomb Riley. All of the poems listed here are presented on one long page, so you'll have to scroll down to each author's section to read their **works.** The poems at this site include "A Child's Garden of Verses," "The Children's Hour," "The Pixy People," "Armies in the Fire," "Tartary," and more.

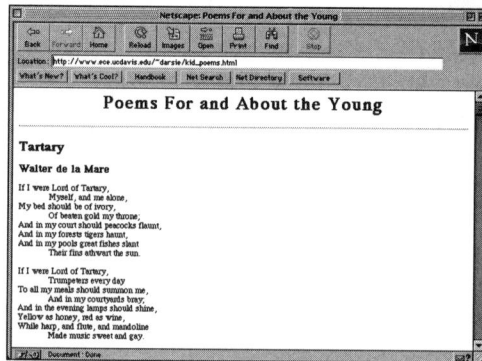

VERy CooL

Netscape: Poems For and About the Young

Location: http://www.ece.ucdavis.edu/~darsie/kid_poems.html

Poems For and About the Young

Tartary

Walter de la Mare

If I were Lord of Tartary,
     Myself, and me alone,
My bed should be of ivory,
     Of beaten gold my throne,
And in my court should peacocks flaunt,
And in my forests tigers haunt,
And in my pools great fishes slant
     Their fine athwart the sun.

If I were Lord of Tartary,
     Trumpeters every day
To all my meals should summon me,
     And in my courtyards bray,
And in the evening lamps should shine,
Yellow as honey, red as wine,
While harp, and flute, and mandoline
     Made music sweet and gay.

Mythology

MythText

http://www.io.org/~untangle/mythtext.html

Myths are stories that have been a part of world culture since the beginning of humanity, and you can find links to **mythology** and information on ancient cultures right here. Sections in this site include Frequently Asked Questions about mythologies ranging from classical **Greek** to **Egyptian** (and a lot in between) and a good list of books associated with them. If you're really **curious** and want to venture farther into the world of myths and legends, check out stories and fables from ancient Greece, Egypt, England, and the Middle East.

wAY CooL

Netscape: Welcome to MYTHTEXT:Mythology Site

Location: http://www.io.org/~untangle/mythtext.html

Mythtext: *Mythology from All Over The World*

© 1996, 1996 Untangle Incorporated

(Last Updated:Sunday, February 18, 1996)

Greek Mythology

http://www.intergate.net/uhtml/.jhunt/greek_myth/greek_myth.html

If you're interested in learning more about the Greek gods, **this is the place for you.** See how Greek mythology is different from Roman mythology, check out the Heroes and Creatures section, and read profiles of Gods and other selected stories. If you want to know how **the gods** are related to each other, delve into the Family Trees section. You can also use this section to look up descriptions of the gods because the names in the tree are linked! Scope out the Other Internet Sources section for links to more information.

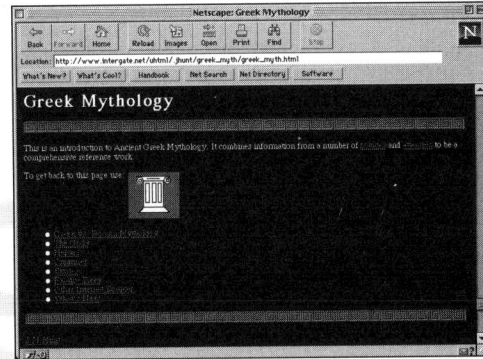

Science fiction

Linköping Science Fiction & Fantasy Archive

http://phttpd.www.lysator.liu.se/sf_archive/

Reading science fiction and fantasy stories and books is a fun way to imagine living in other worlds, traveling **thorough time,** and having fantastic adventures. The Linköping Science Fiction & Fantasy Archive is a great place to find out more about science fiction. The fans at this site have come up with a great information source, with links to reviews from across the Internet on specific authors and book series, special science fiction **magazines available** online, and lists of good books to read.

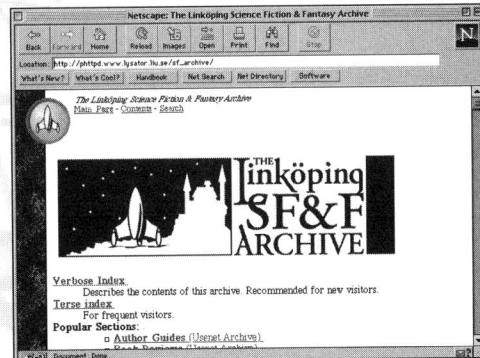

CONTINUED →

http://phttpd.www.lysator.liu.se/sf_archive/

The Main Contents page is definitely the place to check out for **new stuff** in the science fiction/fantasy world. It's loaded with lists of author and book directories and science fiction movie information. Use the book index to find reviews on specific books and stories that you like. If you're **into science fiction magazines,** see the Special Series section, with more reviews and original stories and artwork.

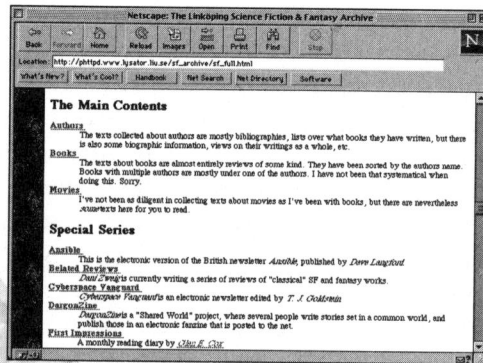

Check out the Authors section for info on your favorite science fiction authors. It's easy to navigate—you can **go directly to any author** by just clicking on a letter. You can also get a chronological list of authors (that's a list that separates the older authors from the modern ones), which will take you to separate author pages with short biographies, information on their books, and independent reviews. This is the place to find out more about your favorite author(s) and other books they have written.

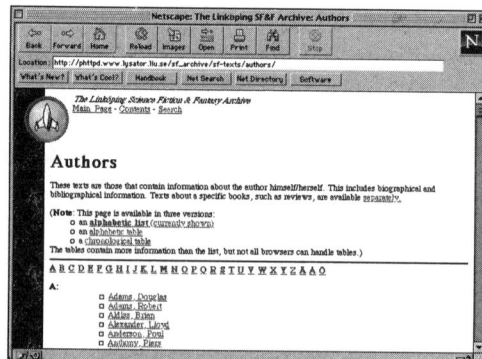

YAHOOLIGANS!

The Science Fiction Resource Guide is one of the **coolest sections** of the Linköping Science Fiction & Fantasy Archive. You'll find science fiction and **fantasy sites** from all over the Internet here. Read the introduction and **Frequently Asked Questions** sections to help get you started, and check out the **huge** collection of links to science fiction archives (picture and sound files), award lists and contests, online bookstores, fan sites (conventions and science fiction club information), and TV show pages. You can also explore the many links to science fiction publishers' pages, fiction sites, and science fiction zines on the Net. Cool worlds and fantastic adventures are out there for you to **investigate!**

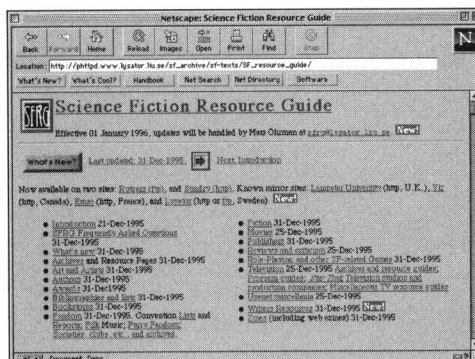

Storytelling

The Storytelling Home Page

http://members.aol.com/storypage/

This is a **major place** for storytelling and storytellers. It's got everything—story resources you can look up, personal pages for **storytellers**, and Internet Discussion Forums you can join for tips and help from other interested people. This site also has information on The National Storytelling Association and other organizations and guilds listed by state. See the **Festivals & Performances** sections and the **Regional Event Calendars** (for Los Angeles, San Diego, Texas, and Washington, DC) for **more** information on what's going on in your area.

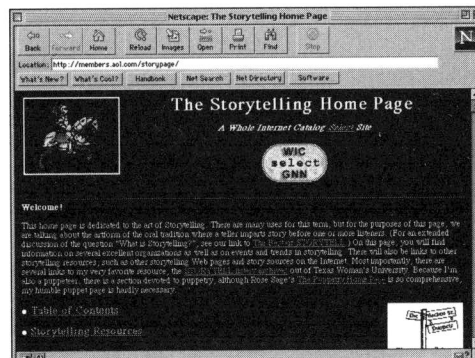

CHAPTER 3

Games & Software

One of the biggest benefits of the Web is the games, games, games! Check out the game sites for reviews of upcoming games, with pictures and sound clips, tips from expert players, and links to game software companies. There are also game directories that can show you where to download cool games (in lots of categories), and official sites for the big game companies. Besides games, the Web can also provide you with a lot of cool shareware and demo software, like graphics utilities, communications programs, screensavers, and more. There are special sites that can help you find almost any kind of software to download for your system.

Board games, card games, game site indexes

Rulemonger's Jyhad/Vampire: The Eternal Struggle Page

http://www.math.sc.edu/~sjohnson/jyhad/

A good unofficial site to Wizards of The Coast's cardplayer RPG, Vampire: The Eternal Struggle (formerly Jyhad). **Control your vampires against other predatory bloodsuckers, and watch your neck!** Find out about basic rules (including an online rulebook and information on how to play the game), expansion sets, and online discussion/trading groups. There's also a local feedback board where you can post and respond to messages with other players, and selected links to other sites with more information. You can also leave messages for the page maintainer and the game creators directly from here.

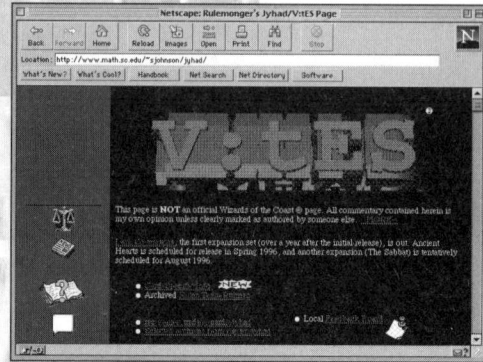

Hyper@ctive

http://hyperactive.com/games/

Very cool site for this international gaming magazine. Check out areas like **Buzz** and Fast Forward for news and previews, Zoom and Play for features and reviews (listed by platform), and a Dump section with links to downloadable software. You can also **poke around** in The Vault for other information, receive and send letters in the Mail section, and check out their good collection of descriptive links to game platform information, new game companies, and upcoming technologies.

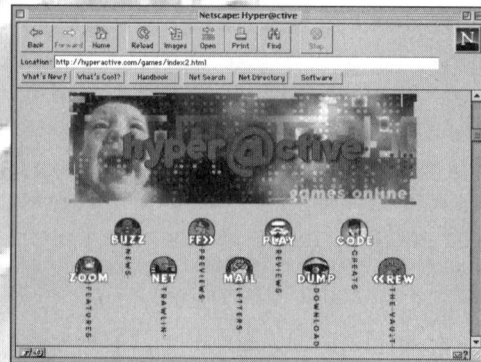

Games by title

The Maxis Home Page

http://www.maxis.com

Here's the page for the creators of all of
those popular Sim games, such as SimCity,
SimTower, SimAnt, SimFarm — you get the
picture. There's a **cool** What's Hot section
(where you can find out more about the
latest games, add-on software, and **contests**),
a product information section (where you
can get the details on specific games and
access online technical support), and an
FTP/General Store area (with links to patch
and utility software, and online order forms).
You can also **check out** the Sim-Business
section for more information about the
company and its products.

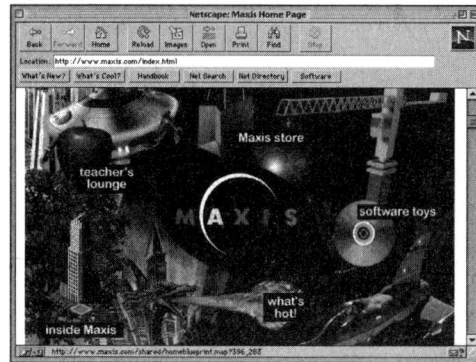

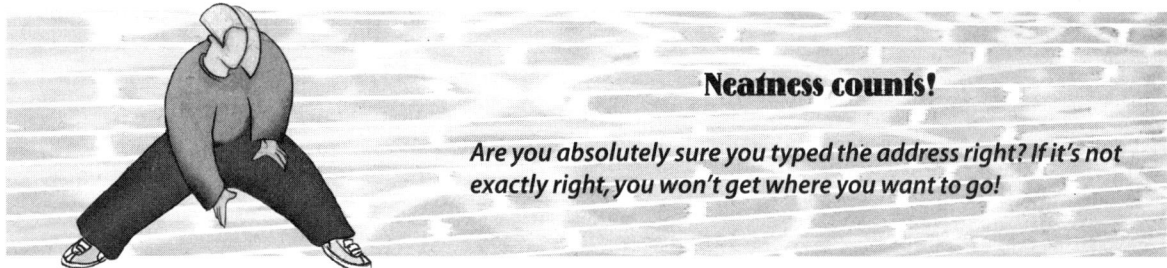

Neatness counts!

*Are you absolutely sure you typed the address right? If it's not
exactly right, you won't get where you want to go!*

Kali (www.kali.net)

http://www.kali.net/

This is the official site for Kali, a shareware
add-on program for your Internet account
that lets you play sophisticated multiplayer
games over the Web. If you have Kali, you
can **play games** like Doom, Hexen,
Mortal Kombat, Descent, Comanche, and
Mechwarrior 2 with other players all over
the Internet. The Kali site has a section
on downloading and installing the Kali
software, as well as a list of current games
that go with it, plus links to other Kali home
pages. It's **cool stuff** — join in!

Role playing & video game sites

Morph's RPG Page

http://www.dreamworld.com/~morpheus/rpgs.html

This is a big set of links to sites for RPG (role-playing games) gamers, including Web pages for games like RuneQuest, Ars Magica, Cyberpunk, Shadowrun, Battletech, and Warhammer. See the list of RPG resources for alphabetical sections on game sites, major game companies (like Chaosium, Steve Jackson Games, and Wizards of the Coast), player home pages, FTP sites, and newsgroups. You can also explore separate Netbooks with information and links to sites for Advanced Dungeons and Dragons, Cyberpunk 2020, Storyteller, and RIFTS, **neat science fiction and fantasy role playing** games set in future times and other worlds. Check it out!

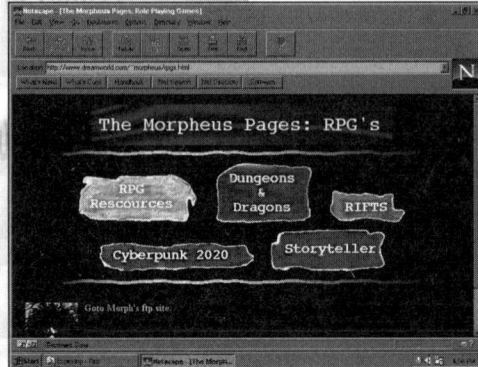

Cybertech

http://digitalcity.web.aol.com/users/j/jeffg/games.html

Cybertech features information on such platforms as 3-DO, Sony PlayStation, Sega Saturn, and Nintendo Ultra64. Each section has a good set of FAQs (**game hints, secret codes, and walkthroughs**), links to other sites from the hardware manufacturer to top software companies, and lots of other information such as interviews with game designers, galleries of art from selected games, and game news. You'll also find links to game-related FTP directories, online gamer magazines, and game stores. If you want more information on certain vendor games like Namco (Ridge Racer and Tekken and Soul Edge) and Game Tek (Robotech Ultra64), be sure to check out the vendors' games sections. Or you can add your own reports!

YAHOOLIGANS!

The Electric Playground

http://www.elecplay.com/

The Electric Playground is a **great visual gamer magazine** with good reviews, features, and news on games for computers and consoles, and in arcades. See the New section to find out about what's coming out. For example, a recent issue had good video clips and still pictures from Time Warner's arcade hit Area 51. Plus you'll find lists of new games for most platforms, hardware updates, and more — even music reviews! The Feature section has interesting articles on games and related topics, such as wish lists from people in the game industry. Pop the Thought Drop to **slap a note** to the Playgrounders.

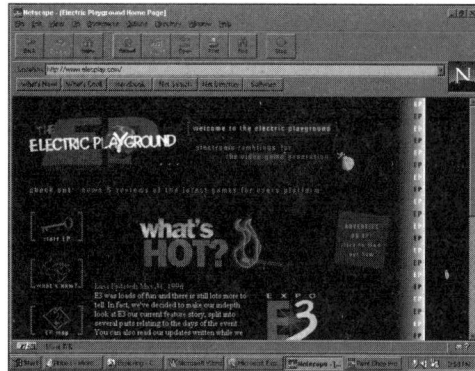

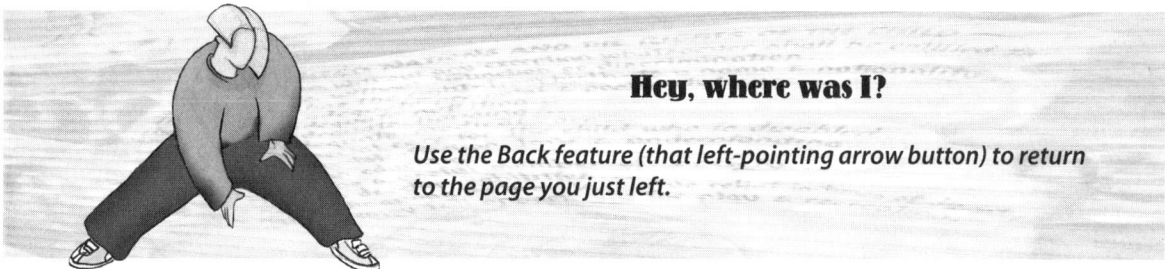

Hey, where was I?

Use the Back feature (that left-pointing arrow button) to return to the page you just left.

Atari Jagwire

http://www.atari.com/jagwire/menu.html

Don't miss the sections on Hot Flashes, Jagwire, and HyperLinks. Hot Flashes has information on **new stuff** from Atari and other game manufacturers, plus press releases. Jagwire covers illustrated hardware and software pages, Lynx info, and ordering information. And HyperLinks sends you to official Atari news sources and other Jagwire sites for software manufacturers and game fans. Don't worry if you get lost or stuck — check out the online help system. You'll see contact information, too, which will help if you want to drop Atari a line.

Software & related sites

OAK Software Repository

http://www.acs.oakland.edu/oak.html

This is a **good** place to find PC DOS, Windows 3.1, and Windows 95 programs on the Internet, including graphics and sound files, game demos, and shareware. Try the search engine that can let you look for programs by name or by description. You can download the programs or read other people's ratings of them.

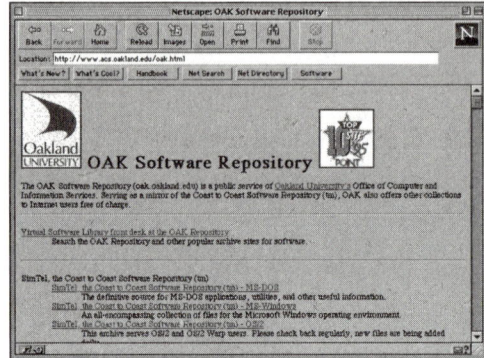

Hold it right there!

If you're in the wrong place, or if you get tired of waiting for the computer to do something and you want to do something else, click the Stop button.

MECC (Minnesota Educational Computer Corporation)

http://www.mecc.com/

A great site from the makers of the Oregon Trail program. You can also find out about the Inter@ctive Explorer series and other cool MECC programs (like Maya Quest and Blue Ice: Focus on Antarctica). The Products section has lots of cool graphics from the different programs, as well as **downloadable** sound clips and (large!) demo files. The site also features good links to **technical support** (free installation and **troubleshooting** information), a What's New section where you can find out about new releases, and a Dealer Locator to help you find a store that carries the programs.

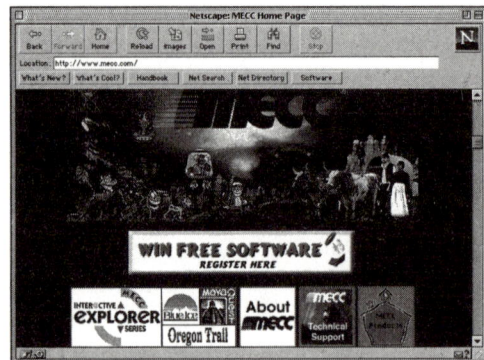

YAHOOLIGANS!

Info-Mac HyperArchive Root

http://hyperarchive.lcs.mit.edu/HyperArchive.html

This site is a **great** place to find Mac software for downloading lots of files, in categories ranging from applications software, **graphics tools**, and communications utilities to educational software and games. You can read a brief description of a file before you download it, and there's also a way to search for specific files.

VERy CooL

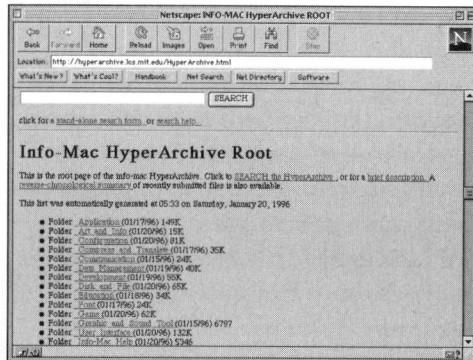

OTS Mac Software Archives

http://www.host.ots.utexas.edu/mac/main.html

This University of Texas site features easy-to-use listings of Mac software in areas like applications and **communications**, games and graphics software, and system utilities. You can also sort the directory lists by author, date, or product name. Check out the section for Internet software and services, with links to useful Mac World Wide Web **sites and programs** for use with your Internet connection. The descriptions of the files are clear, and include shareware fees, file sizes, and system requirements, as well as a direct link for downloading the actual files.

wAY CooL

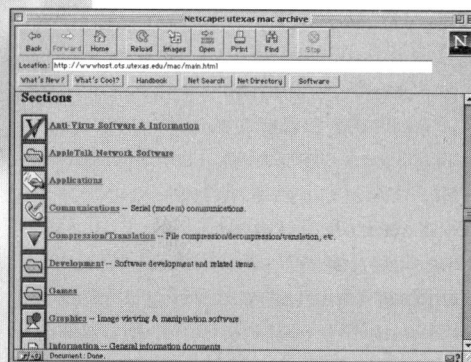

MacWare Revue

http://piazza.com/

This is a great review of Mac shareware and freeware available over the Internet. The **brief reviews** are very good, they're updated frequently, and they feature direct downloading links to the software itself. There are also sections with links to previously reviewed software (in shareware and freeware categories) and a feedback area for discussing selected programs with other readers and the editor of the Web page. If you're using a current version of Netscape (2.0 or later), you can also appreciate the **cool frames** version of the MacWare Revue.

wAY CoOL

Harvest Broker

http://rd.cs.colorado.edu/brokers/pcindex/query.html

The Harvest Broker doesn't look very cool, but it does provide a good way to use six large PC software collections. You can search through more than **35,000 programs** (and the list keeps growing). The instructions are kind of difficult to follow, but you can search for a specific program by name and look for files on a particular software site on the Internet. The Harvest Broker also gives you the ability to look for files by date (so you can look for new stuff), and you can change how many choices the computer sends you.

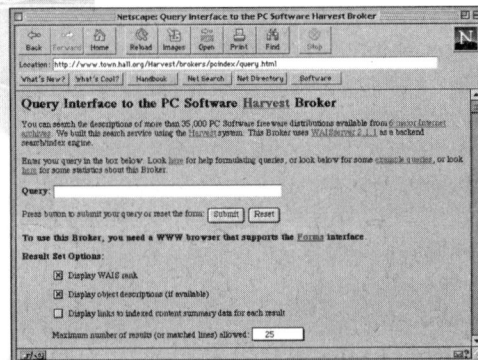

VERy CoOL

Shareware

Jumbo!

http://www.jumbo.com

Jumbo! is a monster Web shareware site for all kinds of computer platforms, including PCs and Mac systems. **Jumbo!** features thousands of file links in areas like home and personal software, games, utility programs, and graphics/word processing software. And, what's more, it's all laid out in alphabetical order, so that you can find stuff fast. **Jump right in!**

Each Jumbo! section is broken down into files for specific computer platforms. Just go to the section for your own computer type, and you'll see direct links to software areas organized into categories. It's super easy to **browse interesting files** in a particular subject. The lists of files have cool descriptions and links for direct downloading.

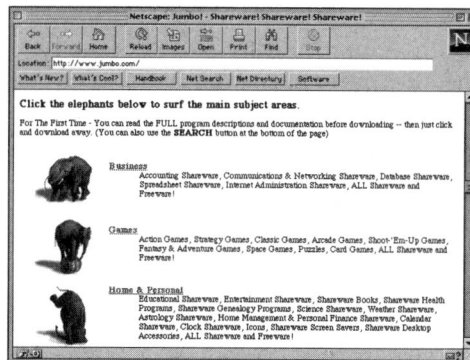

CONTINUED →

http://www.jumbo.com

The link subject areas on Jumbo! also have
special sites, like online game reviews and
tips in the Games section. These sites get
you going in the right directions fast. And
get this: Jumbo! also has lists of new games
so you can **see what's new and popular.**

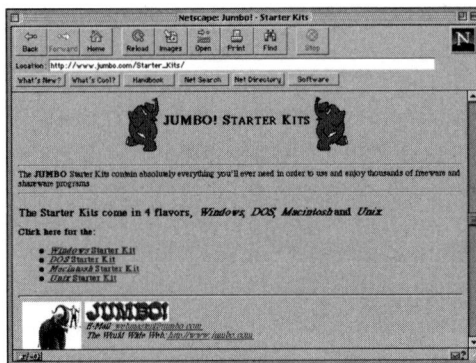

Take some time to investigate the section
with an online Super-Easy Jumbo Getting
Started Kit that can help you out if you're
new to the site (you can download it directly to
your computer), plus a search index you
can use to look for particular files. Jumbo!
makes shareware easy, and the **Jumbo!**
people keep adding more every day. See
what you can find here!

Shareware.com

http://www.shareware.com/

This is a big directory to more than 160,000 shareware files on the Internet. It features a good, adjustable search index that lets you find a file by name or description, by your computer type, and also by date. You can also browse a selection of the most **popular** recent downloads, new software arrivals, and a subject index. Shareware.com also features a **daily software review** (on a selected PC and Mac title) and a Survival Kit section with downloading tips and tools for PC and Mac platforms.

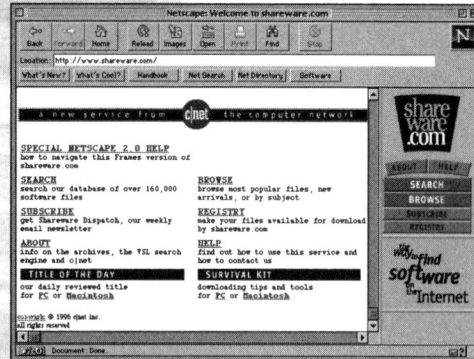

CHAPTER 4

Hobbies

Everybody collects something, whether it's baseball cards, dolls, or postcards. For every hobbyist, there is someone else out there who shares your enthusiasm. Find the group on the Web that likes the same hobbies you do! Or if you're looking for a new hobby, find out more about things like model rockets, origami, or stamps online before you actually commit yourself to anything offline. You'll also find arts and crafts pages and tons of information on what hobbyists all over the world are playing with.

Activities

Hocus Pocus Palace

http://www.teleport.com/~jrolsen/

The Great Mysto will perform his Internet **magic tricks** at your command. Choose any of the tricks, follow the directions, and be amazed at the Great Mysto's powers of deduction. You'll definitely want to go to the links to learn how Mysto performs his tricks. Check out the Virtual Magic Shop, too. Also on this page are **neat sound and video clips**, with links to the utilities you need in order to hear and view them.

Jasper's Origami Menagerie

http://www.mit.edu:8001/people/jasper/origami/menagerie/origami.html

The Origami Menagerie is a picture archive of origami animals. Not only are the many images on this page beautiful and fun to look at, they are organized into picture galleries, which make it easy for you to find any particular animal in its origami form. If you're looking for **paper bugs**, you won't be disappointed. For something a little different, go to the A. A. Milne gallery and check out Tigger and his friends in their best origami **disguises**. Since all the pictures in the galleries are very small, all you have to do is click on them to get full-size viewing of the folding details. Amazing.

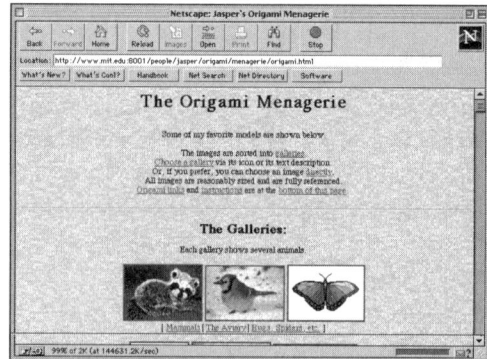

Juggling Information Service

http://www.hal.com/services/juggle/

The Juggling Information Service is the **hottest** place on the Web to find anything to do with juggling. This site has the most complete list around, so you'd be smart to look here first for links to juggling associations, information on where to buy, juggling clubs, or where to go to learn the basics of juggling. If you're a juggler, you may want to look into the International Jugglers Association, the world's **oldest** organization of jugglers. There are **festivals** and competitions; books, videos, and magazines; tips for beginners; and of course a *huge* list of other juggling home pages.

Kite Education

http://www.tyrell.net/~dellis/

Don't you wish *your* teacher held classes on a grassy field, flying a kite? Dave Ellis is a third grade teacher who uses kites, kite making, and kite flying to teach his students. His site has links to his own local kite club and to **clubs** around the country. Joining a kite club can be a great way to learn more about **kite flying**. The site also has a link devoted to web pages designed by kids, as well as a list of links that would be of interest to teachers. Other interesting kite sites are linked as well.

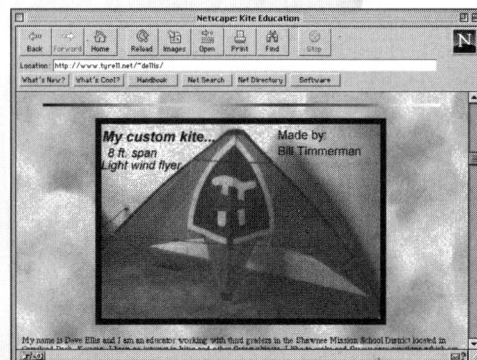

Kite Paradise

http://www.hermes.de/KITE/Hello.html

Kite Paradise is indeed a paradise for the kite lover, but it is also a really cool site that can show you enough of what kiters love about their hobby to get you hooked. It's also a **paradise** for your eyes — the layout, the colors, and the graphics make this page really stand out. Not every Web site you visit will go to a lot of trouble to make sure you get the best possible experience out of it. On some sites, if you aren't using the proper browser, you simply won't be able to see the graphics, and it'll be your tough luck. Here, you are given instructions on how to set up your system to get the most out of the site. If you are using a very current Web browser, you should be able to view the **nifty** bits of animation included here.

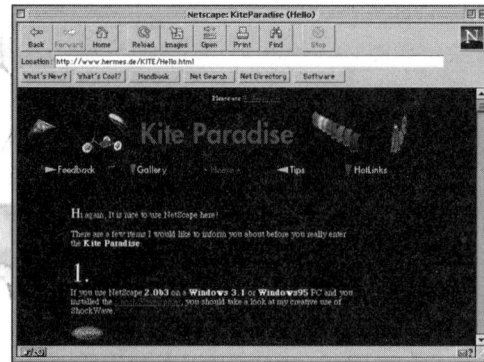

Go to the map of the site for a great overview of what you're going to find. This site is pretty big, but the map makes it easy for you to get around. You'll probably want to start at the Basics icon. Make sure you choose the right option (text only, standard graphics, or **ShockWave-equipped**) for your system. The Basics page offers solutions to problems you may be having flying your kite. There are illustrations of what your kite may be doing wrong, another illustration of the way the kite should behave, and a link to how you can fix the problem. All the problems are listed at the top, so you can go directly to your solution.

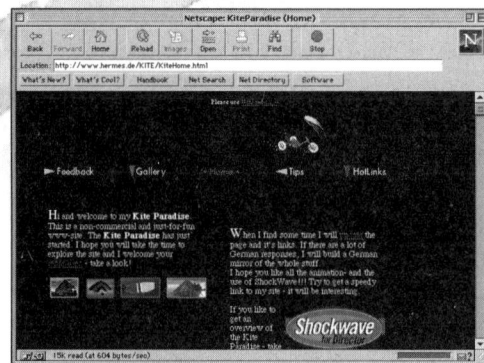

YAHOOLIGANS!

For pictures and descriptions of different kinds of kites, go to the My Kites link. You'll find many very different styles and sizes of kites, with pictures and descriptions and statistics on each kite. Each kite has a small picture you can click on to see a full-size drawing, and you can find out what kinds of kites are good for **stunt flying**, which are better for low wind conditions, and which give the best pull.

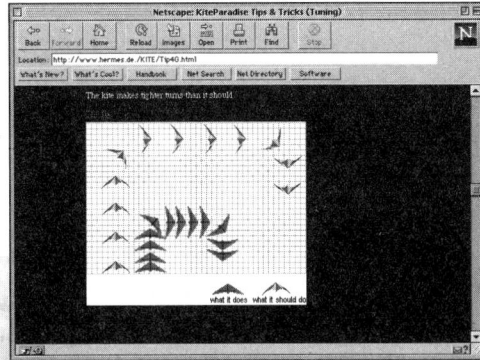

Go to Power Kiting for a completely new look at what kites can do. Power Kiting is simply the sport of letting a kite pull you around, whether you're on your feet or in a specially designed **buggy**. This kind of kiting is very different from flying a standard kite, or even from flying a stunt or racing kite. You need to know a little about sailing, and a little about surfing, and a lot about wind and kites. Just hang out at the Power Kiting page, look at the great pictures, read up on the methods, and you'll almost be able to hear the wind whistling past you.

Magic [Christian V. Andersen]

http://www.daimi.aau.dk/~zytnia/eg.html

If you're a budding magician, Christian's Magic Page is a great place to learn about your chosen **hobby**. You can check out other amateur magicians' pages and then go look at the sites dedicated to the great professional magicians. There are links to magicians' magazines on the Web and to sites devoted to **magic and illusion**. Magic-related news groups and documents are listed as well.

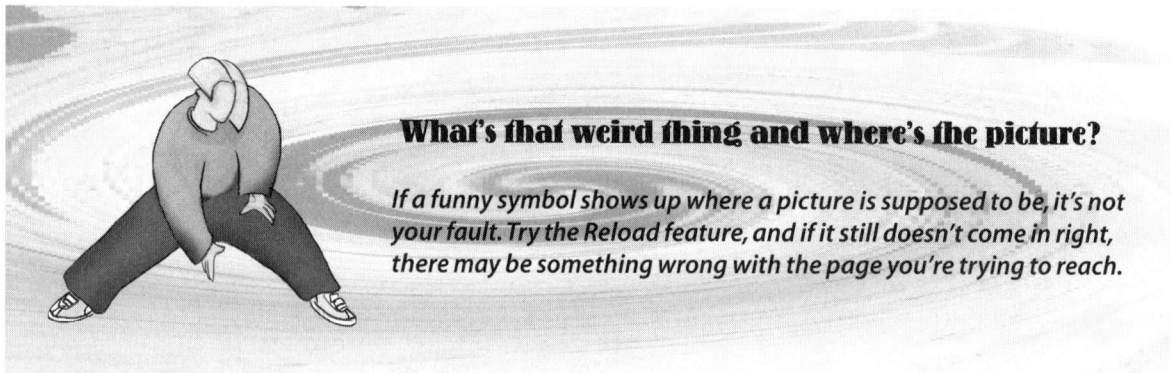

VERY CooL

What's that weird thing and where's the picture?

If a funny symbol shows up where a picture is supposed to be, it's not your fault. Try the Reload feature, and if it still doesn't come in right, there may be something wrong with the page you're trying to reach.

Millefiori

http://wjh-www.harvard.edu/~jenea/artbox/millefiori/howto1.html

wAY CooL

If you've ever wondered how artists make those brightly colored earrings, buttons, and pendants out of clay, the Millefiori page will show you exactly how it's done. The **illustrated instructions** on this page are first rate, showing step-by-step changes in the clay and revealing tips on how to get the best results (the picture shows step 4). If you become **fascinated** with the process, go to the list of links to find out where to buy polymer clay and how to get more information on designs you can follow and groups you can join to talk about your millefiori obsession.

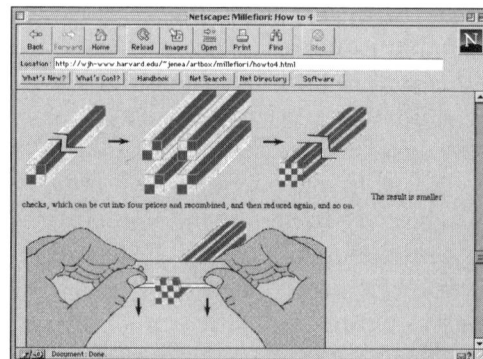

Paul Gray's Model Rocketry For Beginners

http://www.webcom.com/pmgray/

Paul Gray has been building and launching model rockets since he was seven, so he is sort of an expert on getting kids into model rocketry. His Web page is an easy-to-follow guide to building model rockets, with very simple designs and very **exciting** results.

wAY CooL

The beginner's page has good advice on what kinds of models you might want to build if you're a newcomer to model rocketry. It explains the different skill level ratings you'll see on the packaging, and recommends a couple of good starter kits. Be sure to read this page, even if you already know what you're doing. You never know when the advice may come in handy. Your next step is the Basics page, where you'll find out what tools you'll need, what kind of glue to use, and how important it is to **get your fins on straight**.

CONTINUED ⟶

http://www.webcom.com/pmgray/

Now that you have a **rocket**, you need to fly it. There are detailed instructions for the best way to find a place to launch your rocket and how to take the weather into consideration. Safety is always important, but it is most important at the actual launch, so plenty of **safety** guidelines are laid down. You'd be wise to follow them.

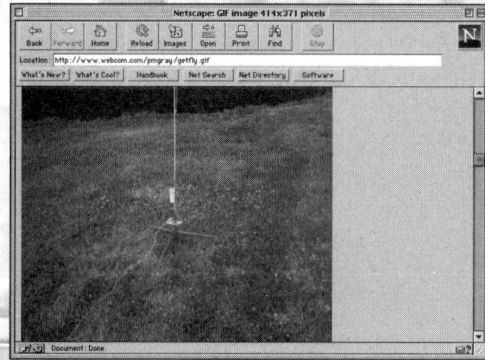

The flight of your rocket is not the end of the story. There are bigger and better models to build and fly, so once you've got the basics down, go to the list of model rocket dealers to shop for your next kit. And when building your next rocket, you can always return to this page for **tips and pointers** that you may have missed on the first go-through.

Tad's Model & High Power Rocketry Page

http://www.primenet.com/~tmorgan/rockets.html

If you **love** rockets, Tad's Rocketry Page is *the* place to check out. It's loaded with lists of model rocket vendors, rocketry exhibits, and clubs for rocketry fans. If you're just getting started in rockets, there's a list of FAQs (frequently asked questions) and a list of **cool rocket words** that you may not be familiar with. Check out the Upcoming Launches for dates and locations of club meetings where rockets will actually **go up in the air**. The launch list is linked to the site for that launch, so you can get even more info.

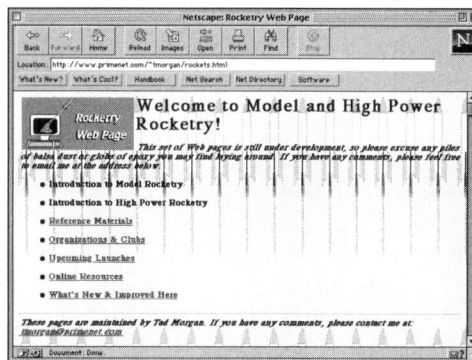

Puppetry

http://www-leland.stanford.edu/~rosesage/puppetry/puppetry.html

For puppet information of all types, you've found the right page. There are **links galore** to all different types of puppets, from hand puppets to shadow puppets to marionettes. Puppet theaters, plays, exhibitions, and museums all have numerous links. Go to the puppetry resources to find out where you can get **puppet-building materials**, ready-made puppets, or puppet magazines. The worldwide list of puppet performances and production companies is huge, so you might want to go to the What's New link for a list that's a little closer to home.

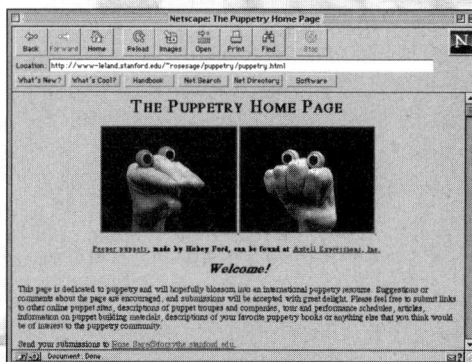

Rockhounds Information

http://www.rahul.net/infodyn/rockhounds/rockhounds.html

So what's the big deal about rock collecting? A rock is a rock, right? Wrong! Rockhounds, or rock finders and collectors, can tell you the differences between hundreds of different types of rocks, gems, and mineral formations. The Rockhounds page takes you deep into the rockhound universe on and off the Web. Visit the Smithsonian's dazzling archive of pictures of gems and minerals, dig into earth sciences all over the globe, **check out dinosaur fossils** (fossils are rocks!), or browse through other rock-hounds' pages. You can be sure, if it's rock-y, it's linked here.

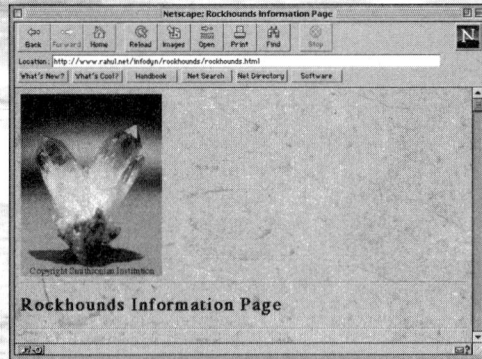

World Wide Webs

http://www.ece.ucdavis.edu/~darsie/string.html

The World Wide Web page is devoted to detailed instructions on how to create dozens of different **string figures** on your hands. There are great drawings of *every* figure, so you always know how it is supposed to turn out. Be sure to read the description of how the instructions are written so you won't get confused halfway through. If you've never played Cat's Cradle, you might want to start with some of the simpler figures, but even if you're already good with string, you'll want to do some of the basic figures just to **practice** following the instructions. Then you'll be ready to move on to the really complicated string figures like the Turtle or Laia Flower figures. (The picture shows one called Many Stars.)

YAHOOLIGANS!

Collecting

Learn About Antiques & Collectibles

http://www.ic.mankato.mn.us/antiques/Antiques.html

So your great-grandmother gave you a Chinese box that she told you was given to her by her father. You know it's old, but is it a real **antique**? You might not want to sell it, but it might be interesting to find out more about it. Maybe it is rare and worth a lot of money to a collector. You can go to the Antiques and Collectibles page to find out. Learn how to talk about antiques so that people won't take advantage of you. Find out where you can go for more information. This page won't actually tell you how much your box is worth, but you *will* find out enough to know whether it is a **valuable** antique.

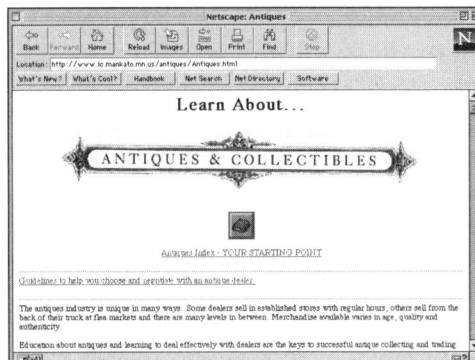

Coin Universe

http://www.coin-universe.com/

Coin Universe has everything the coin collector needs to get started in the hobby or to continue successfully. Along with a **chat** room for coin collectors and coin classifieds, there's a dictionary of coin terms and a listing of coin clubs you can join. Coin Universe is updated often, so you can drop in and see what's new. As we write, there are new links to a coin display products manufacturer and to a vendor of **U.S. and Confederate paper money.** Check out the links to other coin collectors' home pages and see what your fellow collectors are doing on the Web.

Collectible Trader

http://158.93.29.52/Trade.html

This is the place to go if you're in the market to buy collectible **toys**, or if you're selling toys from your collection. You can post a free ad and browse the ads already posted. Check out what people are willing to trade. You'll find links to the Collectible Trader's favorite collectibles—**American Flyer Trains**—and also a list of links to other collectibles pages. Remember, if you want to buy or sell anything over the Net, make sure you have your parent's permission.

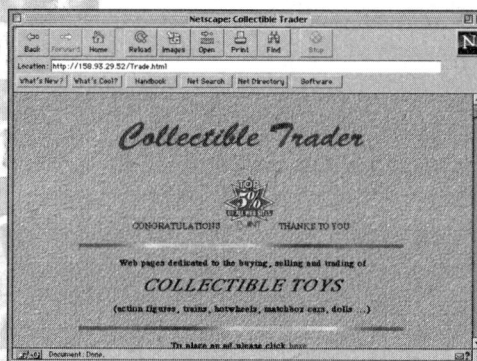

The World Wide Web Virtual Library: Collecting

http://www.antika.com/collecting/

If you can't find what you're looking for on this list, you haven't looked hard enough. Anything that is collectible is listed here, with links to various sites for that particular item. All the biggies are here, like stamps and **trading cards**, but you'll also find paperweights, candy bar wrappers, and cereal boxes. If it can be collected, someone collects it, and it is represented here. You'll find lots of references to Yahoo!, but you'll also find stuff unlisted anywhere else. This site is a *find.*

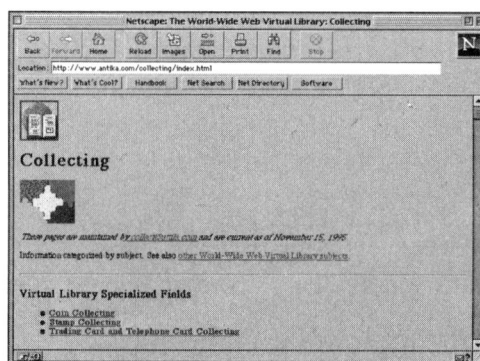

Joseph Luft's Philatelic Resources on the Web

http://www.execpc.com/~joeluft/resource.html

Stamps! This is the **mega** list of resources for both the serious stamp collector and the beginner. There are dozens of links to different countries' stamp pages and a huge list of general stamp collecting links. Want to find out more about collecting first day covers, or do you just want to know what the heck a first day cover is? Look here. The list of other collectors' pages is enormous and includes collectors from all over the world, so if you're looking for people to correspond with, this is a great place to start. There is information on stamp dealers, stamp shows, and plenty of general info on all things postal.

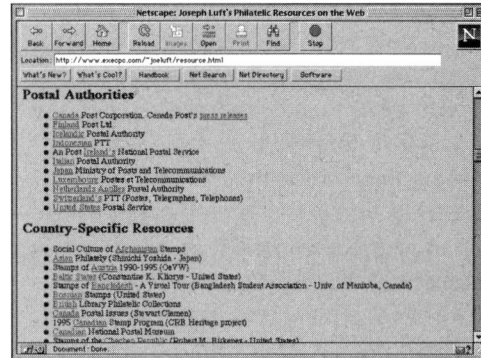

Stamp Collectors

http://www.magic.mb.ca/~lampi/stamps.html

The Stamp Collector page is a good link from one stamp collector to another. The links include other pages maintained by collectors and sites designed by other countries for exhibiting their stamps. The U.S. Postal Service page is pretty cool. There are also links to pages that sell stamps and to software that can help you **organize your collection**. Drop the Webmaster a line if you find an interesting link you think he or she would want to know about!

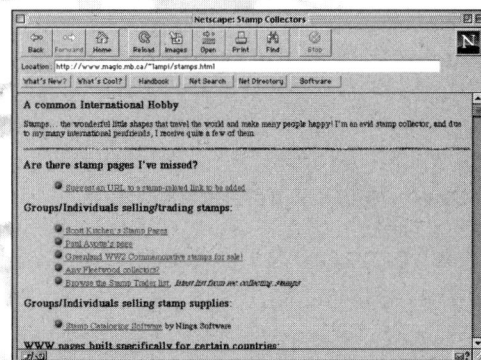

Collectors' Trading Card Universe

http://www.tradingcard.com/

As you can probably **guess** from the name, Trading Card Universe is devoted to people who collect and trade **sports cards** and **nonsports cards**. If you're one of these people, this is definitely the place for you. You can post a **classified** ad and read other people's ads. There's a chat room here just for you and your fellow card trading fans, plus plenty of links to other card trading pages. More links take you to a list of **card trading shows** and card trading dealers.

Dolls, toys, & models

Bearly a Page

http://www.aa.net/~urizen/bears2.html

For teddy bear lovers, nothing else will do. So if you're looking for bears online, go to Bearly a Page. This cool site provides a picture **gallery** of teddy bear photos and original teddy bear art by the Webmaster. Go to the Ursine legends for fun and amusing stories and quotes about bears in their many forms (teddy and otherwise). The page rounds out all these offerings with a list of teddy bear resources on the Net. Find out about teddy bear shows, or **read the story about the very first teddy bear.**

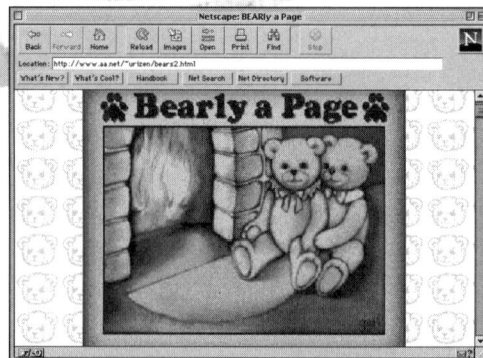

Chatty Deb Dolls N More

http://www.geocities.com/Hollywood/1272

This page has lots of **nifty graphics**, so be patient while it loads. Chatty Deb collects dolls, especially Chatty Cathy dolls, but she also provides links to collectors' pages for other kinds of dolls. There are some great Barbie links and links to some **unusual** sites, like Dream-Land Dollies and an Island Doll Shop in Hawaii. Go to her Guestbook to see what other collectors are looking for or selling, leave your own message about her page, or place an informal classified ad.

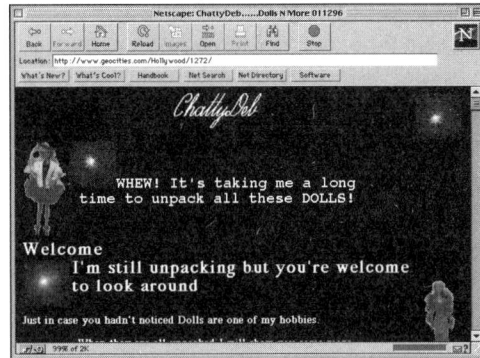

VERy CooL

Model Horse Gallery

http://www.ecst.csuchico.edu/~rebecca/mh/HrblGalmodels.html

wAY CooL

Be warned: if you like horses at all, you're going to want to spend a lot of time at this site. It takes a while to load because of all the great pictures in the gallery, **so be patient.** The Webmaster claims to have more than 1,000 pictures on display, but if it were only pictures of plastic horses it would be pretty dull. **What keeps the site exciting** is the variety of pictures, the way they are organized, and the other features available. One entire gallery is devoted to horse equipment and other stuff, one is for different breeds, and one is only for horses in performance settings. If you're a real collector, you'll want to check out the link to the Northwest Congress Gallery, a competition among model horse collectors. **This site is a must-see for every horse lover online.**

National Model Railroad Association (NMRA)

http://www.mcs.net:80/~weyand/nmra/

The NMRA promotes the hobby of model railroading, so its site is a good place to start if you are just getting interested. The site offers links to NMRA magazines and to model railroad convention information. The NMRA also sponsors an online achievement program that allows its members to **earn certificates** toward becoming a Grand Master Model Railroader. You can also get railroad kits and modeling supplies through the NMRA. Even if you don't join, you can enjoy their huge list of links to other model railroading sites.

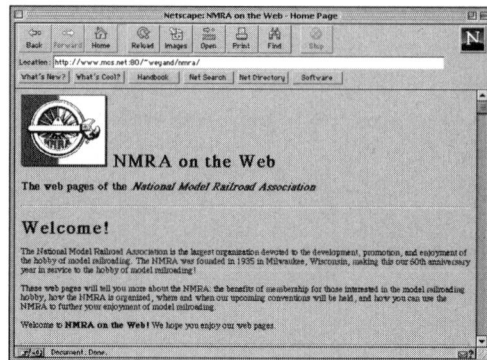

Saving your favorite places

Start your own personal list of favorite sites! Every time you go somewhere you want to visit again, add a bookmark to your list. Next time you want to go there, look in your bookmark list and click on the name of the place: it takes you right there!

Ornithopters

http://www.bucknell.edu/~chronstr/orn.html

An ornithopter is a machine that **flies by flapping its wings.** The ornithopter page has plenty of great pictures of these flying machines, plus information on their history and how they work. Follow the links to see movies of ornithopters in flight, or to see a listing of other ornithopter sites. Designing and building these unusual models takes skill and patience, but making something that can fly like a bird is a powerful reward for the work. Check out the link to the Ornithopter Modelers' Society to find out how you can get started building your very own ornithopter.

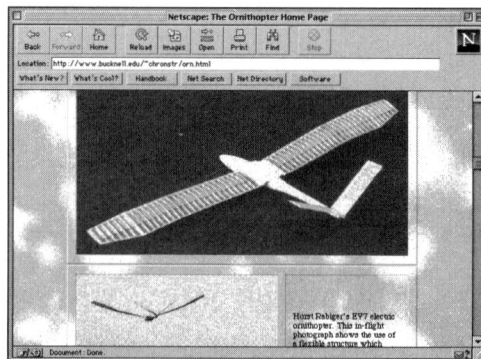

Paper Airplanes

http://pchelp.inc.net/paper_ac.htm

The Paper Airplane page lists different types of **paper airplanes**, with a brief description of each. Just click on a description of the plane you want to build to get a picture of it and complete instructions on making that airplane. New planes are added monthly (more or less), and previous month's planes are listed, so you can always go back and make an earlier one. If you want, you can print out the instructions and fold offline.

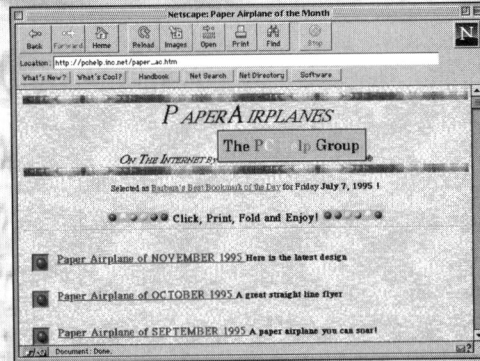

PEZ

http://www.csif.cs.ucdavis.edu/~telford/pez.html

For kids who love PEZ, this PEZ lover's page is a **tasty treat**. Do PEZ, the little oval candies you eat from a cartoon dispenser, have any nutritional value? Go to the PEZ map and find out. The PEZ page has a terrific gallery of PEZ pictures from the Webmaster's collection, including Flint-stones figures, Looney Toons, Disney, and Muppets characters, and various other **cartoon figures**. The pictures aren't very big or very clear, but you get the idea. Go to the FAQ (frequently asked questions) link for more general information about PEZ, the people who **collect the dispensers**, and how you can get started on your own PEZ collection.

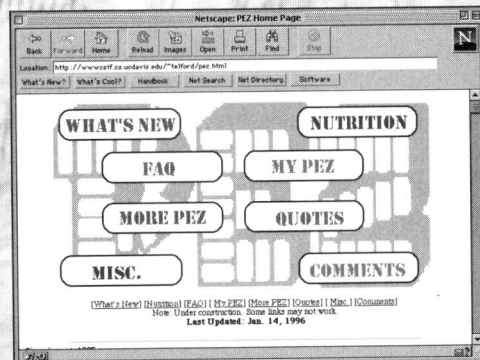

Scale Modeling

http://msowww.anu.edu.au/~dfk/scale_model.html

Ever heard of a scale model? Well, a scale model is a small, but exact reproduction of a larger object, such as a car or plane. The Scale Modeling page is a super resource guide for anyone who enjoys making scale models. There is a terrific 10-part modeling course you can follow and plenty of **kits** you can preview by looking at the plans and reading a review. Go to the gallery for pictures of completed model kits of cars, boats, planes, and other scale model figures. You'll find all kinds of other information here, like how to match your paint colors to the original plane or car and where to find **modeling clubs**, manufacturers, and fellow fans.

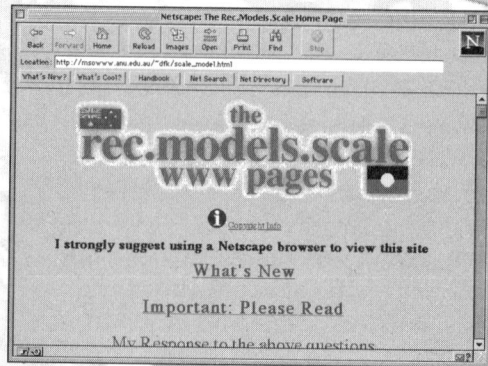

ToyLand

http://www.cwo.com/~syko/toy.html

The information here is kind of limited, but the graphics are really cool (the top of the page has a scrolling **trivia** question that changes constantly), so go to this site to see the pictures and check out the Hot Wheels history. You'll also find links to a couple of other car collecting sites and information on Hot Wheels sets for sale. You can e-mail the Webmaster if you have **Hot Wheels** info you'd like to see on the site.

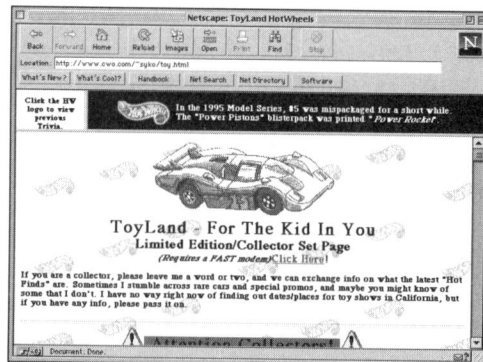

Webville and Hypertext Railroad Company

http://www.he.tdl.com/~colemanc/webville.html

Don't let this site's description of itself confuse you. Although it says it is "the site for the archiving of historical and informational documents and **binaries concerning Railroads, Railfanning, and Model Railroading,**" what it *really* is is a **totally cool** railroading site. It's packed with information for beginners and enthusiasts alike, and it contains neat graphics and a cool layout.

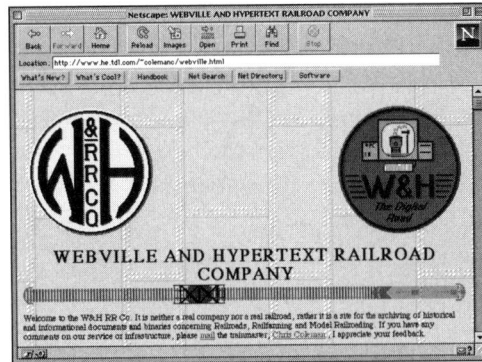

The **various** pages on this site are named for the different railroad places they resemble. For instance, the Front Office is where you'll find railroad discussions, and the Interchange Yard is for links to railroad sites. You might want to start in the Main Yards, though, to read up on a wide variety of railroad-related articles. You'll find information on monorails and locomotives, histories of railroads and railroad companies, and even a list of railroad **jokes**.

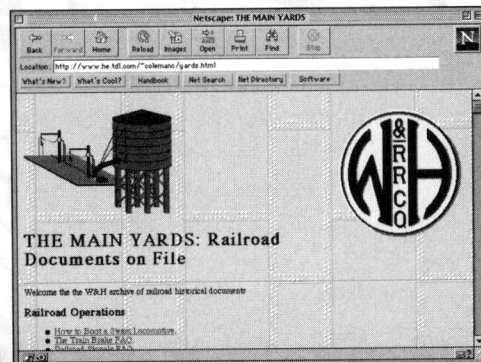

CONTINUED →

http://www.he.tdl.com/~colemanc/webville.html

Test your knowledge of railroad trivia at
the Right-Of-Way railroad multimedia page.
Each month (mostly!) there is a new multimedia
feature here. Links to utilities for your
particular system to view the multimedia
format are here, too. There is also a trivia
question based on railroad signs, signals,
and company affiliations. Can you **solve
the mystery** of the Hued Herald? If you
get it right, you'll get your name posted to
the page!

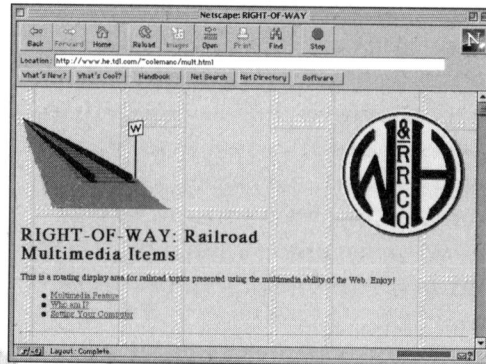

The Narrow Gauge Branches page is an
enormous list of linked topics about
different sizes and scales of **model trains**.
There are definitions of all the major types
of models and links to clubs all over the
world for each kind of railroad model.
Companies that make model railroad
supplies are listed here, too, as are other
model railroad sites. If it has to do with
model railroads, you will find it here. Go
check out the Model Railroad Museum in
San Diego, CA, or find out about building a
scale model of the West Jersey & Camden
Railroad. You'll have to visit this site again and
again to take advantage of all its great resources.

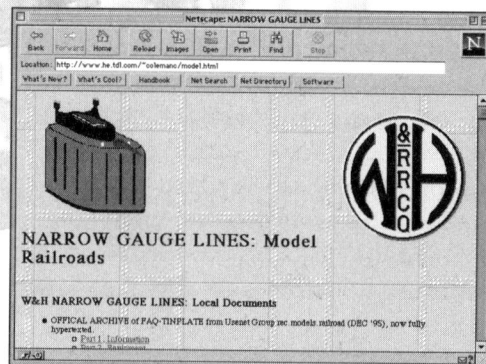

Handicrafts

Aunt Annie's Craft Page

http://www.coax.net/annie/

If you're looking for a project, start here. The activities on this page go from easy and quick to more complicated and time-consuming, but you're sure to find *something* to do. For example, you can make cards, gift bags, and **nifty suncatchers** to hang in your window. If you have a favorite project you'd like to share, send it in to Aunt Annie's Craft Exchange and get it described on the page. And even though new projects are added every week, you can always look at the list of past projects and find one you missed.

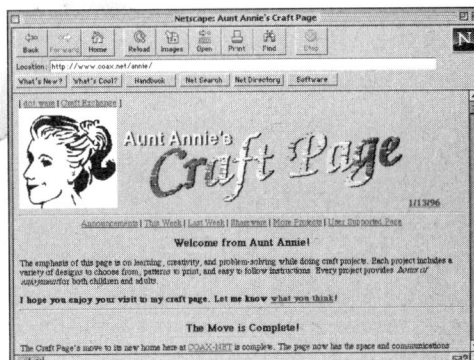

Creativity Connection

http://www.connect2.org/cc/

The Creativity Connection is a terrific resource for craft **ideas** and craft business information. Different types of craft projects are outlined, from **beadwork** to clay to crocheting. You can search a list of craft-related events by state to find out if and when a craft show is coming to your neighborhood. This page also lets you search for craft stores in your area. Everything is here for you to get started on a craft project. **Go for it!**

The Knotting Dictionary of Kannet

http://www.ida.his.se/ida/~jan/knopar.eng.html

Using easy-to-understand rope graphics, this page teaches you every knot you'll ever need to know for **scouting**. Even if you think you know this stuff already, you'll find knots on this page that would tie up even the experts! The instructions on how to tie each knot are simple and often funny; learn the difference between a *knot* and a *bend*. This site describes what you can do with each knot, and it even shows you drawings of what some of the knots look like if you tie them wrong. There's also a link to other **knotty** pages (and you probably thought there was only one).

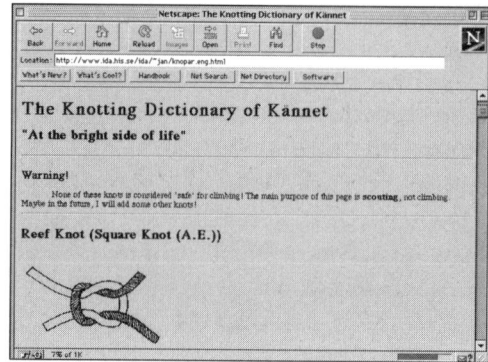

WAY CoOL

Netscape: The Knotting Dictionary of Kannet

Location: http://www.ida.his.se/ida/~jan/knopar.eng.html

The Knotting Dictionary of Kännet

"At the bright side of life"

Warning!

None of these knots is considered 'safe' for climbing! The main purpose of this page is scouting, not climbing. Maybe in the future, I will add some other knots!

Reef Knot (Square Knot (A.E.))

Online rush hours

Getting a slow connection? Try surfing after 5 p.m. (when businesses are closed) and you might get a faster connection.

Alex and Sara's Raptor Page

http://www.csif.cs.ucdavis.edu/~pomeranz/raptor.html

Raptors are the big birds, the birds of prey, and they get their own big page. Look here for fabulous pictures of **eagles, hawks, owls, vultures, and more**. Different raptor centers are linked here; learn about how raptors are rescued when they are injured and how they are released into the wild. The California Raptor Center, a British School of Falconry, and SeaWorld's Birds of Prey pages are just a few of the dozens of places you can go from here. Read reviews of bird books and follow links to conservation and wildlife sites. Whether you already love to watch the **soaring and diving** of hawks, or you want to find out more about what that vulture is doing circling over your backyard, this page has something for everyone.

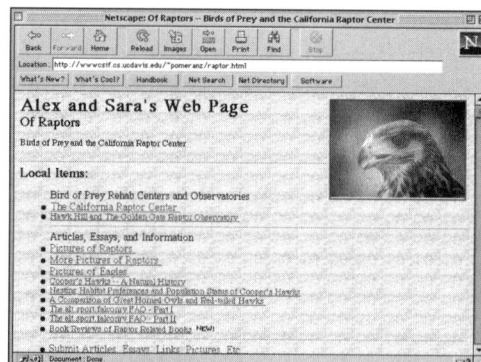

VERu CoOL

Netscape: Of Raptors -- Birds of Prey and the California Raptor Center

Location: http://wwwcsif.cs.ucdavis.edu/~pomeranz/raptor.html

Alex and Sara's Web Page
Of Raptors

Birds of Prey and the California Raptor Center

Local Items:

Bird of Prey Rehab Centers and Observatories
- The California Raptor Center
- Hawk Hill and The Golden Gate Raptor Observatory

Articles, Essays, and Information
- Pictures of Raptors
- More Pictures of Raptors
- Pictures of Eagles
- Cooper's Hawks -- A Natural History
- Nesting Habitat Preferences and Population Status of Cooper's Hawks
- A Comparison of Great Horned Owls and Red-tailed Hawks
- The alt.sport.falconry FAQ - Part I
- The alt.sport.falconry FAQ - Part II
- Book Reviews of Raptor Related Books NEW!
- Submit Articles, Essays, Links, Pictures, Etc.

Birding

http://compstat.wharton.upenn.edu:8001/~siler/birding.html

Bird-watching, or birding, has become a popular hobby, and those who pursue it will tell you there is nothing like it. One birder put up this page devoted to the subjects birders want to know about, like what is going on in the birder world, answers to FAQs, and a Hot List of birds sighted all over the country. This site is constantly being updated, so check the Hot List any time you want to know what **rare and unusual** bird is visiting your neck of the woods. You can post your own sighting, but you'd better be prepared to defend it by knowing all the standard field marks. Checkout the classification page if you're not sure about bird identification markings. You can find links to other birding pages, lists of events and references, and links to the American Birding Association and the Academy of Natural Sciences.

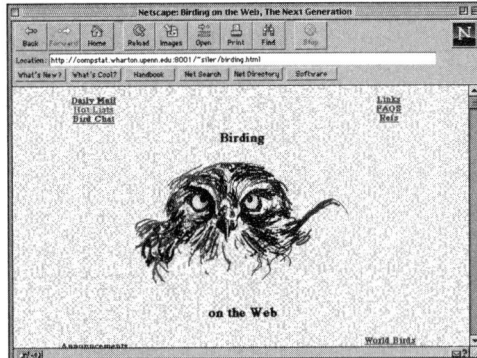

Jason's Snakes and Reptiles

http://www.shadeslanding.com/jas/

Cool pictures of snakes and other reptiles is only the first reason to spend time on Jason's Snakes and Reptiles site. Jason has been a snake fan for more than half his life (he's thirteen now) and wants to share the links he discovered while searching for reptile info on the Web. His list of links will keep you busy for a while! If you're interested in **owning a snake as a pet**, be sure to check Jason's Snake Care page. You'll also want to see the coverage he's gotten on his local news stations and the pictures of his own pet reptiles.

Petscape

http://www.hisurf.com/petscape/

Designed to look like the popular Netscape Web browser's home page, the Petscape index is a Net/pet lover's dream come true. Pets of all kinds show up here, from the usual dogs and cats to ants, rabbits, and, yes, **hedgehogs**. Links have short descriptions of what's on the page, even when it's obvious. What else could be on the Poodle Page but "Poodles! Poodles! Poodles!" Submit your own favorite pet site to be included on the Petscape list.

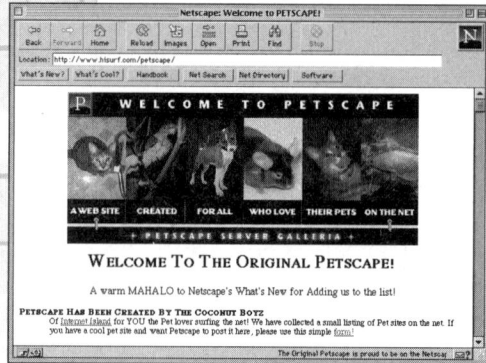

Petnet

http://www.inch.com/~petnet/

Petnet is *the* site to go if you want to see photographs of real pets, or if you want to have your own **dear Fido** included in the picture gallery. Petnet posts (for free!) your cat, dog or bird photos, with a title and your description of your pet. The cute cartoon kitty (or **doggy**, or **birdy**, depending on which part of the site you're on) guides you easily through the slide show. Once you've enjoyed the show, check out the links to other pet sites on the Web.

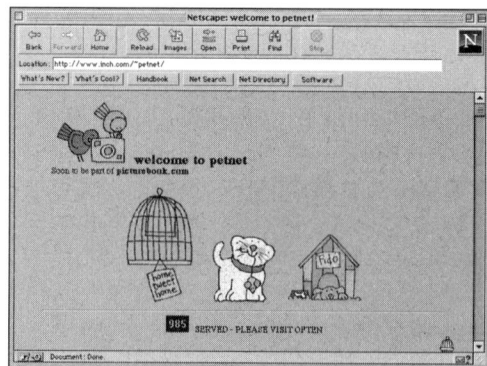

Up At Six Aviaries

http://www.upatsix.com/

This is *the* page for the bird fancier. Start here if you're just getting your first bird, or even if you think you already know everything about your feathered friends. Up At Six has links to all the usual things, like FAQs, classified ads, and bird organizations, but it also has mailing lists you can subscribe to, software on living with birds, and lots of links to other pages that are devoted to birds. There is extra information specifically for **parrot fanciers** and an opinion posting page for bird fanciers who are a little over enthusiastic in their dedication to their birds. You'll definitely want to visit this site many times for all the exciting information it has on it. You can then go to the "**Rate Your Bird Addiction**" quiz to find out if this page has turned you into a **bird fanatic**.

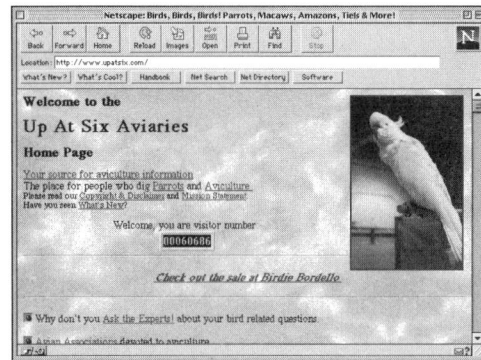

CHAPTER 5

Movies & Entertainment

N o, the Web isn't only about computers! There's also a whole lot of entertainment stuff, including sites for movies and TV, comic strips and comic books, and amusement parks. Check out the sites for your favorite TV shows and movies, where you can find out about new movies (with sound and video clips), look up movie reviews, and read online entertainment magazines. The comics stuff includes comic book publisher Web sites and online review magazines, with information on upcoming comics and release dates, as well as online comic strips (like Dilbert!). See the amusement parks section for links to your favorite parks, rides, and attractions!

Amusement parks

Index – Theme Park and Amusement Park Links

http://www.mcs.net/~werner/parklinks.html

This page from Yesterland is a good list of amusement parks with home pages on the Web. See the sections for Paramount's Great America, Knott's Berry Farm, Universal Studios, and Six Flags. These include links to official and unofficial Web pages with more information on the parks and their attractions. You can also find pages for Theme Park history and **various attractions**, like HERSHEY PARK in Pennsylvania. Visit the Yesterland home page (you can get there from here) for a great history of Disneyland past, and see the big collection of links to other Disney sites on a separate page.

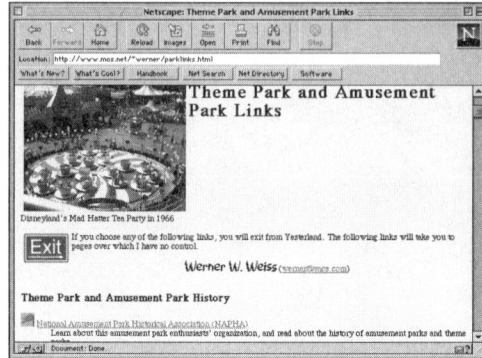

Comics, cartoonists, & comic strips

ComicsWorld

http://www.farrsite.com/cw/index.html

If you like comics, **this is the place for you!** See the News and Reviews sections for great pictures and lots of information on upcoming comics, including artist changes, special issues in the works, new TV shows, and more. There's also a separate page for **new comics releases** and links to other comics resources. ComicsWorld is an independent Web magazine, and it's not hooked up with any comics publisher, so its opinions are fresh and independent.

Reviews give you the scoop on what's good and bad in the **top comics series** and special issues out today. Find out what's happening to your favorite characters (you might be surprised!). It's also a good way to see what's worth buying, for readers and collectors. Special issues and series with limited edition covers can be worth more and sell faster than regular books, and you might need to know when they go on sale so you don't miss them.

So you want to be an astronaut? Check out the Internet Kosmos!

The Net is even in outer space! When NASA has a space shuttle mission going, check the NASA home page at http://shuttle.nasa.gov for a live connection that is out of this world.

Other things to check out here include interviews with top people in the comics world. Top artists and writers tell you how they got started doing comics and what inspires them to come up with their neat books. You might get the inspiration yourself! Then, go track down the links to art and writing sites on the Net (on Yahooligans!), and **make your own comics**. You can also find a lot of Web sites for comic book publishers at Yahooligans!

CONTINUED →

http://www.farrsite.com/cw/index.html

ComicsWorld even has a fun trivia contest you can play, to see how much you know about comics. Do you know which vampire got cured by drinking Spider-Man's blood? There's also a helpful comics shop locator you can use to find out if there's a shop in your neighborhood and where its located. Comics are a lot of fun, and you can get a little deeper into them at ComicsWorld's place on the Web.

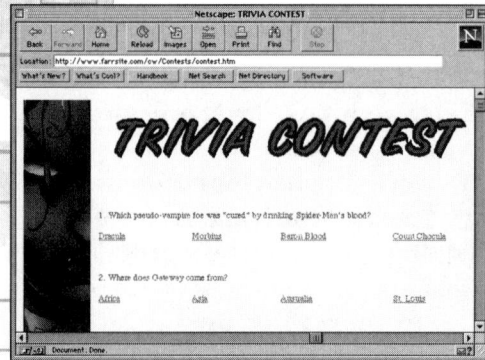

Mike Allred Fan Page

http://www.geocities.com/Paris/2346/

This is the page for fans of Mike Allred, the artist who does Madman Comics for Dark Horse. It's **cool stuff**, and this site has lots of info, including a biography, a comicography (find out what else Allred has done), and an Art Gallery (with plenty of cool graphics!). See the Other Links section for sites on the Web that are related to Madman, including pages from Dark Horse and other comic book companies, as well as reviews, pages for other Madman fans, and a good set of comic-related links.

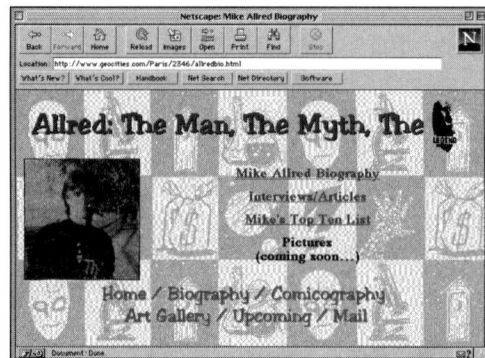

YAHOOLIGANS!

Comic Book Net

http://www.cris.com/~Xenozoid/ComicBkNet.html

This is a great source of information from the comic book industry, including news, reviews, and special feature articles. You can read the magazine online or download it to read later. These guys really seem to have the **inside scoop** on what's coming out, and you can also find a big collection of past issues available from here (so you can look for information on past titles you might be interested in). See the links at the top for connections to cool comic book companies' Web sites that Comic Book Net recommends.

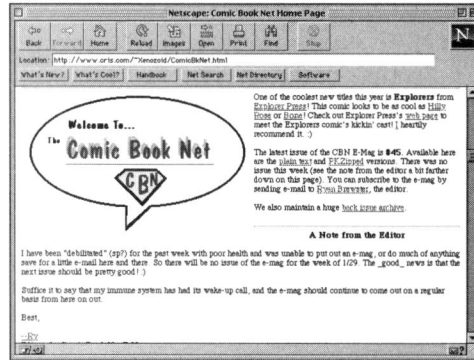

The Fortress of Solitude

http://www-scf.usc.edu/~dsilvers/supes1.html

Okay, Superman fans, this is your place! Find out what's up with that strange visitor from the planet Krypton and the big changes he's been through in the past few years. There are lots of reviews and interviews here and **cool artwork**. Find out the main Superman story arcs, visit the Rogues Gallery (to look in on those **annoying villains**), and check out the links to Superman in the movies and on TV. There's also **comic book price guide** information and links to other DC Comics heroes' Web pages.

You Can with Beakman and Jax

http://www.nbn.com/youcan/

Beakman and Jax give you a great start with **neat science stuff** on their Web site. This is an excellent place to find interesting science experiments (including stuff you can do at home), answers to science-related questions, and ideas for school projects. There are also great space pictures from the Hubble Space Telescope located here. Find out about what's coming up for the Beakman's World TV show and future editions of You Can with Beakman and Jax. It's neat stuff!

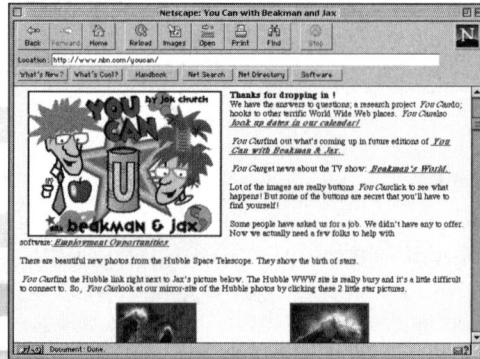

Comics N' Stuff

http://www.phlab.missouri.edu/~c617145/comix.html

This is a megasite to find comics on the Web. They have a good policy: if you can't read the strip in your Web browser, they won't link the site, so you won't waste your time (too many fan pages out there with no content!). The strips and comics are listed alphabetically, with notes on how **frequently** they're updated (daily, weekly, or less). There's also a search engine you can use to look for comics by name and an FAQ (frequently asked questions) for new users that might come in handy. Check out the Comics N' Stuff WebChat link, where you can talk with other comics fans over the Internet!

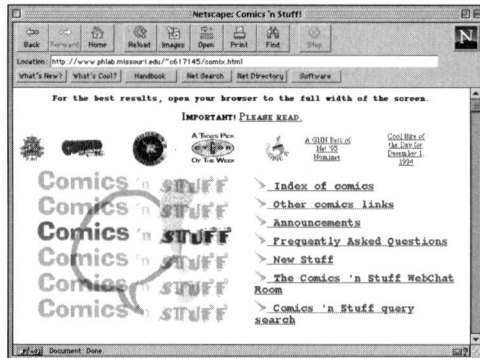

Humor, jokes, & fun

Mr. Potato Head

http://winnie.acsu.buffalo.edu/potatoe/

You'll have lots of Big Fun with Mr. Edible Starchy Tuber Head, the guy who looks a lot like a potato. You can click on different parts and make your own version of Mr. ESTH in the online game, and you can also view funny pictures and animations online. Read the Authorized biography! **See Mr. Edible Starchy Tuber Head's Worst Nightmare!** Don't miss the online PotatoCam section with live pictures from Mr. ESTH's journeys around the country. This place is fun!

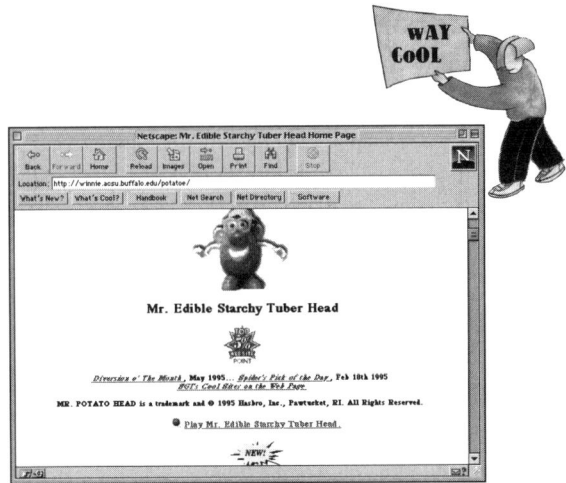

Snax.com

http://www.snax.com/

Find out about that junk food you love right here. Check out all the funny games you can play (can you tell what that crunching sound is?) and interesting party recipes for stuff like chip dips and chocolate-smothered potato chips — yum! You can also participate in an online contest and win snack tins and T-shirts as prizes. There's almost no nutritional value here (your Mom's probably not gonna like this), but the site is very funny. There's also a snack gallery with close-ups of various snack foods (don't forget to feed your computer!)

Magazines

Arbor Heights Cool Writer's Magazine

http://www.halcyon.com/ahcool/home.html

This is one of the better-looking magazines for kids ages 7 to 12. It's produced by the Arbor Heights Elementary School in Seattle and it's filled with interesting articles written by students on many different subjects, including animal stories, historical subjects, and poetry. There's also a section with writing aids for young authors and a good set of links to general subject areas on the Internet that kids can use for writing projects. You can even play a maze game and a puzzle here. **This is one neat site!**

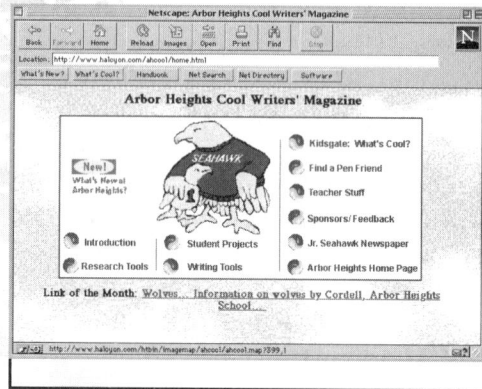

CyberKids

http://www.mtlake.com/cyberkids/

CyberKids is a free magazine by and for kids. The main site features links to the online magazine issues (with kid fiction and reviews), information on a writing and art contest kids can enter (winning entries are published online), and CyberKids Interactive (where kids can post and read messages from other kids). The magazine has a good format, with lots of pictures and artwork. There are also games and **puzzles** you can play here and some free stuff to download.

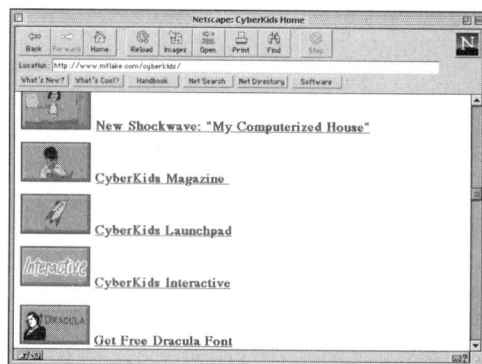

KidzMagazine

http://www.thetemple.com:80/KidzMagazine/

Okay, this is kewl: got it? It's totally produced by and for kids. There are feature articles, video game columns, and reviews you can read, and short fiction, too. You can see who's been around in the **Guest Book** section (and add your own comments), read TV and entertainment news in the Tidbits, and check out a list of the Coolest Web Sites. Look for an expanded version of this site that will include even more articles, reviews, and fiction, and even an online kids' poll.

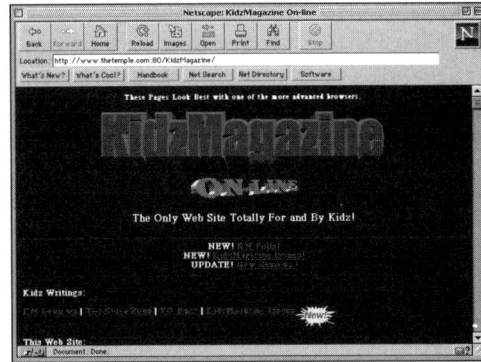

MidLink

http://longwood.cs.ucf.edu/~MidLink/

MidLink is an electronic magazine for the middle grades. It's got a **kid-friendly** look and is actually the result of many ongoing projects from middle schools across the Internet. The interesting subjects include science exploration, environmental awareness, and global peace efforts. See the cool stuff (like design-an-Alien) too! There are also good lists of kids' Web sites picked by kids themselves and links to middle school home pages all over the Internet. There's also information on how your school can get involved in the ongoing projects. Get your teachers interested, and sign up!

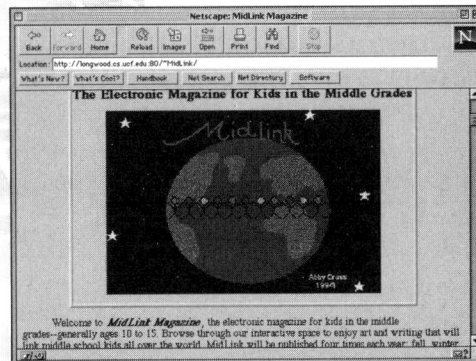

Parents and Children Together Online

http://www.indiana.edu/~eric_rec/fl/ras.html

Parents and Children Together Online is a good place for families to promote reading. Most of the articles and stories are perfect for kids in the 4th to 6th grades, and each one also features a **good** illustration and author info. It's also nice that the articles are linked to other resources on the Internet on the same subject. If you find an interesting story here, you can immediately jump all over the Internet to find a lot more information. There's also an interactive story section kids can join in on, book reviews, and links to other resources for parents and kids.

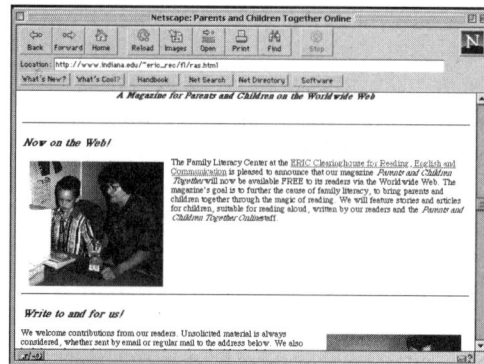

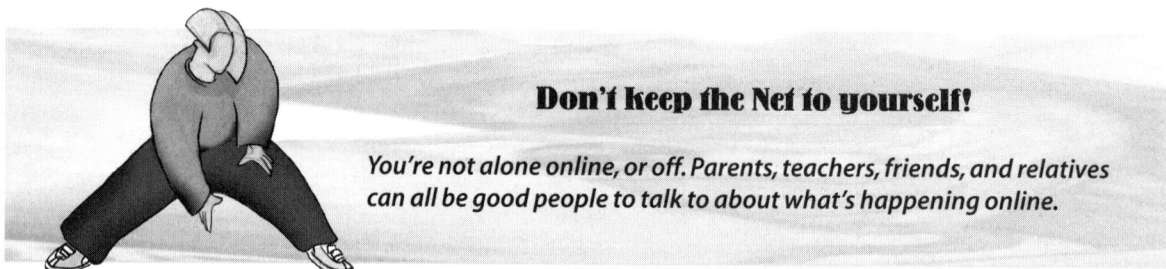

Don't keep the Net to yourself!

You're not alone online, or off. Parents, teachers, friends, and relatives can all be good people to talk to about what's happening online.

Lift Online

http://www.lifted.com/

This is a really cool monthly picture magazine/Web site with a **cutting-edge** style. Read the exclusive interviews with upcoming bands, including sound links (so you can play their tracks while you read!). There are also special features (like "70's Galore," an exposé on the Seventies, complete with **rollerboogie** pictures and a disco sound clip). See the neat restaurant reviews too, with some of the coolest places to eat profiled. Lift Online has a nice layout, so explore and enjoy!

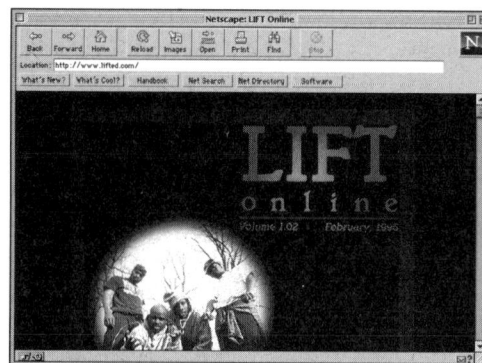

Spank!

http://www.cadvision.com/spank/spank.htm

Spank! is **in-your-face** Youth Culture Online (just like they say they are!). This site has interesting columns and articles on a lot of subjects, including hot bands, cult movies, music, and more. See the Random Taggings section for your chance to **express yourself** (in 25 words or less), and see what others have written (almost as soon as they write it!). Check out the Creative Imaginings section with youth fiction, artwork, and poetry, and also the **Music Words Film** section (with up-front reviews you can use).

Miscellaneous cool sites

PlanetKeepers

http://galaxy.tradewave.com/editors/wayne-pendley/plankeep.html

Find out what you can do to protect your planet because it's the only one you've got. PlanetKeepers provides you with news on the current global environment, including status reports and editorial information, and links to environmental agencies and other resources. Find out how to get involved here, and see how much you know about the state of the planet you'll inherit in the PlanetKeepers Quiz. They also have good tips on what you can do today to help **conserve** resources. This is important stuff, and you'd be wise to pay attention to it.

StreetSpeak

http://www.jayi.com/jayi/Fishnet/StreetSpeak/

Find the hip street talk here and learn how to be **cool**, so you don't come off like a **dinkle farf lamer** (stupid or uncool). Lots of good examples of how to be really hip are arranged here in an index that's easy to use. If **"Hey, man, can you dig it?"** isn't in any more, you and your friends can add your own words and phrases. The site also has handy examples of how the phrases should be used. How you say phrases is also very important, and sound files are mixed in with the listings to help you out.

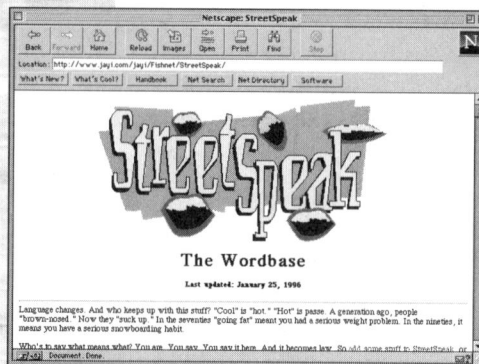

Movies & films

Internet Movie Database (US)

http://www.msstate.edu/Movies/

This is the central movie database for the Internet. Come here if you like movies a lot; you'll find a **ton of information** on your favorite films, actors, and directors. You can look for a film in the search index (by name, year, or type) and you'll then see (usually) a cast list, a viewer rating, and a brief plot summary. Some **films** also have more information, like movie trivia and release dates. What's really neat is that the film cast listing is also linked to the database; just click on a stars' name and you'll get a list of all the films they've starred in, and you can go to the pages for those films from there!

Movie Makers Club

http://www.el-dorado.ca.us/~dmnews/mmguild.html

Check this site out if you're interested in learning how to make your own movies. The Movie Makers Club is especially for kids and it shows you how to **make a storyboard** (this is what filmmakers use to develop the visual elements of a film). This site also includes a sample script that shows how film scripts are supposed to look and how they relate to the storyboard. Also see the links to sites that can show you how to start making short films on your Mac or PC. Ready to write/direct/produce your first movie? There's nothing stopping you from trying it!

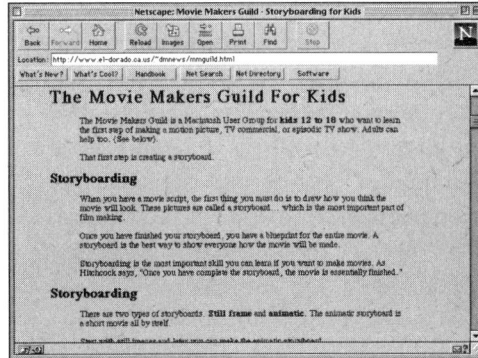

MovieLink – 777FILM Online

http://www.777film.com/

MovieLink is a big commercial site for the latest hot movies in the theaters. Just click on your area on the big map, or enter your zip code, and the site will find out what's playing near you. You can then **check showtimes** and even order tickets online! The site also has posters and movie clips you can download, so you can watch film trailers right on your computer (if you don't have the right software to play these movies, the site will show you where to get it). It's updated frequently, and the new movies are here. Come check it out!

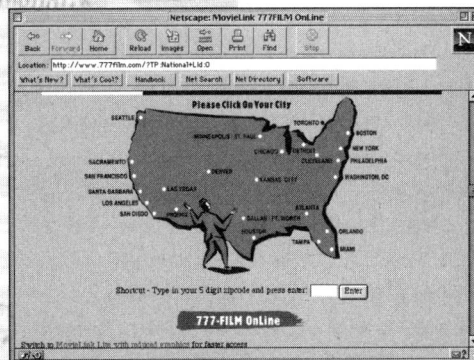

TV Tonight Network and Cable TV Schedules for Tonite

http://www.tvtonight.com

This site has useful information on the shows that are on right now, including capsule reviews of continuing series, TV movies, and specials. Each review is also linked to sites for the show or to the network that it will air on. See the network list to find out **what's playing** at what time and check out the daily highlights. The site is updated constantly, and you should always be able to find out more about what's on right here.

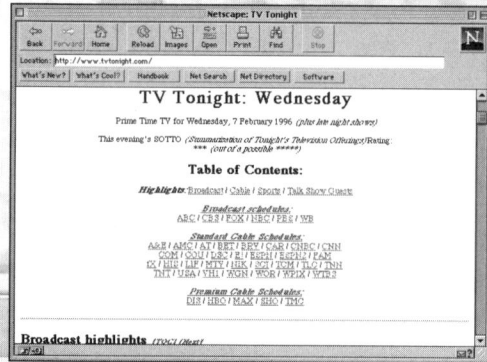

Clarissa Explains It All

http://www.ee.surrey.ac.uk/Contrib/Entertainment/Clarissa/

This site for the Nick show gives a good overview and includes an episode guide, cast list, and general background information. There are also video and compact disc release details, special interviews, and a trivia section. Have you ever wondered where Clarissa's family lives or how she developed over the years? Or are you curious to know the story behind her career plans? For **clues** and answers to these questions, be sure to see the detailed discussions area for more reports and general ramblings from your fellow Clarissa fans. If you like Clarissa, you'll find all the information you need right here!

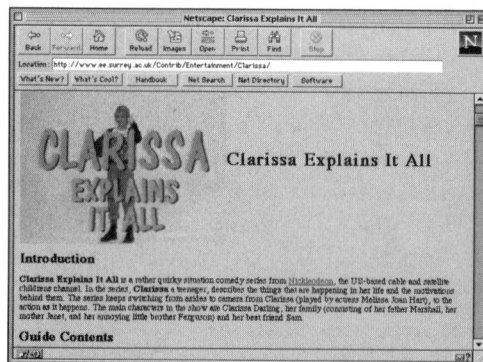

Nye Labs Online

http://nyelabs.kcts.org/

Science Rules! There's no question about it, especially at the Bill Nye The Science Guy site. There's a lot here, including an e-mail center where you can write Bill and read letters from other **science buffs**, online demos and science experiments, and a live Nye Chat room. Nye is the guy who knows science, and this site can show you how much fun it is! NyeLabs Online is a Web site that actually compares to the great TV show. **Jump in!**

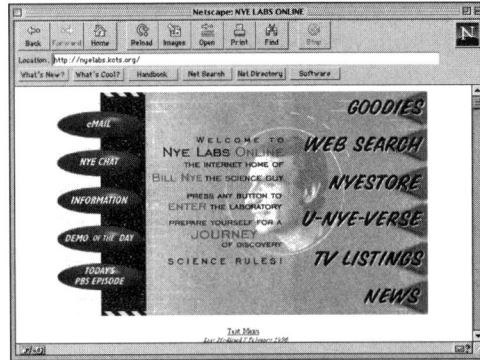

You can go straight to the Goodies section for Sounds of Science, the Photo Album, and the Screening Room, where you can view **animation** and film clips. These areas lead directly to examples of cool science principles in action, so you can see and hear how science works. It's a good way to learn those basic concepts that make up our physical world. You can also **download** the picture and sound files to use later.

CONTINUED →

http://nyelabs.kcts.org/

Try the Demo of the Day for your own **hands-on** science experience. These demos let you try at home the same experiments that Bill does on the show. Each **demo** has a good explanation of the scientific principles behind it and a list of the materials you should have (usually household stuff). The demos also tell you whether you'll need an adult to help out. You can also look up past demos by date and subject.

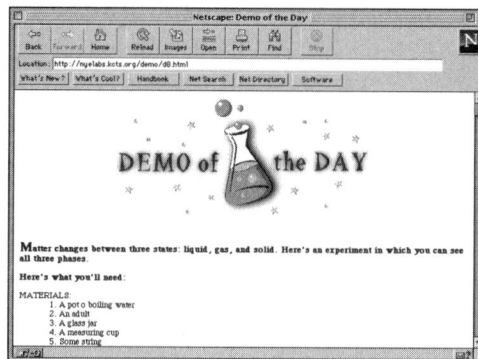

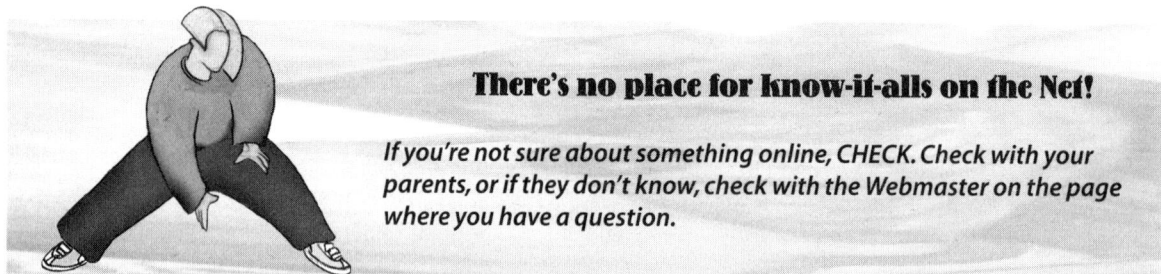

There's no place for know-it-alls on the Net!

If you're not sure about something online, CHECK. Check with your parents, or if they don't know, check with the Webmaster on the page where you have a question.

Take a look at the **U-Nye-Verse** for more information on the Science Guy TV show, which has an episode guide and news on upcoming shows. Also, see the Web search section for a great collection of links to sites in the physical sciences, planetary science, and life sciences. This can be a terrific resource for doing homework and writing papers and for just finding out more about science. Nye Labs Online is a first-rate Web site. **Science does rule!**

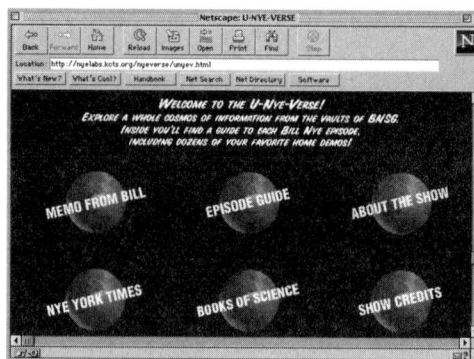

The Farnsworth Chronicles

http://www.edge.net/noma/philo/index.html

Did you know that a 13-year-old farm boy from Utah invented television? Find out the real story of how Philo T. Farnsworth followed his dream and built the first working television system. This site is an excellent overview of the struggles the **great** inventor had to fight to maintain his vision. There are also **great pictures from the early days of television,** including the first systems, trial versions that didn't quite work out, and lots of neat equipment. You won't believe **these funny machines actually worked!**

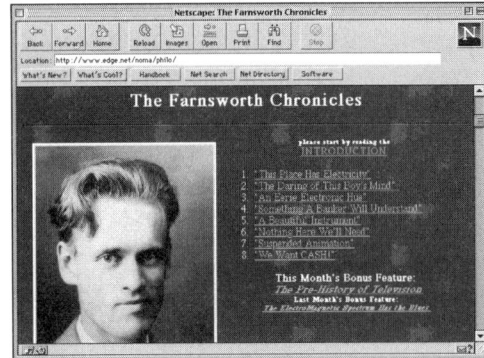

CHAPTER 6

Music

Whether you play an instrument or you just like listening to the radio, a music site out there has your name on it. Tons of bands have official sites, and plenty of fans have put up loving tributes to their favorite musicians. Check out sites that list new music, or go to sites that are all about classical or jazz. Find out about world music, or drop in on a folk festival's page for a touch of down-home music. There's something here for every music lover and for all the music lovers to be.

Music & musician indices

RockWeb Interactive

http://www.rockweb.com/

If you've got a system that can handle it, RockWeb Interactive will rock your world. The top panel on this **visually exciting** page is a guide to the rest of the site, with links to musicians' listings, the chat room, a What's New page, and lots more. One side panel is dedicated to news about rock musicians, reviews of concerts, and interviews. The main panel has links to RockWeb's mailing lists, user surveys, and audio services. Using the RealAudio Player (there are instructions on where you can download it), you can listen to music clips, interviews, and other features. Pretty cool.

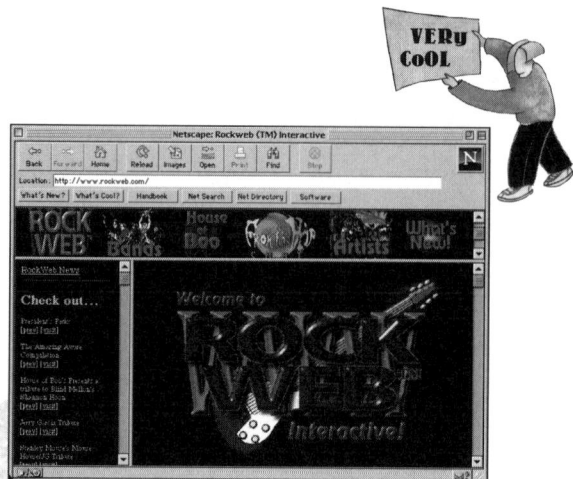

Music Artists Mammoth Music Meta-List

http://pathfinder.com/@@VhEOeVBt6wEAQDuF/vibe/mmm/music_artists.html

If you know the name of the band you're looking for on the Web, check out this alphabetical list of pop, **classical**, jazz, and many other groups. There's even a category for marching bands! Some of the listings have brief descriptions of what kind of music the band plays or where they're from. Sometimes there's a list of what's included on the site This is a well-organized list without a lot of frills, but it's easy to find information here, and you can select lots of different kinds of music. If you find something on the Web that you think should be on the list, drop the **Webmaster** a line.

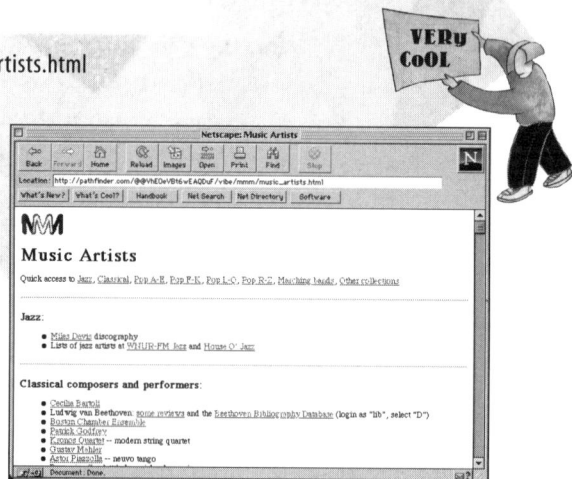

The Ultimate Band List

http://american.recordings.com/wwwofmusic/ubl/ubl.shtml

The **Ultimate** Band List page claims to be the "largest interactive list of music links" on the Web, and it may be right. It's *humongous*, so rather than look at the whole list (your system would probably crash), go to the kind of music you want or to the name of the band you're looking for. File sizes are listed to make it easier for you to decide **if you really want to wait** while the tons of megabytes load! There's another listing by resource, which means if you want to see what's available in sound files, you can go to the list of digitized songs. The add-a-band feature is easy to use, so you can link your band's home page. For a repeat visit, go straight to the What's New list to see who has added the latest bands and information.

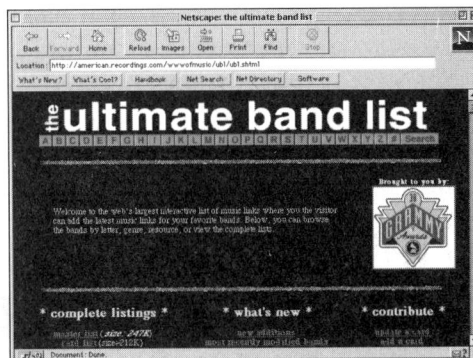

Index—Composers' Pages on the Web

http://molbiol2.anu.edu.au/DixonGroup/Cameron/Composers.html

This site has some useful information, if you can put up with the way it's laid out. Some of the lists are not alphabetized (**Yikes!** You may have to search for a long time), and the links are listed twice (why? no one knows), but there's a ton of information on **famous** and not-so-famous composers from around the globe. Some of the entries on the list describe a little of the content, like whether picture and **sound** files are available at the site. There's even a list of other lists if you don't find who you're looking for here.

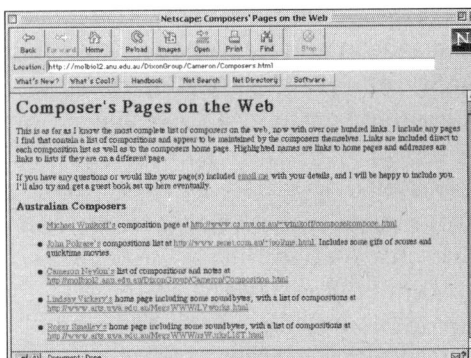

World Band

http://co-nect.bbn.com/WorldBand/CoNECTMusic.html

You're closer to your fellow musicians than you might think! The World Band Project is all about getting students to create live **performances** without actually having to sit in the same room. **World Band** lets kids to **write, produce, and perform** digital music in concert with kids in schools all over the world. Go to this site to find out more about the project, how you can get one going in your school, or simply to learn more about digital and electronic music.

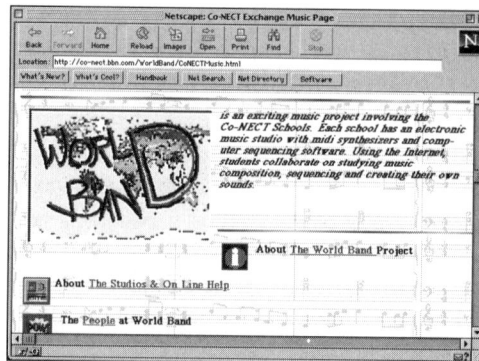

VERy CooL

You can make your own Web page

Kids like you are making their own Web pages. Check them out. You may wind up doing one yourself!

Concerts & general information

Worldwide Internet Live Music Archive

http://www.wilma.com/

VERy CooL

Another concert search service? Sure. The Worldwide Internet Live Music Archive (WILMA) has lots of extra goodies that make it **more** than just a **concert date finder.** For instance, like at other sites, you can search by band, **location,** or date, but here the database includes lesser-known bands and smaller venues. Also available are reviews written by your fellow concertgoers. Add your own opinion! **Sign up to join the Intergalactic Freak Club** and you may win CDs or concert tickets.

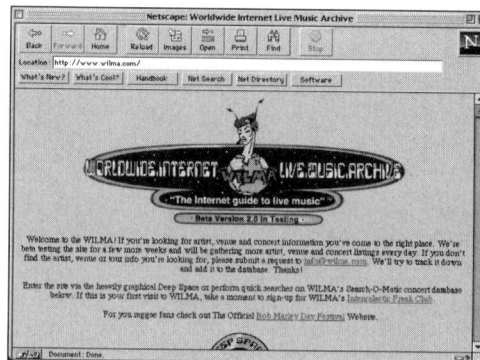

YAHOOLIGANS!

Harmony Central

http://harmony-central.mit.edu/

Harmony Central describes itself as an "Internet **resource** for musicians," and that's exactly what it is, and more. Harmony Central tries to make it easy to find the kinds of **things musicians are looking for** on the Net. Information is arranged under topic headings so you can go straight to what interests you. The headings are described so you can decide if that's what you're looking for before you go there, and every topic has lists of links that take you further into your chosen area. Guitar, keyboard, and **computer-related music** are all well represented, but there's also plenty of other interesting stuff—like bands, drums, music jokes, classified ads, you name it—to keep you surfing around for hours.

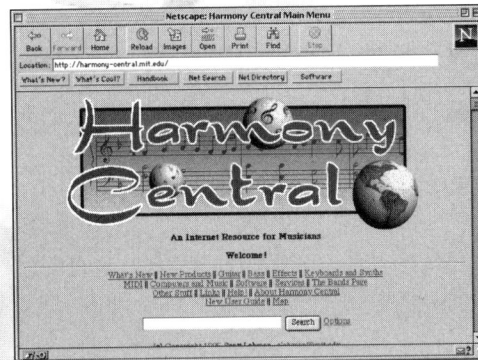

Musician's Web

http://valley.interact.nl/av/musweb/

The Musician's Web plans to link *everything* about music, musicians, and musical instruments. This page features a music **product of the month** from one of the page's sponsors, but that's just the tip of the iceberg. Each area of music gets its own page. For instance, the Drummer's Web has drum news, drum ads, where to look for **different** drums, interviews with professional drummers of **all types** (rock, classical, etc.), and tips for better drumming. Check back if you don't see what you're looking for: **new stuff is added to this site constantly.**

Music styles

The Country Page

http://infoweb.magi.com/~jamesb/country/country.html

Fans of country music will love James' Country Page. It's got great pictures of all the big-name artists. Even the background is a wallpaper of country singers! Click on a name for a brief bio and list of that artist's work to date, or click on the picture for a full-screen shot of the singer. There are links to other fans' pages for different artists and a few pointers to other country sites. Even if you don't know who **Garth Brooks** is, a visit to this site will give you a head start as you begin your exploration of country music.

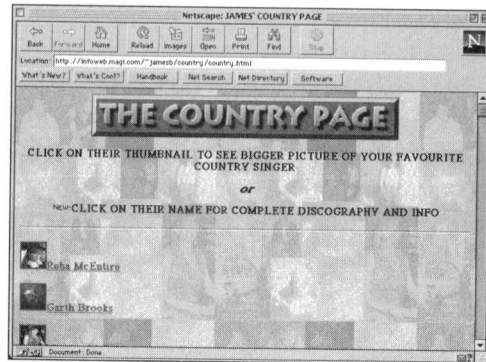

Folk Music Home Page

http://www.eit.com/web/folk/folkhome.html

There's a little bit of everything on the Folk Music Home Page, so stop in and stay awhile. The stuff you'd expect is right up front—like concert listings for **folk festivals,** where to find folk music, links to newsgroups—but if you go a little further you'll find some really cool links. There are **links to guitar music,** interviews with famous folk musicians, and plenty of links to other folk music sites on the Web. Funny songs, jump rope songs, a magazine called **Dirty Linen**—everywhere you turn, this page is full of surprises.

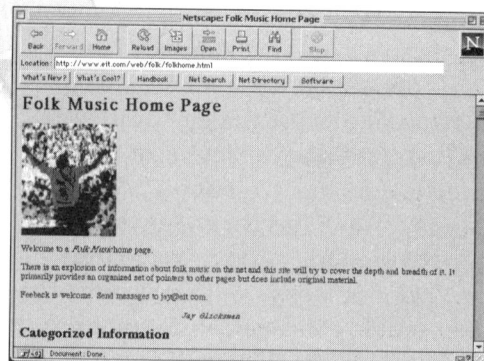

Reggae Down Babylon WWW Homepage

http://www.nyx.net/~damjohns/reggae.html

This index of reggae information has everything the reggae fan could **want** and everything the reggae beginner could **need**. Links take you through a **dictionary of Rasta terms** and FAQs (frequently asked questions), just to get you talking the talk. Then you're ready to explore the reggae sound files, **pictures of reggae artists,** other reggae home pages, and the links to specific reggae artists. Magazines, sheet music, lyrics, even a link to a reggae page in Japan—it's all here. The yellow and green print is a little hard to read, but this page has so much good information it's worth straining your eyes to get at this great stuff.

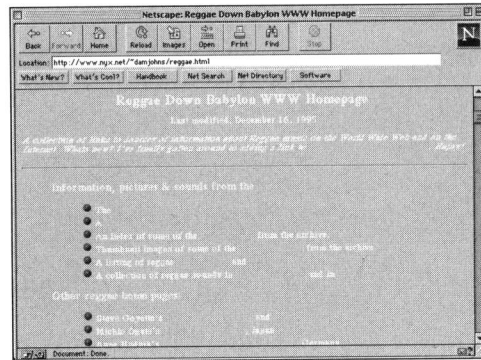

Musical Instruments & lyrics

Clarinet Player's Home Page

http://www.windplayer.com/wp/clarinet.html

If you're surfing the Web when you're supposed to be practicing your clarinet, stop in at this page so you can at least say you were working on your music. Read up on famous clarinet players (jazz and classical), browse the woodwind instruments for sale (or list your own), and find out about how professional clarinet players make a living. Or if you're considering changing instruments, go to the Windplayer home page for a look at the other winds you could be blowing. And then you really should get back to your clarinet.

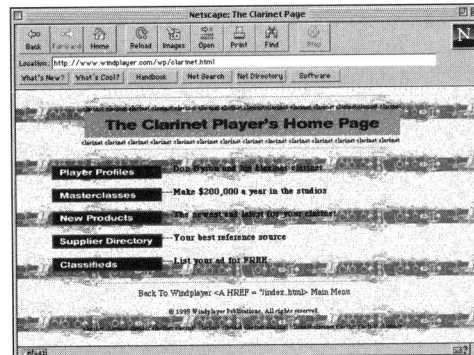

Drums and Drumming

http://www.magna.com.au/~mwilcox/drums1.html

Whether you're just getting into drums, or if you've been beating a rhythm since before you could walk, you need to visit the Drums and Drumming site. This is mostly for those interested in drumming on drum kits (like in a band), but all drummers will find something of interest at this site. Read through the tips of the trade—how to sit, how to hold drumsticks, what kind of drums you might need—and then check out the links. Other drum pages are listed, along with a link to a drum instruction page. Finally, get a giggle at the Drummer Jokes page, and don't forget to take the Drummer's Quiz.

The Drums and Percussion Page

http://www.cse.ogi.edu/Drum/

All kinds of drum and percussion instruments and artists are given space on the Drums and Percussion Page. You'll want to go first to the Announcements page to see what's new, and then on to the list of links. Links are organized by topics, like People and Companies, so you can find exactly what you're looking for. For beginners, there's a list of How-To guides; for veterans, there are grooves you can print out and play on your own drums. There's also a big list of sound files of hand drum rhythms you can download and play. Just make sure your system can play MIDI (Musical Instrument Digital Interface) files.

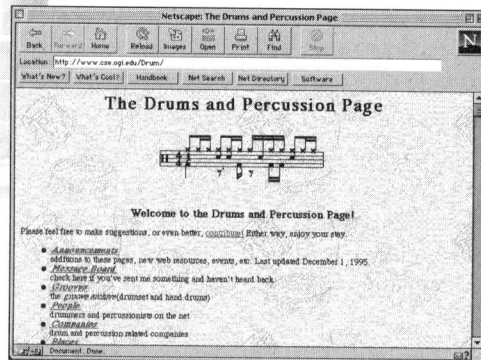

YAHOOLIGANS!

Guitar Net

http://www.guitar.net/

It's all here, everything a guitar **player** or guitar **lover** needs, including guitar music, guitar tips, and links, links, links. Find out more about how guitars are made by visiting The Guitar Maker and learn how best to take care of your own guitar. **Jazz Guitar** Online is linked here; it's a great starting place for anyone interested in jazz guitar. OLGA's link, the On-Line Guitar Archive, is packed with guitar music, lessons, **lyrics**, and even more links. Guitar Net plans to provide some exciting goodies, like a live chat line with guitar players from around the world and free live guitar lessons online. You'll definitely want to visit this site again and again.

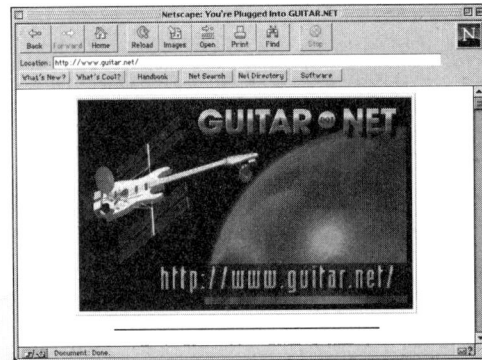

Web Guitar Resources

http://www.wfire.net/~trevize/guitar/

This site is **a good starting point** for guitar resources on the Net. It has plenty of information for beginners, like the FAQ list and the lists of places to buy a guitar, and it has even more stuff for the experienced guitarist. These links will take you everywhere, from software to magazines to places where you can get guitar lessons. Bass guitar links get their own page, as do guitar societies you can join and guitar products you can **buy.** You can search the site for anything specific you might be hunting for, or you can quite happily browse the links for hours, finding things on your own.

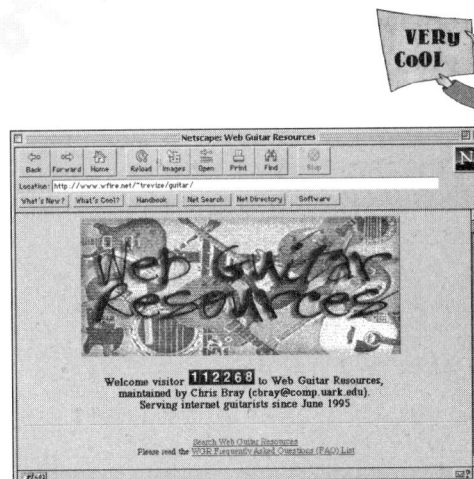

The Piano Page

http://www.prairienet.org/arts/ptg/homepage.html

You may not be in the market for a piano, but that doesn't mean the Piano Page won't have something for you. True, there's a lot to think about when it comes to choosing and buying a piano, but you can also find out about **piano teachers in your area** or who you can call to get your piano tuned. Check out the newsgroups and mailing lists for fellow piano lovers that you can talk to. There's also a good list of more Internet piano resources, including more on **digital music** and **computer software** that helps you compose and write your own piano music.

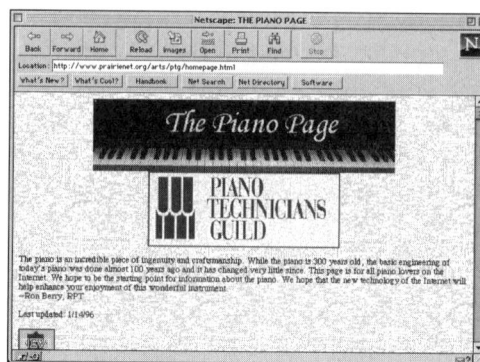

CoOL

Trumpet Player Online

http://www.trb.ayuda.com/~dnote/Trumpet.html

This site has everything for the trumpeter. You'll find **trumpet lessons online**, tips on how to improve your playing, trumpet sound files and even **movie clips you can download.** If you don't play one yourself, you can still read up on famous trumpet players, check out the reviews of trumpeters in concert, and follow the trumpet links to other places on the Web that cater to trumpet lovers. Be sure to visit the **Trumpet Picture of the Month** for a photo and a bio of a famous (or not so famous) trumpet player.

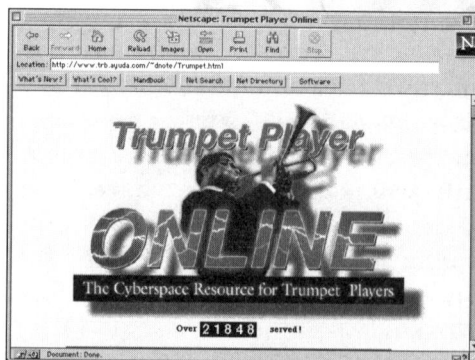

VERy CoOL

Fiddle

http://www.cs.brown.edu/people/gwk/fiddles/Fiddle.html

Fiddle around for a while on the Fiddle page! Different types of fiddle (violin) music are listed and described, with links to sites for Celtic (Irish), bluegrass, jazz, and other styles of fiddle music. If you want more in-depth information on your favorite fiddler, check out the Fiddlers on the Web, a list of links to other violin pages full of fiddle music. Sound files are here and there throughout this site, and you'll find fiddling societies and information on fiddle concerts linked, too. All in all, this site is a terrific resource for anyone who loves **foot-stomping,** hand-clapping fiddle music. So, what are you waiting for? Stop fiddle faddling around and pick up that bow and fiddle!

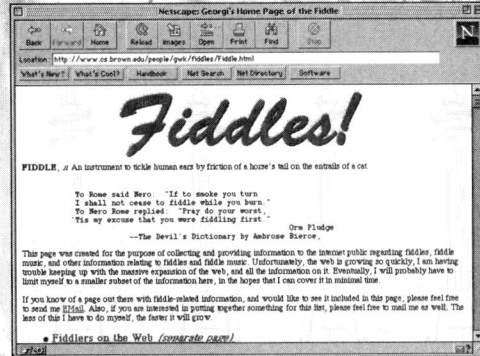

Miscellaneous

George and Ira Gershwin

http://www.sju.edu/~bs065903/gershwin/homepage.html

This is your chance to **meet** and learn about George and Ira Gershwin, two of America's most famous composers and song writers. The Gershwin brothers have written some of the most popular musicals ever performed on stage or screen. Classics like *An American in Paris* and *Porgy and Bess* are reviewed along with the Gershwins' entire body of work. CDs of Gershwin music are listed, and there are links to biographical information, memorable quotes, and pictures. If you care at all for American musicals, you need to **spend some time** getting acquainted with George and Ira Gershwin.

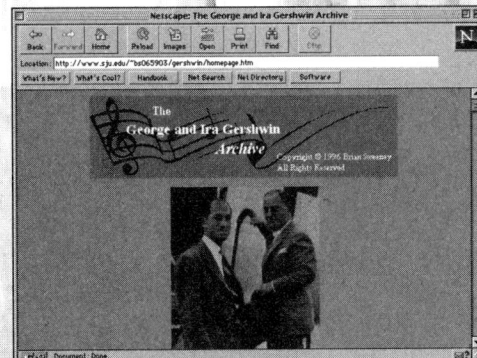

Kerry's List of Marching Bands

http://www4.ncsu.edu/eos/users/k/klsmith2/mosaic/bands.html

Kerry's List of Marching Bands is an index of many of the marching bands that maintain a Web presence. You'll find serious precision marching bands here, but you'll also come across **"scramble bands"** that perform more for fun than for prizes. Be sure to check out the **World's Worst Marching Band!** If you have a favorite band that you don't see listed here, you can get it added. Even if your band doesn't have a home page, you can get it listed here by filling in the form.

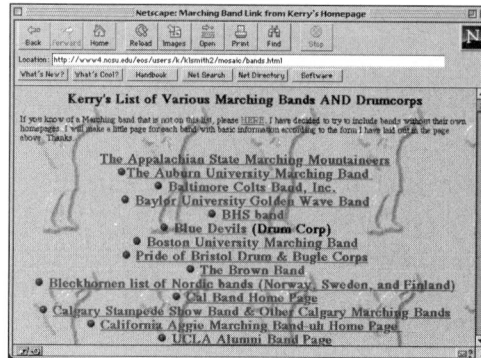

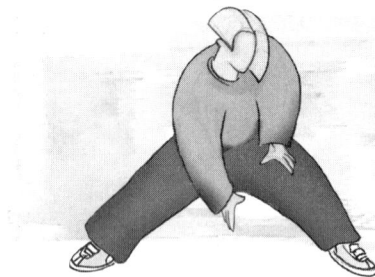

CoOL

Patience is genius!

Don't get frustrated. The Internet is a huge place, and you won't be able to see it all in a hurry. Take your time, see a few things, and then come back another day.

Music Notation and Music Notation Programs

http://www.scubed.com/Staff/O-Neill/

This site does one thing and one thing only, but it does it pretty well: it compiles information on programs that **help users write music on a computer.** The Webmaster has a very strict policy of not reviewing the products or expressing a personal opinion about them. There is, however, a list of helpful questions and answers for anyone getting started in musical notation on their computer and further information on prices and availability of the software.

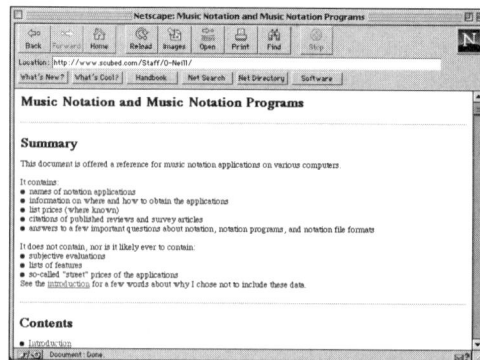

VERy CoOL

YAHOOLIGANS!

Music Video Resource Page

http://www.well.com/user/mdg/FEED/Video_Feed.html

The Music Video Resource Page is for people who enjoy watching music videos and for people who are interested in **producing** music videos either for their own band or for someone else. Up-to-the-minute news and press releases about video-related subjects are available, as are links to other sites for music video. There's a long list of video clips you can download and plenty of lists of resources for producing and enjoying music videos.

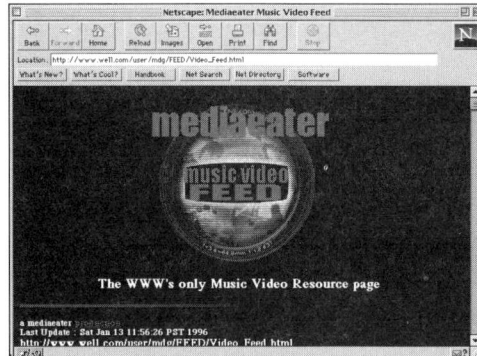

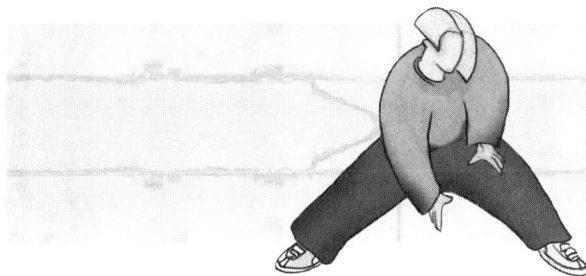

Crack the world in a nutshell— through the Web!

The Internet is connected all over the world. Surfing the Web can really give you a global perspective!

Young Concert Artists

http://www.arts-online.com/yca/

If you need a reason to get serious about your music, go to the Young Concert Artists site for inspiration. Through international auditions, YCA selects and sponsors a few new musicians every year. Find out what it takes to be a **world-class** cellist or pianist; look in to taking classes with YCA selections or going to one of their concerts. Remember, this year's winners include a 14-year-old violinist!

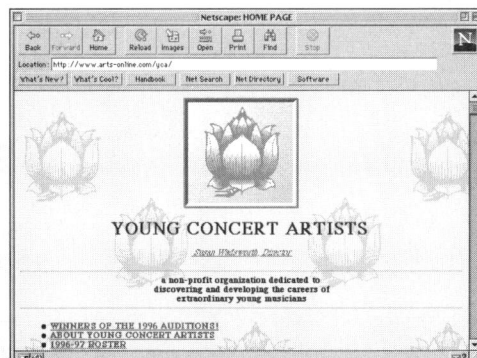

CHAPTER 7

News & Reference

If you're interested in what's going on in the world around you, you need to know the news. Guess what? The Web has a whole lot of online newspapers and news services you can use. Get the latest current events, sports, and entertainment news right here, complete with pictures and sound files. You can even make your own custom Web newspaper and publish your own news stories on the Web! See the reference section if you need help with your writing or if you want to look up something interesting—it has links to useful online dictionaries, translators, and electronic libraries.

Calendars

Literary HyperCalendar

http://www.yasuda-u.ac.jp/LitCalendar.html

If you're into books, you'll enjoy this site. It has a **big calendar** for the current month and includes information on literary events that happened on those days in the past. Just click on the date and you'll get a list of events in literary history arranged by year. It's a nice-looking site, and they'll be adding more ways to **look up individual months** and events soon.

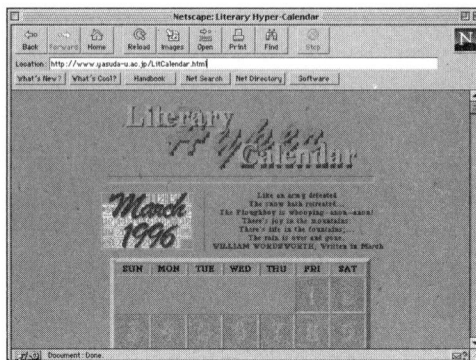

The hotlist situation

Most browsers let you set up different hotlists or bookmark lists. Keep your math sites separate from your favorite rock group sites!

Calendar Information Page

http://www.panix.com/~wlinden/calendar.shtml

Check out a whole lot of different calendars at this site along with **what happened on this date in history.** There are links to calendar and time information from all over the world and **beyond** (try the links to views of the planets in their current orbits)! You can also check your horoscope here, read up on world population reports, and look for the **ever-scary** National Debt Clock (showing how much the U.S. owes other countries, a bill *you'll* have to pay in the future).

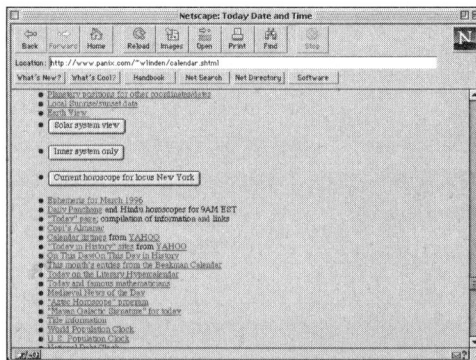

YAHOOLIGANS!

Dictionaries & words

Acronym List

http://curia.ucc.ie/info/net/acronyms/acro.html

Tired of all those confusing computer terms, the ones you run across whenever you surf the Net? Check out this site! You can look up difficult terms and get a clear answer. You can also look up a list of acronyms (funny names made from the first letters of words) and see what they stand for (like ROTFL means "rolling on the floor laughing" in an e-mail message). The great part is that you can add your own terms to the site, making the list even bigger!

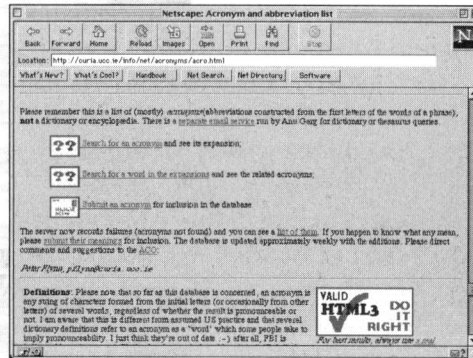

Listing of Acronyms, Abbreviations, and Definitions

http://www.umiacs.umd.edu/staff/amato/AC/main.html

Go to this site to find lists of confusing Internet terms and abbreviations that you can look up just by scrolling down the pages. It's split between technical and nontechnical sections for an easier search. There's also a section that explains what different parts of an Internet address mean (for example, you can see what country a Web site is located in), and there's a short section of Latin abbreviations. Improve your NetSpeak here!

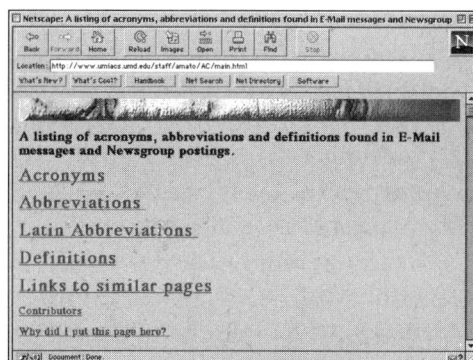

The LOGOS Dictionary

http://www.logos.it/query.html

Parlez-vous français? This is a helpful foreign language resource that can really help you out with those strange words that people speak in other countries. Just enter a word in English and you can see possible matches in Italian, Russian, French, German, Spanish, Chinese, Turkish, Dutch, Norwegian, Portuguese, Swedish, Finnish, **Hungarian**, Czech, Danish, Greek, or even Latin. You can also enter a word in one of these languages and see the matches in English (and in other languages, too). More words and languages are added all the time, so this site should keep getting better!

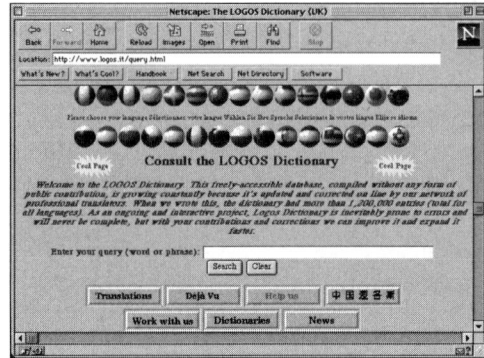

Hypertext Webster Interface

http://c.gp.cs.cmu.edu:5103/prog/webster

A dictionary is where you look up the hard words, and *Webster's Dictionary* is one of the best. **This site lets you look up words right over the Internet.** Just type in your word, and you'll get a short explanation of what the word means. Even **better**, each word in the explanation is also linked to the dictionary. There's also a **direct link to a thesaurus page** for your word, where you can find a list of words that mean the same thing or close to it.

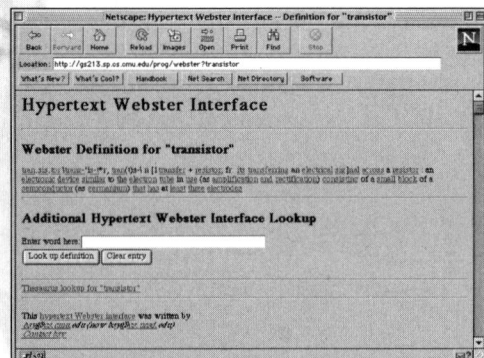

YAHOOLIGANS!

Online Rhyming Dictionary

http://www.cs.cmu.edu/~dougb/rhyme.html

Need a rhyme in time? This site's just right! Don't think you're a nerd, just enter a word! It gives you a list that shows what you've missed! If you're **writing a poem**, this place will show 'em. For words you submit, some rhymes will emit. Each rhyme is distinct with a **definition** that's linked. If you need to move a song along, this place can help you find words that belong. You don't have to be shy, just give it a try!

American Sign Language Dictionary

http://home.earthlink.net/~masterstek/ASLDict.html

The American Sign Language (ASL) is the language used by many of the hearing-impaired. **It's a language that lets you communicate with hand and body movements.** The basic alphabet and number system are described here, along with a lot of commonly used words and phrases. This site has some good pictures that explain some of the more **complex movements.** Use the alphabetical index to jump between sections, and pretty soon you and your friends will be Signing!

Main Sanitary Nag (Anagram Generator)

http://www.infobahn.com/pages/anagram.html

Jumbled-up words (anagrams) can make fun phrases, and this place **does it for you!** Just enter your name (or any other word) and hit the Mama Gear Sank (Make Anagram) button—you'll get a list of fun word combinations. You can also limit the number of words to use in the phrase it makes up. The results are mostly nonsense, but you'll be surprised at what it can come up with! Did you know that "homework" can become "work me, 0h!"? And remember, **Rave Same Grin Lane!** ("Anagrams Never Lie!"—well, hardly ever!)

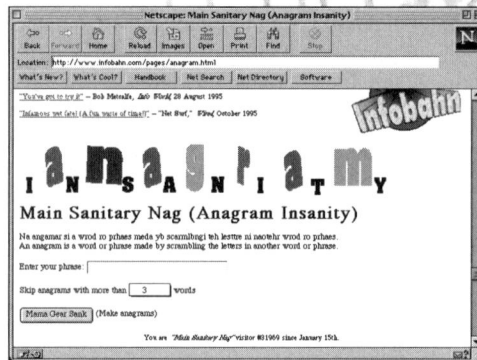

A Friend In Need Is "De Ennid Neirfa" Backwards (Palindromes)

http://www.infi.net/~rvance/plndrome.html

Palindromes are phrases that are the same spelled backwards or forwards, such as **"Flee to me, remote elf!"** These can be a lot of fun to read and to make yourself. Check out these Web pages for general palindromes (ordinary ones like "a man, a plan, a canal—Panama!" and others that are a little bit weirder) and **Palindromatic Art** (plays and poetry in the frontwards-backwards style). You can also add your own phrases to the site (they're hard to make up, but fun to try!). A Fool, A Tool, A Pool; LOOPALOOTALOOFA!

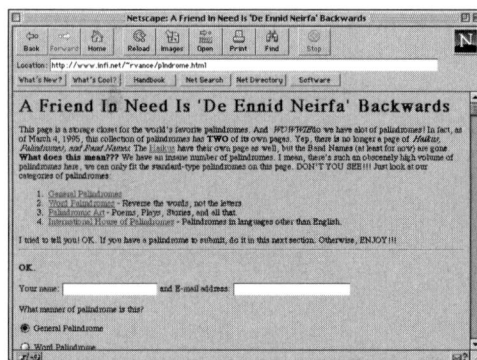

YAHOOLIGANS!

WordNet Vocabulary Helper

http://www.notredame.ac.jp/cgi-bin/wn.cgi

"WordNet is an on-line lexical reference system whose design is inspired by current **psycholinguistic theories** of human lexical memory." Huh? We know this sounds really weird, but you can get lists, definitions, and different ways to use words and short phrases through the WordNet Vocabulary Helper. Check out the hypernyms, holonyms, **meronyms,** and coordinate terms for your word! No, we don't know what those terms mean either, but the cool word lists that pop up on the screen under those categories really hold a lot of information on words you look up!

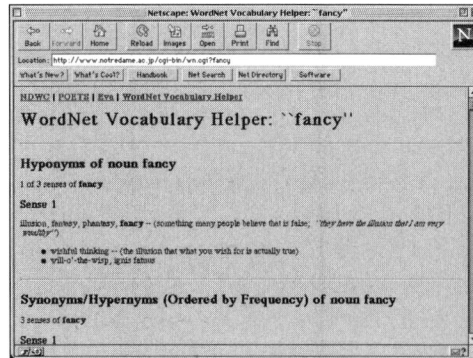

Roget's Thesaurus Search Form

http://humanities.uchicago.edu/forms_unrest/ROGET.html

A thesaurus is a reference book where you look up words that have the same or similar meanings as other words. You can use a thesaurus to help you expand your vocabulary, impress your friends, and make the reports and stories you write more interesting. This place lets you search for words with the same meaning just by entering the word or by looking at a list of subjects (headwords). **You'd be surprised** at what a thesaurus can do for your writing, and this online thesaurus will work wonders!

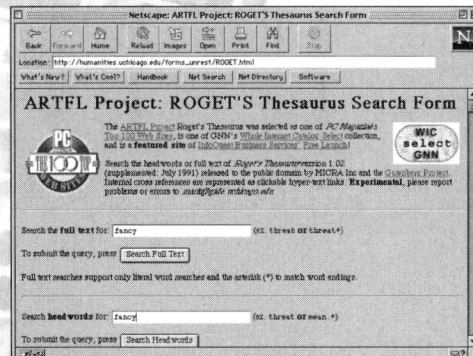

Libraries

Library of Congress

http://www.loc.gov/

The Library of Congress is one of **the world's best libraries,** and it has a great site on the Web. You can find sections for General Information (get tips for visiting the library if you're in Washington and find info on library publications), Government, Congress and Law (search for government and legal information), Research and Collections Services (browse the Library's **historical collections and online** Reading Rooms), and Events and Exhibits (find out about online exhibits).

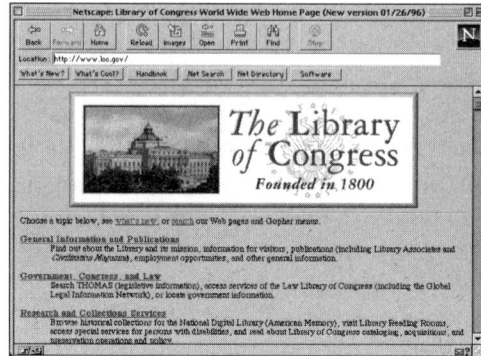

The General Information and Publications section also has documents on the history and purpose of the Library of Congress, including *Jefferson's Legacy: A Brief History of the Library of Congress* (yep, it was Thomas Jefferson's idea!) and a report from the Librarian of Congress. Check out **25 of the questions people ask most** about the library (read this first!) and telephone numbers for visitor information.

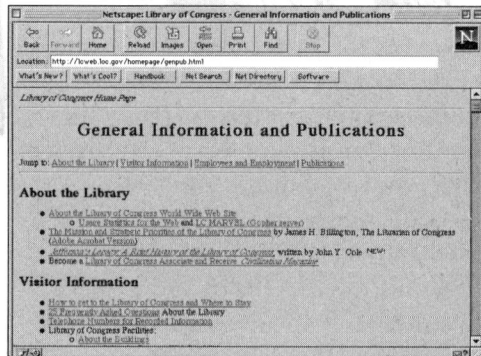

YAHOOLIGANS!

Dig right in to the federal resources in the Government, Congress, and Law section. This is where you can search big databases for all kinds of government information. The law is what makes the country tick, and it's a good idea to find out what it's all about even at your age. You can also find government resources for info about different federal agencies, like the Justice Department and the Military, arranged by Library subject specialists (the people who **know** this stuff the best).

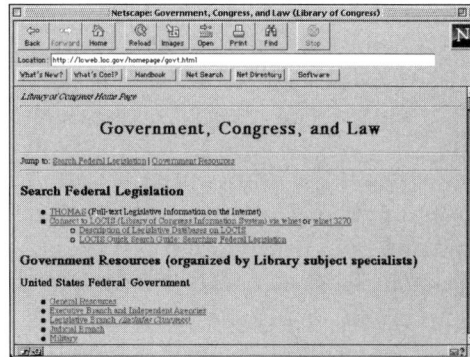

The Research and Collections Services section **has the most Web-based information** at the Library of Congress. That means there's a lot you can see here in your Web browser, including historical collections from the National **Digital** Library's American Memory project and studies on America from the Federal Research Service. You'll also find reference materials (info on how to use the Library for research and frequently asked reference questions) and special online Reading Rooms. Check out the Prints and Photographs Room, the American Folklife Center, and a good collection of links to Newspapers and Current Periodicals.

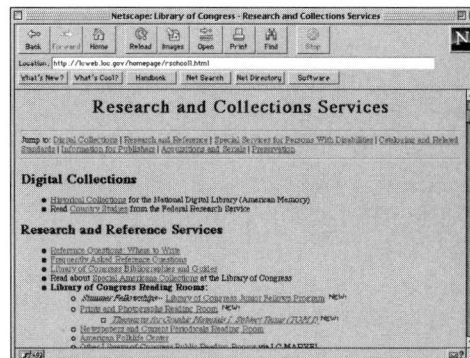

Internet Public Library

http://ipl.sils.umich.edu/youth

The **Internet Public Library** (IPL) has sections just for kids your age! Go straight to the Youth section to find online story hours, book reviews, science and math answers, and children's writing contests. You can even write to kids' book authors and illustrators here (send e-mail to people like Jane Yolen and Robert Cormier). For older kids, try the Teen section, too. While you're at the IPL, you can also check out the Reference section, the exhibit halls, and the Reading Room for special Web books, book reviews, Internet resources, and more.

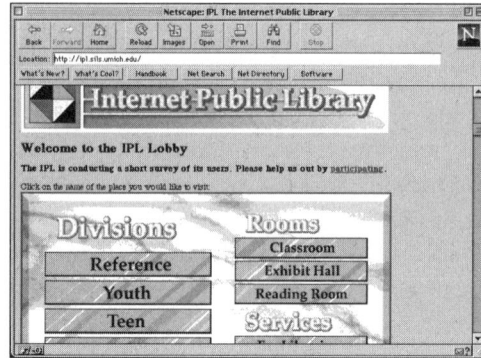

Miscellaneous sites

The Quote Archive

http://apsc7.rescomp.arizona.edu/~ollisg/quote/

Quotes are snappy sayings that other people have made up or fun bits from movies and TV. This place lets you look up any subject for a hip quote that relates to it. You can pick your quotes from a lot of categories (like computers, history, **literature**, movies, TV, music, politics, sports, or even Star Trek!). Also, if you know the author of a quote or you want to get a list of all the quotable things a person has said, you can look them up here.

Nobel Prizes

http://mgm.mit.edu:8080/pevzner/Nobel.html

A Nobel Prize is **one of the highest honors a person can receive,** and this award is given to **high achievers** in literature, medicine, economics, physics, chemistry, and peace. This site describes the prizes, tells you about the new winners, and lists past awards and the people who got them. It's something to strive for, and it's interesting to see what the Nobel Foundation thinks is high achievement "for the **benefit of mankind.**" If you want to see the reverse side of the Nobels, try the link to the IgNobel Awards (given by the Annals of Improbable Research to the dummies of science whose achievements "cannot or should **not** be reproduced").

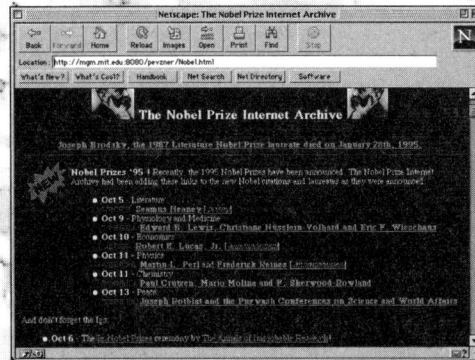

News & reference

Knut's News-Links

http://www.carleton.ca/~kmenard/news.html

This site provides a basic list of newspapers and news services you can get over the Internet. **But what a list!** Lots of links for countries ranging from Australia to Zimbabwe and points in between are here, plus an alphabetical list of newspapers by name (better have your foreign language skills handy, not every paper is in English!) and a new sites section. Check out the Sports section for links to **worldwide sporting news.** There are also links to monthly and weekly news publications along with cool zines (electronic magazines).

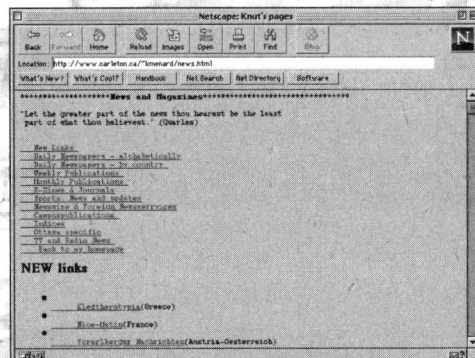

Media-Link

http://www.dds.nl/~kidon/media.html

Real Media on the Real Web! This is a good index to magazines and newspapers on the Web, in easy-to-use sections. They're arranged by country and town, with a separate page for the huge number of U.S. newspapers. You will also find a lot of listings for **TV stations** and **networks**, **film studios**, and radio sites. You'll be surprised at how much of the world is covered! Check out the small flag icons for each country section (can you match up the countries with their flags?).

TV on the Web

TV shows and movies have some really cool Web pages. Your favorite show may already have a fan club on the Web!

The Nando Times

http://www2.nando.net/nt/nando.cgi

Nando is neat-o! **The folks at the Nando Times have gone to a lot of trouble to make a really cool Web news site.** Just click on the pictures to go to current news sections on current events, sports, and politics in America and around the world. It's updated every day, so the news is fresh. You can also go straight to sections covering entertainment news, health and science issues, and technology. Don't forget to check out the Sports Server for lots more sports info from your favorite teams.

YAHOOLIGANS!

Newsroom Resource Guide

http://www.evansville.net/courier/scoop/

Let Scoop Cybersleuth, the Internet's ace reporter, take you on a tour of the **hot news sites on the Web!** There are links to interesting stuff going on right now, like the Telecommunications Law. This site has all the words to the Telecommunications Law. (This is the law that could limit your rights to free speech on the Internet, so **you better know about it!**) You can also go to sections that will help you look for **specific** information, with links to sites in areas like federal, state, and local government, environmental issues, and law enforcement. Don't forget to check out the Education and Children's sites section for **a lot of cool kid links** to gamer sites, online museums, and more.

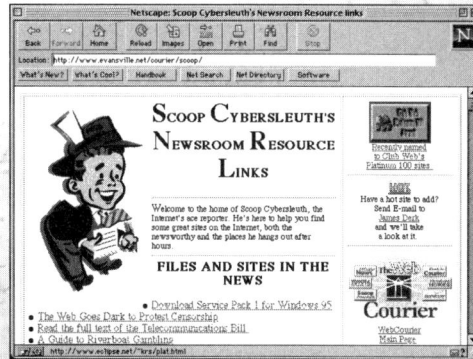

News Search—The Internet Sleuth

http://www.charm.net/~ibc/sleuth/news.html

Here's another cool way to get news from the Web. The Internet Sleuth has lots of links to news services and newspapers. **All you have to do is type in the subject you want to read about,** click the Search button, and you'll get a list of good news articles. Newspapers linked here include the *New York Times,* the *Daily Telegraph* (from London), the *San Francisco Chronicle,* and the *Boston Globe.* Going straight to the news sources is a good idea, and you can also search news services like CNN and the Federal News Service for info.

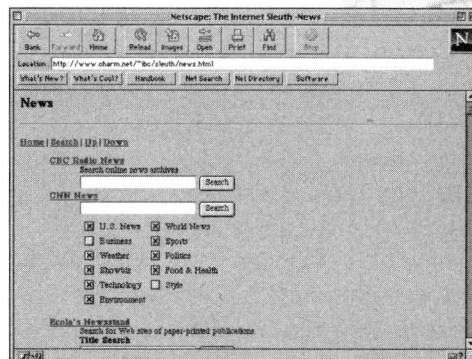

Small Hours/News

http://www.aa.net/~rclark/news.html

This is yet another newspaper/news service index for getting a lot of good current information from sites all over the U.S. and the rest of the world. You can find links to stories from big news agencies like Reuters and CNN, news updates from the Red Cross and the **Environmental** News Network, and UN disaster reports. The newspaper index is listed by state and city, with direct links to back issue archives and local search pages **(to your hometown classifieds, for example).**

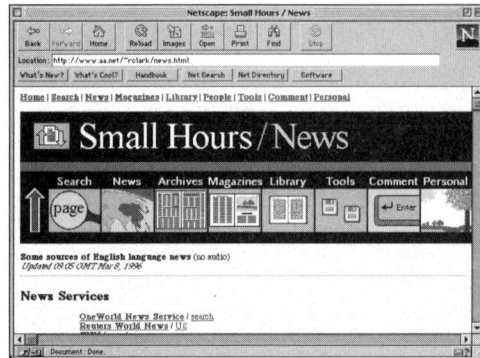

United States Information Service

http://www.usia.gov/usis.html

Want to find out more about the U.S.—its policies and its history? Come right here for the official word. The USIS site has information on issues and events affecting Americans, including **background information** on stories in the news right now, info on educational and cultural exchange programs, and research links. Do you want to know more about U.S. history and where this country came from? You can find a good section on it right here. **Check out the Special Events section** for more info on upcoming elections, nuclear test ban treaties, and foreign policy plans.

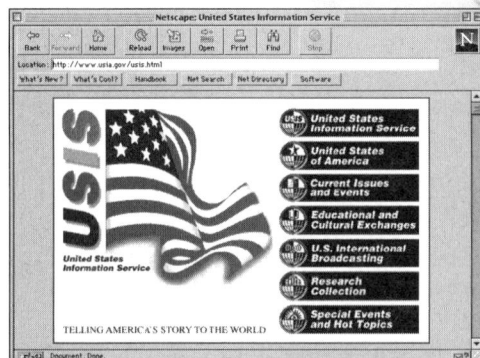

WWW Library, News Resources (International Affairs Network)

http://www.pitt.edu/~ian/Resources/iat-news.html

Stop here for links to interesting international news resources, directly from the countries themselves and major news agencies. This is where you can **dig up information on what's happening** on the world scene. See links for the China Digest, News on India, German news, and Russian affairs. If you want to know more about how the U.S. deals with the international community, see the links to U.S. foreign policy articles and the **Voice of America** international radio information. **If you want to see something really scary,** check out the links to the Military and Arms Transfer and Nuclear Proliferation News digests.

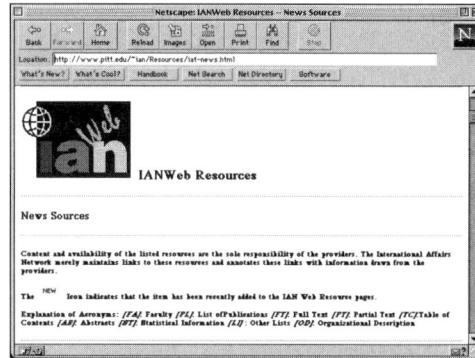

Politics & social studies

News and Current Events—Social Studies

http://www.execpc.com/~dboals/news.html

This site is part of the History and Social Studies page **for K-12 teachers,** and it's also a great news reference **for kids.** It has links that are grouped around specific events (like Bosnia, current elections, and **political assassinations),** with clear explanations and pictures. There's also a huge amount of news source links from all over the Internet, including newspapers, news services, and research organizations. This site does a good job of explaining the links in a clear way. **Go gather some info!**

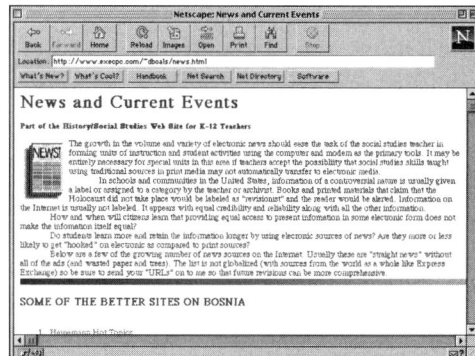

PoliticsUSA

http://www.politicsusa.com/

In America, **we live in a democracy,** and it's important to see how it works. In our political system we elect other people to represent us. This site shows how our government operates and what influences it. Check out the sections covering current elections, campaign news, and **hot political issues.** Pull on the voting booth lever to take part in a daily vote on a political issue. There's even a section where you can check out what U.S. politicians have voted on in the past, so you can see if you like what they're doing.

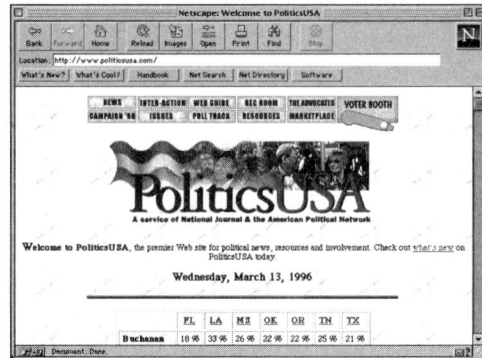

Scout it out!

Scout troops and Councils are on the Web! Check them out for info on upcoming events, online talk, and virtual cookie sales.

School sites

International WWW School Registry

http://web66.coled.umn.edu/schools.html

A lot of schools have their own Web sites, and this is a good place to look them up. **Jump to schools in your area by clicking on a big state map.** The sites are listed by city and will point you to cool student newspapers, **computer clubs,** creative writing classes, and **general school information.** Each school runs its own site, so you never know what you might find, but most of them are pretty interesting! You can also look up schools in other countries and add your own school site to the big list.

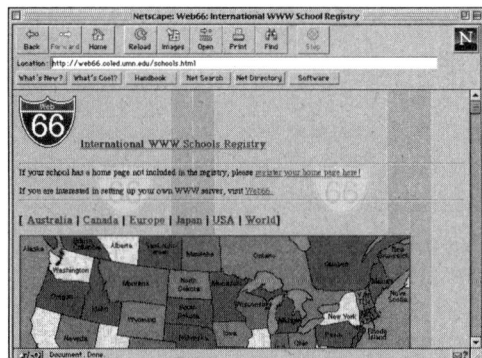

Student newspapers & organizations

International Student Newswire (ISN) KidNews

http://www.vsa.cape.com/~powens/Kidnews3.html

Want to write your own news stories, book reviews, and personal essays? This Web site will publish them for the entire world to read! You can write about stuff from several categories, including news and features, profiles (write about **a famous person in history** or someone you know who's really cool), **sports,** creative writing, and reviews (tell the world what you think about the last book you read or movie you saw). Go straight to the Submit Writing section to find an easy-to-use form you can use to send your story to the site. You can also **read all the different stories** that other kids are writing, right here.

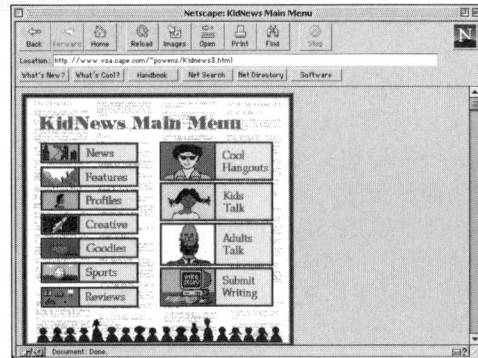

On-Line High School Student Publications

http://eb.journ.latech.edu/Schol_Journ/HS_pub_web.html

Want to see what the kids in higher grades are doing? Check out this list of high school (and some junior high school) newspapers on the Web. It's arranged by state and city, and you can go to each one just by clicking on the link. This is a good way to **gather some ideas for starting up your own newspaper** and find out what's happening at schools across the country. **It's amazing** what kids can do with the Web, and the inspiration is here!

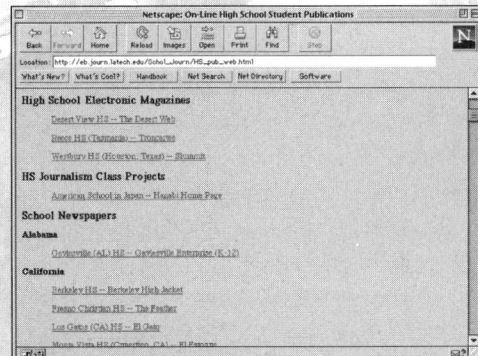

CHAPTER 8

Science & Technology

The world of science is all around you—pick up all kinds of cool scientific information right on the Internet. There are top sites for space exploration, oceanography, and biology on the Web, with interactive demos and multimedia tours you can check out right in your Web browser. If you're into the hard stuff, try the sites for chemistry, physics, and robotics. There are also cool math sites that can help you with your homework and links to the most interesting science museums on the planet!

Agriculture & ecology

AGropolis

http://agcomwww.tamu.edu/agcom/agrotext/agcommap.html

Texas A & M University's AGropolis is the place to find out about the greater world of agriculture, including info on how to grow your own gardens and food, prepare healthy meals, and take care of pets and **farm animals**. This Web site emphasizes how to be good to the environment. It also has an area on how to deal with home and family stress. The AGropolis "town" is centered around a map of places you can visit directly, including a farm, food center, animal yard, family house, and a visitor's center.

Picture perfect

If the pictures you're seeing in your browser don't look quite right, check to make sure your computer system is set to display at least 256 colors.

Gaia Forest Archives

http://forests.lic.wise.edu/forests/gaia.html

The Gaia Archives offers thousands of online articles relating to forest conservation. These articles are broken down by country, but you can browse the entire list and also search the archives to look for information on a particular subject. There's also a section with up-to-the-minute **"action alerts"** highlighting current forest issues that need attention. If you're concerned about what's happening to our wilderness, you can send your own protest over the Internet. Check out the Picture Gallery for some scary images of what's being done to the world.

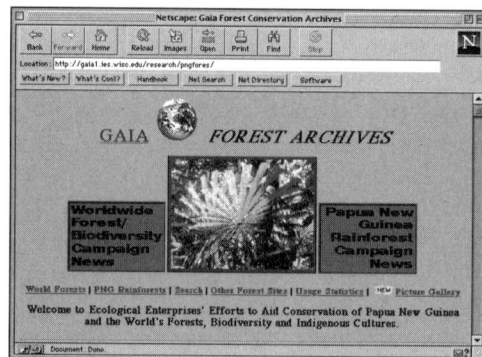

Alternative & amateur science

Dr. Bob's Interesting Science Stuff

http://ny.frontiercomm.net/~bjenkin/science.htm

This fascinating, sometimes **eerie** science and technology site features short articles like "The Death of the Sun" (yep, it's going to blow up in a couple million years!), "**Insect Chemical Warfare**", and "Hole in the Head"— an article about a guy who got a 13-pound steel rod embedded in his head in 1848 and survived! (Yeah, there's a picture!) Dr. Bob also features a neat set of links to other **interesting** science and technology sites. He plans to change some of the stories monthly, so check back often.

Weird Science

http://www.eskimo.com/~billb/weird.html

Oh yeah, it's *plenty* weird here. This is where you can find out about free-energy machines and antigravity generators, Tesla coils, and other **mysterious** devices. There are also sections on odd science journals and newsletters, online archives of weird-ness (including a link to the huge KeelyNet archives), and alternative bookstores. You may also want to check out the links to mail-order catalogs and stores that sell this **stuff**. Travel to the Weird Art section to see what some of the weird inventions really look like.

Beakman's Electric Motor

http://fly.hiwaay.net/~palmer/motor.html

This is a great home page that gives you complete step-by-step instructions on how to build an electric motor using stuff around the house like paper clips, **wire**, a toilet paper roll, and a magnet you can find at Radio Shack. The page's author is a "Beakman's World" fan who created this site to try out an experiment that was featured on that show. Each step of the project is well illustrated, and you can download the instruction sheets directly into your Web browser (and print them, too). **It's fun stuff!** You can also write something in the online Guestbook if you want.

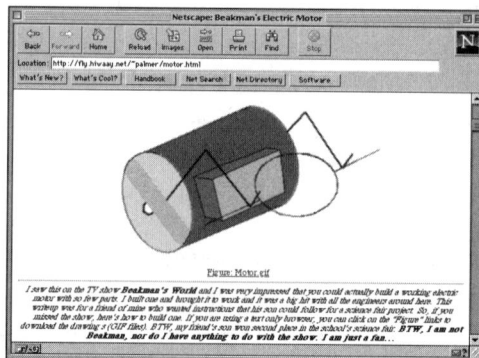

Astronomy

Views of the Solar System

http://bang.lanl.gov/solarsys/

This is a truly **cool** tour through our solar system, courtesy of the Los Alamos National Laboratory. More than 970 images and animations are here along with 200 pages of info on the nine planets, the sun, comets, asteroids, meteorites, and the history of space exploration. Each section includes a historical overview, scientific statistics, and a picture index. The pictures here are well worth the trip! There is also a good solar system introduction section and a set of links to other planetary science sites.

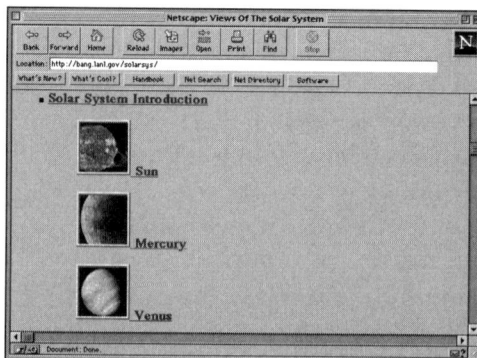

The Nine Planets

http://seds.lpl.arizona.edu/nineplanets/nineplanets/nineplanets.html

The Nine Planets is a multimedia tour of our solar system. It's a terrific source for information on the planets and their satellites along with info on smaller **celestial bodies** (like meteors and asteroids). There's an online Introduction for first-time readers, a What's New section for people coming back to the site, and an Express Tour of the Ten Best Worlds. Each entry includes great pictures and scientific data, as well as sound clips and animation files that you can download. There's also an online glossary (a list of cool words and what they mean) to help you if you get stuck on a hard astronomy term, and there's a set of appendixes with more info on planets.

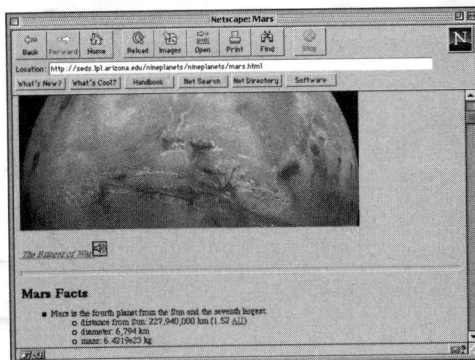

Bioscience: bugs, animals, & chemistry

CELLS Alive!

http://www.comet.chv.va.us/quill/

This is a beautiful site with cool pictures, animation, and video files on cells in action and **crystallography** (the study of crystals). See how your body works on the inside! The site has helpful links to the different sections, and it has pointers to locations on the Internet where you can find the viewers you may need.

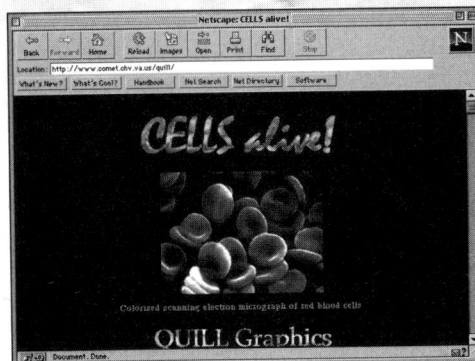

CONTINUED →

http://www.comet.chv.va.us/quill/

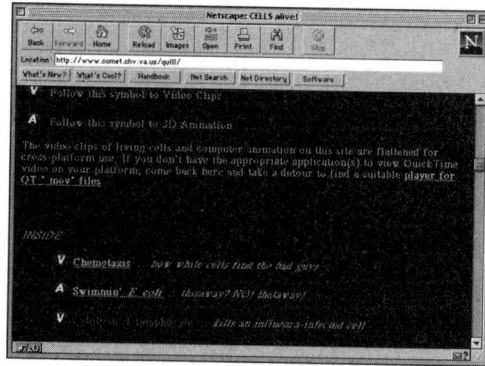

See Chemotaxis (how white cells find the body's enemies), watch T lymphocytes (or T cells) at work, and observe how other cells function—up close and personal! This site offers good, basic explanations of what goes on with cells. Overall, CELLS Alive! is an uncomplicated site with a lot of useful scientific info.

http://www.comet.chv.va.us/quill/

In this example, you can download a QuickTime movie that shows a cell attacking and destroying an invader many times its own size (make sure you have QuickTime installed on your computer). The animation helps to make the demonstration look very real (remember, it's going on inside you all the time), and there are some weird sound effects added (sounds that cells probably don't make in real life!)

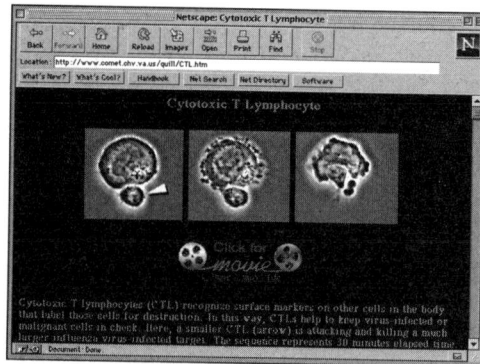

This site also includes good links to other microbiology sites, including the American Society of Microbiologists, the National Science Teachers Association, the Center for Disease Control, and related Web pages. See the Crystals section for beautiful pictures of crystal forms and a link to IBM's **subatomic** research facility (where they build structures one atom thick!).

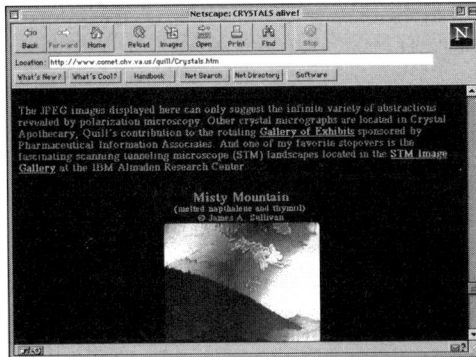

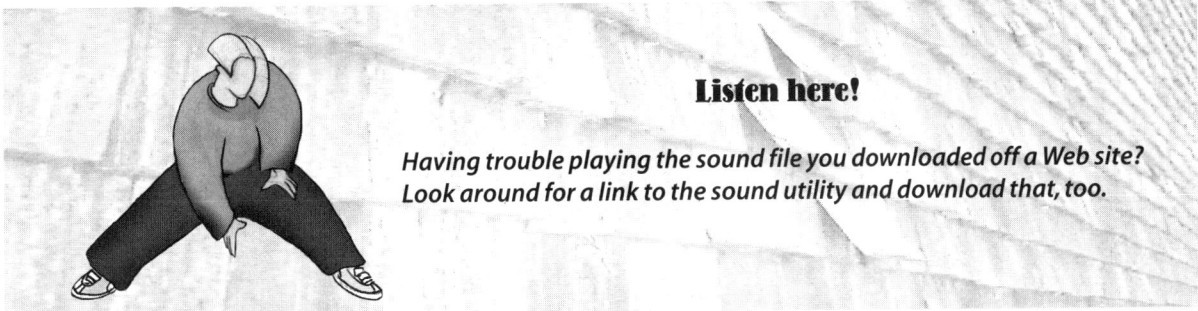

Listen here!

Having trouble playing the sound file you downloaded off a Web site? Look around for a link to the sound utility and download that, too.

Cephalopod Page

http://is.dal.ca/~wood/www.html

See the beautiful worlds of squid and octopi in full color at this amazing marine biology site. Info on these fascinating marine animals is arranged in a separate, **hyperlinked** outline (with short descriptions beside their Latin names and links to awesome color pictures). There is also a short, helpful introduction to the study of cephalopods (squid and octopi are cephalopods), and there are links to related Web sites and Internet mailing lists. This is a good starting point for doing research on these undersea creatures.

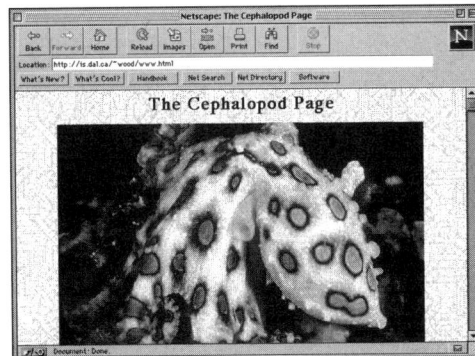

The Mote Marine Laboratory

http://www.marinelab.sarasota.fl.us/

The Mote Marine Laboratory (in Sarasota, Florida) has a great Web page for those who are into the marine sciences. You can read the latest info on marine mammals, like dolphins and manatees. There are articles about other interesting sea creatures such as crabs, octopi, and **sharks**. This site also offers advice for students who are planning to work in marine science plus information on Mote's many educational and research programs. A good list of links leads you to other sites that related to science and nature, including other **marine institutes**, government agencies, and university programs.

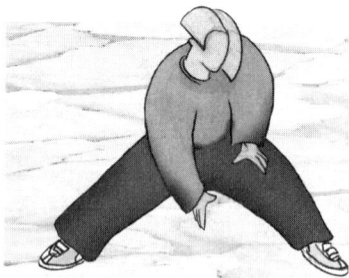

VERy CooL

Netscape: Welcome to Mote Marine Laboratory!

Welcome to Mote Marine Laboratory!

Animation frustration

Animations take a long time to download and need special software in order to run. Make sure you have (or can get) the right software before you spend the time these files take to download!

Bugs in the News!

http://falcon.cc.ukans.edu/~jbrown/bugs.html

This is a great site for finding out just what in the heck all those bugs *are*. Learn about genetic engineering, enzymes, bacteria, viruses (including HIV, the one that causes AIDS), and even the common flu virus. The articles are written in an **easy-to-understand** way—not too technical, but full of information. You can send your comments to the site's author and submit your own microbiology **questions** (you may get a detailed answer online!). There are also links to a small group of the best microbiology sites on the Web.

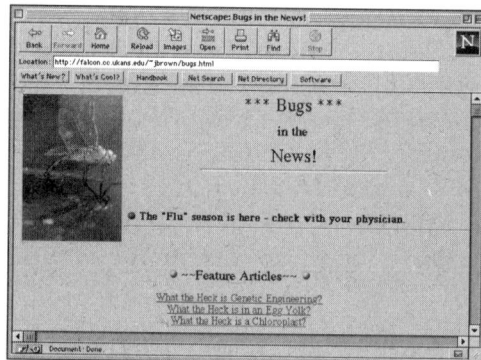

wAY CooL

Netscape: Bugs in the News!

*** Bugs ***
in the
News!

The "Flu" season is here - check with your physician

~~Feature Articles~~
What the Heck is Genetic Engineering?
What the Heck is an Egg Yolk?
What the Heck is a Chloroplast?

YAHOOLIGANS!

I Want To Be A Veterinarian

http://vet.futurescan.com/

This is a career guide sponsored by the Association of American Veterinary Medical Colleges, which does a good job at showing what being a vet really means. The site tells you how long you have to go to school and what kinds of jobs you can get in the field. Look for the **Dear Doctor** section where you can post questions about veterinarian school and get responses. There's also a feature section that zones in on what different vets specialize in (for example, some just work on large animals) and includes interviews about what's good and bad about being a vet.

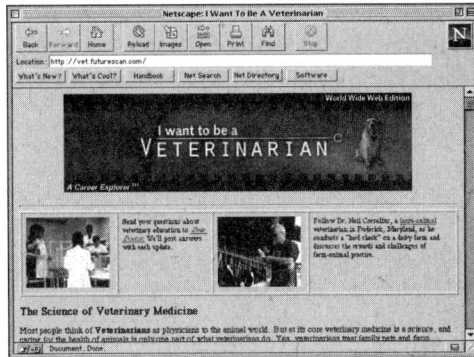

NetVet Veterinary Resources

http://netvet.wustl.edu/

This is a **megasite** for veterinary and animal information on the Net. It has a well-organized directory called NetVet, which tells you where to find info on reference materials, colleges and universities, professional organizations, electronic archives, mailing lists, and animal-related pages on the Web. This is also the site for the Electronic Zoo, where you can find a huge set of links to your favorite **beastie** across the Internet. See the Pick of the Litter section for the best animal-related Web site (updated weekly).

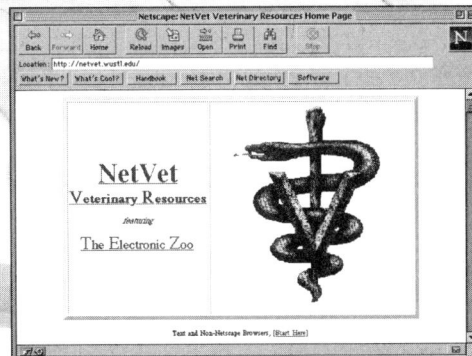

Cyberzoo

http://www.primenet.com/~brendel/

This site features a lot of great information on wildlife, including the order Carnivora (cats of all sizes, **wolves and dogs**, and bears) and the order Squamata (lizards and snakes). Each link contains a full-color picture and a description of the animal. There's also an Introduction to Science, Ecology, and Field Biology you can read to learn more about animals in the wild. Check out the section on unusual partnerships in nature (how different animal species interact with each other).

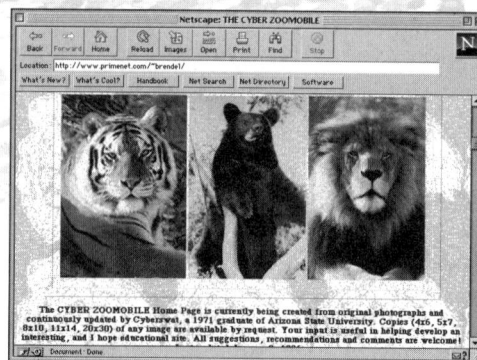

Chemistry Teaching Resources

http://www.anachem.umu.se/eks/pointers.html

Here are chemistry links by the ton! The author tried to **jam** as many chemistry teaching links as possible into one Web site, but you can also use it to find a lot of good info for class work and home projects. There are sections on chemistry talks, lectures, online courses and software, reference materials (including the periodic table of elements), and journals. You can also find pointers to topics in the news relating to **chemistry** and the other sciences.

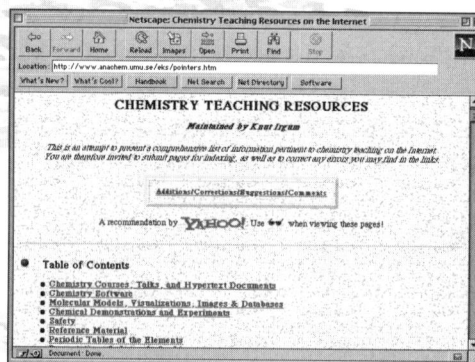

Earth sciences: geology, weather, & ocean studies

Geo Site

http://www.ts.umu.se/~widmark/lwgeolog.html

Check out this Swedish site with it's strong collection of links for beginners interested in the field of geology. See the sections on geochemistry and geophysics, paleontology, **earthquakes**, and volcanology for details on different parts of geology. There are links to museums and rock shops online as well as geology schools and earth science institutes. Look at the links to geology-related newsgroups for more recent info. Then, check out the author's instructions on how to build your own rock tumbler out of a spare tire and small electric motors. (Just leave it in the living room—no one will **notice**!)

Interactive Weather Information Center

http://thunder.atms.purdue.edu/interact.html

Check out this site for the Purdue Weather Processor, which is a great index of information on the atmosphere and weather, including satellite pictures, surface data maps, upper air and **radar** data, and multiple forecast models. If this gets a little confusing, you can go directly to weather information for your area just by clicking on the current surface/radar weather map, or you can do a text search by filling out a simple online form. The main site also features a helpful introductory section and a gallery of the best **atmospheric** images. Be sure to scope out the short movie clips and see how weather patterns move about.

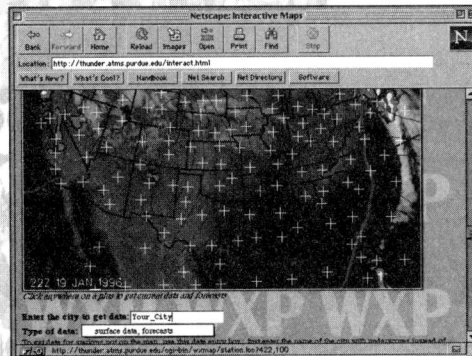

WeatherNet

http://cirrus.sprl.umich.edu/wxnet/

WeatherNet is another good site for
weather information, including U.S.
weather reports and reports on weather
conditions in other countries (look under
the Travel Cities section) along with satellite
pictures and maps. The site has many links
to weather-related sites on the Internet, a
section on PC/Mac weather software you
can download, and good skiing info. Check
out the WeatherCam area for links to **live
cameras** on the Net, listed by city. Go and
see what the weather's really like in other
places!

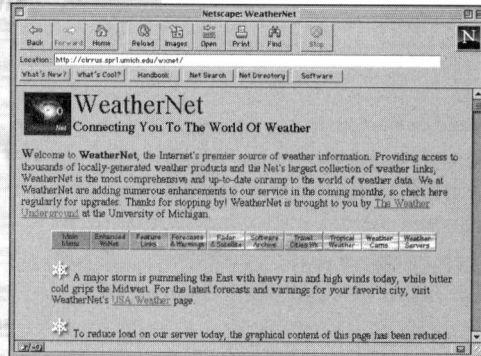

Oceanographic & Earth Science Institutions Directory

http://orpheus.ucsd.edu/sio/inst/

The Scripps Institution of Oceanography
Library site lists links to oceanographic
and earth science sites across the Net. It
includes sections on government, universities, private companies, **aquariums**, museums, and other organizations that deal with
the ocean and earth. Each list is made into
an outline, with links at several points
clearly spelled out so you can easily find a
site. You can also find a list of oceanographic and earth science sites around the
world, arranged by country.

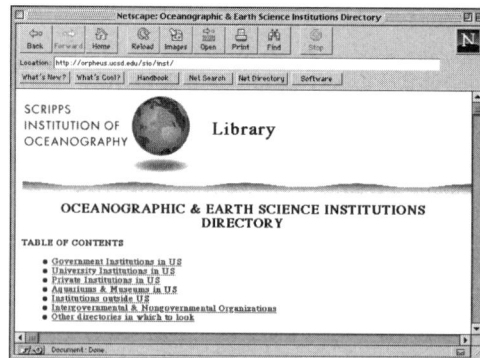

Dinosaurs

Dinosaur Hall

http://ucmp1.berkeley.edu/diapsids/dinosaur.html

This is a great interactive dinosaur museum. There's a whole series of articles with pictures on dino subjects (including myths, definitions, and different species), and there are hyperlinks to Web pages for each subject. For example, the **Tyrannosaurus** link leads to a separate Web exhibit that has cool articles, pictures, and artwork. You can also search for info on one dinosaur type directly, or you can browse a list of types, a specific dinosaur period, or a list of museum topics on related subjects.

Funky Dinosaur Land

http://www.comet.net/dinosaur/

Funky Dinosaur Land shows you where to find links to interesting articles and sites on dinosaur subjects, like the Hadrosaur skeleton that was discovered in New Jersey in 1858 and started the dinosaur **craze.** Look for new revelations about dinosaur eggs, discussions about how these creatures became **extinct**, and more. This site also has direct links to museums and tours (with descriptions), an art gallery section with cool dinosaur photos (and links to more sites with images and **artwork**), and a reference section for when you need to look up the specifics.

Robots & physics

Robotics Internet Resources Compendium

http://www.eg.bucknell.edu/~robotics/rirc.html

This site offers a good overview of what you can find out about robots on the Net. You can go to sections on U.S. and international robot labs in major universities, robot companies, and government programs. Each section describes related sites and provides a direct link to other sites. There's also an alphabetical listing of the sites in major robotics categories (like artificial intelligence, **humanoid** and metamorphic robotics, machine vision, and hostile environment systems) and a collection of links to other robot Web pages.

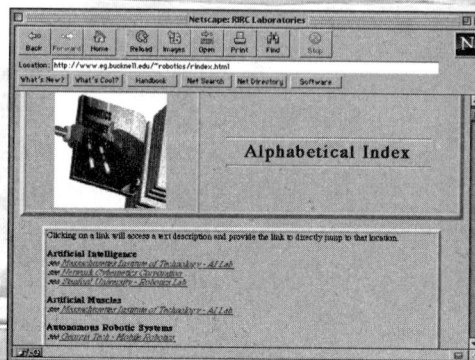

wAY CoOL

U.S. FIRST

http://usfirst.mv.com/

This is the home page for the U.S. FIRST organization, which stands for the United States Foundation for Inspiration and Recognition of Science and Technology. They sponsor an annual robotics competition for high school students, in which teams match their own student-designed robots in several different **contests**. There are links to high school robotics programs, and you can view pictures and videos from previous competitions, go directly to a list of past participants and sponsors, and find out how to **register online**.

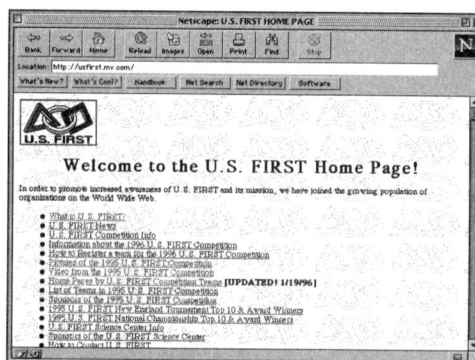

VERu CoOL

YAHOOLIGANS!

Net Advance of Physics

http://web.mit.edu/~redingtn/www/netadv/welcome.html/

Here's where you can find information on the physical sciences, including general physics (physics around the world and basic physics info), space science (galaxies and black holes), research into the nature of the universe (**Big Bang** theories on how it started and what it's made of), electromagnetics (magnetism, optics, and energy physics), and mathematics (general relativity, geometry, and higher math). Each section has a list of interesting articles across the Web. There's also a section on the history of physics and an alphabetical list of all related subjects (use your browser's edit/find command to search this list for topics).

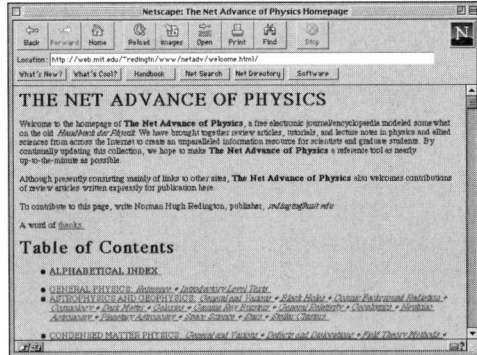

Geography

Project GeoSim–Geography Education Software

http://geosim.cs.vt.edu/index.html

You can find interactive software for studying geography here. There are different sections for population and migration studies (when people move from one place to another) as well as interactive programs showing changes in congressional districts and U.S. county and state populations. Be sure to take the **mental map quiz!** If you get confused, the programs include multimedia tours that explain what they're talking about plus interactive pretend situations you can run. You'll need to download the software first. It's made for Macs and PCs, with links to the **downloading** sites at this page.

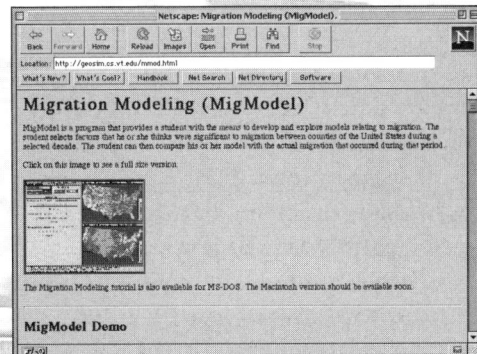

PCL Map Collection

http://www.lib.utexas.edu/Libs/PCL/Map_collection/Map_collection.html

The Perry-Castaneda Library Map Collection at the University of Texas at Austin is a huge collection of online maps (over 230,000). It includes links to maps of areas around the world, listed in alphabetical order by continent and region. Just click on the link to view the maps (but beware that these files are huge and can take a long time to download). Don't miss the section on maps of areas in the news, like the Gaza Strip and Bosnia, and check out the Historical Maps area. The site has a useful FAQ section to help get you started and a set of links to other **cartographic** resources (anything related to maps).

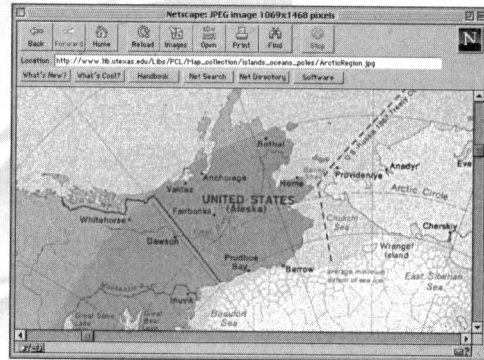

Math

Ask Dr. Math

http://forum.swarthmore.edu/dr.math/dr-math.html

Ask Dr. Math is a service that lets you post your math questions to Swarthmore College math students and get a reply. You can also read **questions and answers** other people have sent and received about algebra, fractions, equations, geometry, and more. The site is broken up into sections for elementary, middle, and high school students (and even college students), so you can go right to the section in your level. You can also **search** this site to **find the math information you need.**

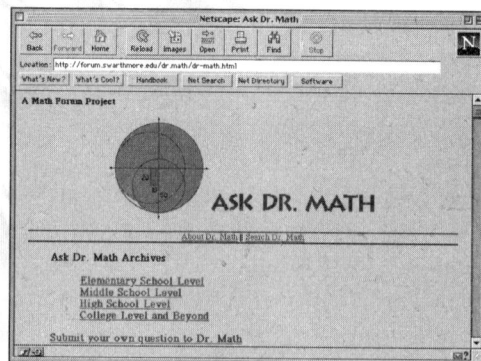

Science news, research, & invention

Psychology of Invention

http://hawaii.cogsci.uiuc.edu/invent/invention.html

The Psychology of Invention site is *the* place to find multimedia articles and links on the invention process. You'll find an interesting exhibit on the development of the airplane, with more than **300** pictures from the Wright collection and a link to a multimedia site describing Alexander Graham Bell's invention of the telephone. You can also **check out** links to related fields here, including an introductory page on cognitive science and a Psychology of Science group. There's also a bibliography for more information on the **invention** process.

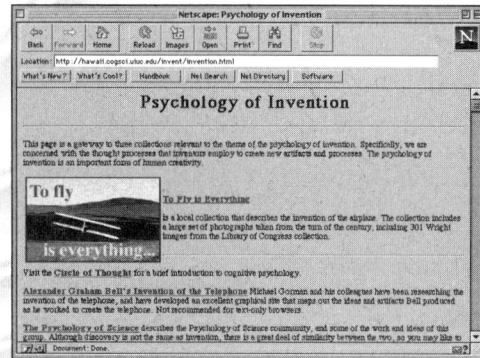

Science Fair Research Directory

http://spacelink.msfc.nasa.gov/html/scifairt.html

This site from NASA has a great set of links to help you with **science fair projects** and science study work. The subject areas include biological sciences (such as behavioral and social sciences), biochemistry, botany, medicine and health, microbiology, and zoology. Also, check out the physical sciences, like chemistry, computers, earth and space sciences, engineering, environmental science, mathematics, and physics. You can surf links from here to other places that will help with your science project, including online dictionaries and databases that you can search directly.

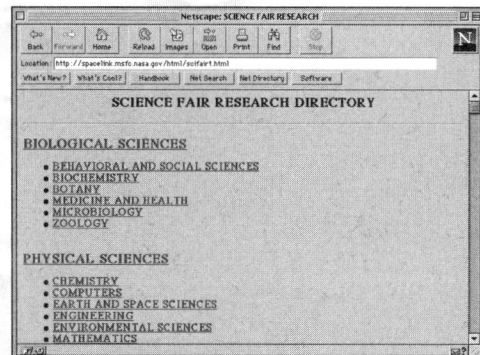

Space

Basics of Space Flight

http://www.jpl.nasa.gov/basics/

This site is the Jet Propulsion Laboratory's online workbook to help students learn about spaceflight and related topics. The Environment of Space covers the solar system, gravity and mathematics, planetary orbits, and electricity. The Space Flight Projects section covers mission planning, scientific **experiments**, spacecrafts, telecommunications, and navigation. You can also learn about space flight operations, including the launch, cruising, and encounter phases of a spaceflight. Use the helpful introduction to find your way around and go to the **online glossary** to look up words you don't know.

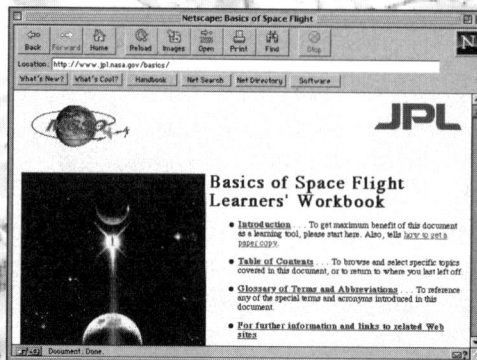

International Space Station Alpha

http://issa-www.jsc.nasa.gov/

Scientists and engineers will begin building the international space station in 1997, and you can learn all about it right here. This site has great graphics, such as pictures showing how the station will be built during shuttle missions. You can also find an overview of the project and information on the international space agencies that are involved (along with links to their Web sites). If you want to **dig** for solid facts, go to the Technical Data Book section. Learn all about the new era in space right here!

YAHOOLIGANS!

NASA Spacelink

http://spacelink.msfc.nasa.gov/

Spacelink is NASA's Educational Affairs
Division Web site, where you can find
information on NASA projects, news,
and **hot** topics. You can also search the
Spacelink library for specific topics and
look into the Educational Resources section
for info on school programs. Check out the
Additional Resources section for a huge list
of links to NASA sites everywhere, including
spaceflight centers, educational programs,
current events, and NASA inventions. See
the NASA Overview for more information
on how the various agencies relate to each
other. If it's related to NASA, it's probably here.

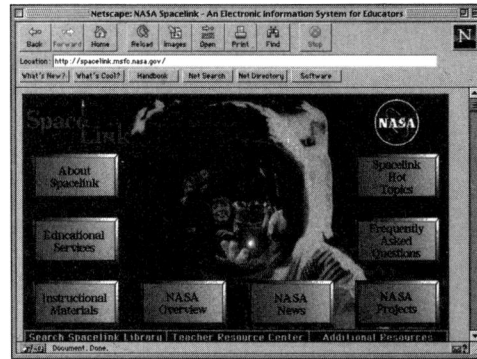

National Air and Space Museum

http://www.nasm.edu/NASMpage.html

The Center for Earth and Planetary Studies
at the National Air and Space Museum has a
site that covers research programs in space
studies that the institute offers. You can find
cool shuttle photographs of the earth here,
and there's an excellent illustrated exhibit
showing the history of the Apollo space
program. You can then go directly to the Air
and Space Museum's site, which features
multimedia exhibit galleries you can
browse with an interactive map, event
calendars, links to different departments,
and a list of educational programs.

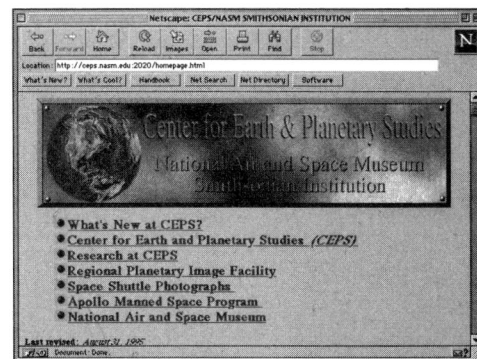

CHAPTER 9

Sports

Calling all sports fans! Sports on the Web are hot, hot, hot. Your favorite professional sports all have great sites, and nearly all of the sports you can play yourself are represented, too. Get the scores, chat with fellow fans, and keep track of your team's statistics. Or, if you're into playing a sport yourself, you can hook up with other players in all kinds of sports, from baseball to swimming, and get tips that may improve your performance. Learn about a new sport (Ever tried wrestling? And no, water polo doesn't use horses!) or brush up on your old favorites. It's all here!

Baseball

Fastball

http://www.fastball.com/

If you're one of those people who follow baseball instead of any other professional sports and count the days until **spring training**, this is *the* site for you, even when the Boys of Summer seem like they'll never come out of the snow. Despite the tendency to favor the Atlanta Braves (OK, so they won the World Series in 1995), Fastball covers it all during the season and throughout the year.

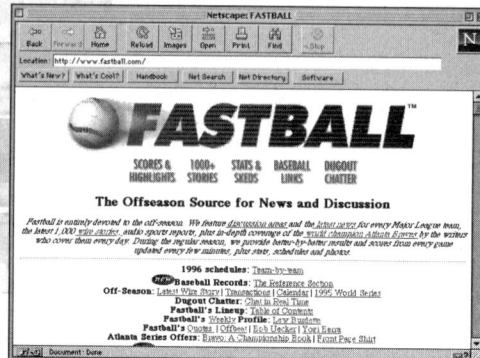

Each team in the National and American Leagues is listed. Go to your team's news option (or to the team you love to hate) and pick up on the **latest coverage**. Every team has a discussion page where fans can chat with other fans and voice their opinions on topics like replacement players and the possibility of yet another strike. You'll find messages posted by your fellow fans, agreeing and disagreeing with the players and with team management. You can add your opinion to the general **hubbub**. Even in the off-season, this site has a ton of information on trades and moves from within the baseball community. Don't let the starting lineups catch you by surprise!

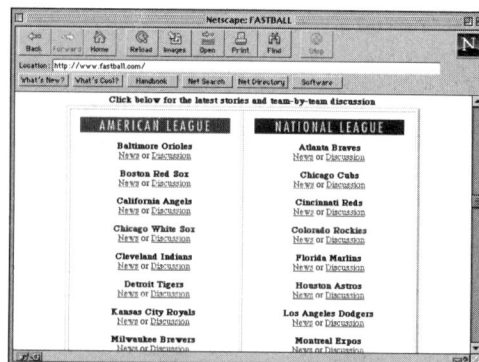

In case you missed all the **excitement**, or you want to relive the moments, you can see photos and read news stories on the 1995 World Series. This site also provides a host of baseball-related links that can take you to other sites put up by baseball fans, sites sponsored by teams, sites devoted to specific **players**, and even a site for Japanese professional baseball information.

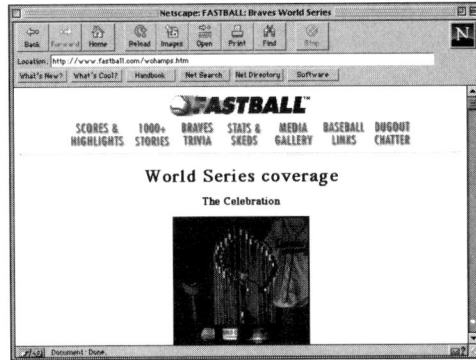

Fastball provides a weekly profile of a famous ball player of yesteryear, complete with photos and statistics. Did they cover your favorite Braves shortstop last week and you didn't get a chance to see it? No problem: the **profiles** are saved so you can see all the past coverage. Fastball is a real shot in the arm in the off-season when you need something to get you through till spring, but it really comes into its own during the summer months, with up-to-the-minute stats and batter-by-batter results.

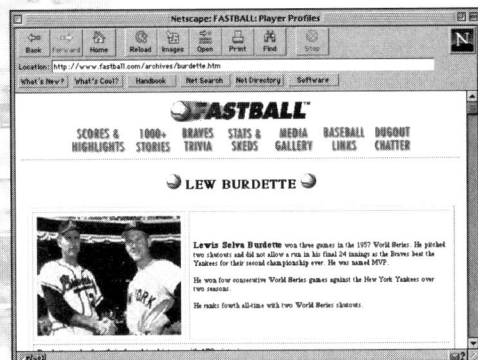

Little League Baseball

http://www.littleleague.org/

Whether you're a player, a follower, or just plain **curious**, the Little League Baseball site provides links and information at all levels of interest. If you're new to baseball this site can answer all of your questions. Find out what you need to do to start up a team in your neighborhood. Need special coaching to improve your baseball skills? Check out baseball **summer camp** programs in your area. You can even browse in the shop for official Little League logo hats and shirts.

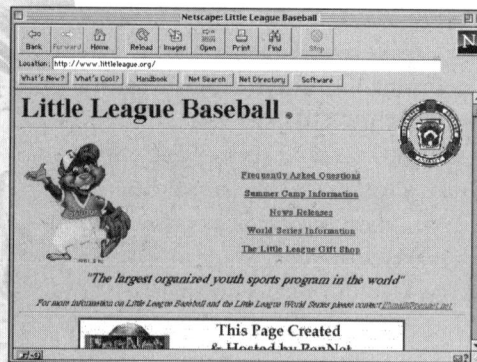

CoOL

Sean's Ultimate Baseball Page

http://www.rain.org/~ssa/sean/baseball.html

VERy CoOL

Fifteen-year-old Sean is a Los Angeles Dodgers fan who really loves baseball. His page has all kinds of cool stuff you won't find everywhere else. For instance, he has a nifty baseball **trivia** quiz that would stump even the experts, and a page devoted to his personal hero, Ken Griffey, Jr., of the Seattle Mariners. Sean's got baseball cards for sale (duplicates of those already in his **collection**), schedules for 1996, and even a link to the Major League Rulebook (in case you need to look up the answers to that trivia quiz). Great backgrounds and plenty of **jazzy** pictures make this page as fun to look at as it is interesting to read.

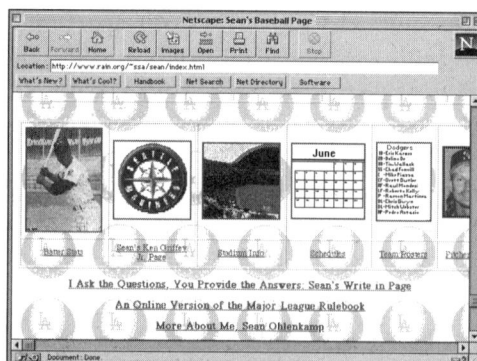

Basketball

College Basketball Page

http://www.cs.cmu.edu/afs/cs.cmu.edu/user/wsr/Web/bball/bball.html

This page may look a little dull, but it has a lot of great information. Along with links to the big sports servers like ESPN and Nando, it offers a *huge* list of pages on individual college basketball **teams** all over the country. This isn't just the big names, it's an A-to-Z list of nearly every college team in existence, including a lot of women's teams. Go to the What's New page for the latest additions to the list. If by some strange chance you don't see your favorite team listed, **drop a line** to the Webmaster, who'd be more than happy to add it to the list.

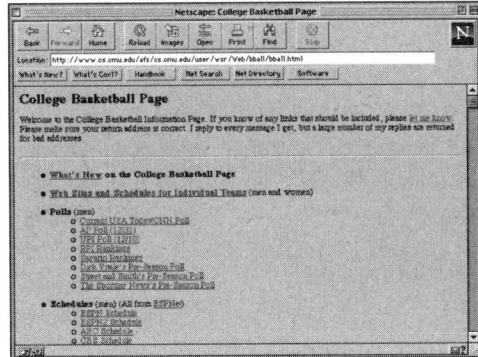

Biking, riding, & racing

The Cyberider Cycling WWW Site

http://blueridge.infomkt.ibm.com/bikes/

This is the most complete list of cycling information available. These links go everywhere! You can see some great views from bicycle trails all over the country without ever leaving home. Plan a biking trip, talk to other cycling **enthusiasts**, and check out the schedule for any cycling events that may be coming to your area. Cycling clubs from all over the country are linked here. Whether you're a cycling fanatic or you can't quite take those training wheels off your **two-wheeler**, you'll be **fascinated** by the places you can go on a bike.

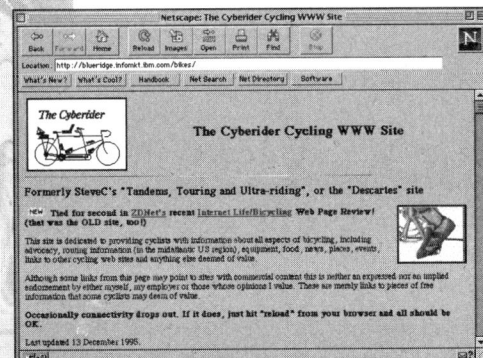

Dirt Central

http://people.cks.com/~spoo/mtb/dirt.html

Dirt Central takes you on the back roads and kicks up some dust. Other cool sites are linked here, along with plenty of neat pictures of bikes in some places you never thought bikes could go. Check out the great shot of a cyclist in **midair** over a flight of steps! The host also posts his own **"ramblings"** about places he's been on his bike. If you love biking, visit this site and enjoy the ride.

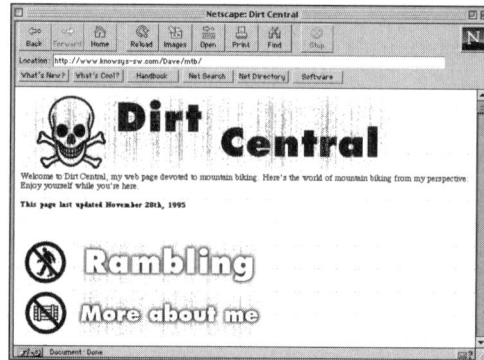

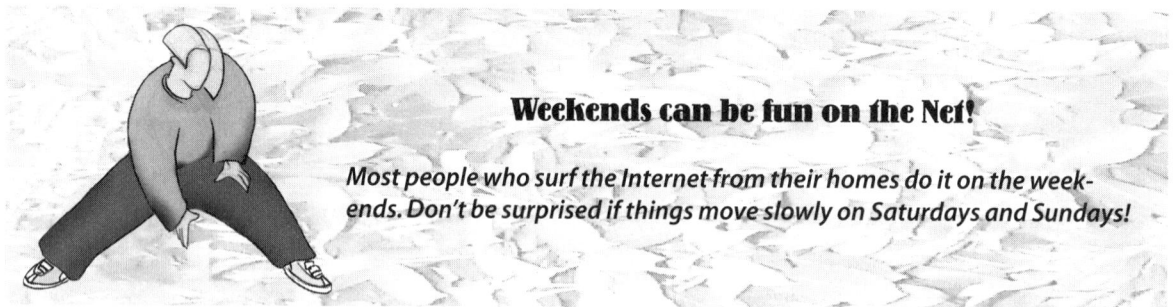

Weekends can be fun on the Net!

Most people who surf the Internet from their homes do it on the weekends. Don't be surprised if things move slowly on Saturdays and Sundays!

The Karting Web Site

http://www.callamer.com/~pete/karting/

Whether you're new to the idea of little single-seater go-kart racing or you're a dyed-in-the-wool karting fan, you need to see the Karting Web Site. The list of FAQs and their **answers** are enough to get you going in the sport. Links can take you all over the karting world, from race tracks to schools for brushing up on your karting expertise. Feeling all alone in your go-kart addiction? This page maintains a free worldwide list of your fellow karting fans.

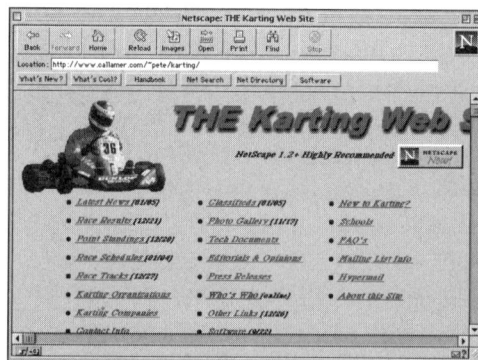

Horse Country

http://www.pathology.washington.edu/Horse/Carroll_horse.html

Welcome to Horse Country. Be prepared to stay awhile because there is so much here for the horse lover that only something as big as the **World Wide Web** could possibly hold it all. You'll find links to horse stories, horse **gear**, horse art, horse sports, and more.

wAY CooL

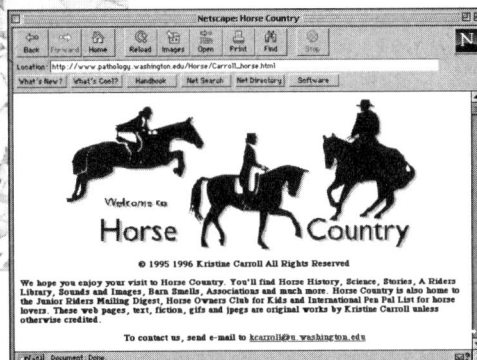

For the hunting crowd, there are pages with information on events, rules, and pictures taken at real fox hunts. The links to horse sports take you all over the professional equestrian world, from **rodeo** to polo to show jumping. If you need help with that report on horse evolution for school, look here for a time line of horse history. If you're looking for new equipment, Western or English, there's a list of places you can browse for saddles, helmets, or boots.

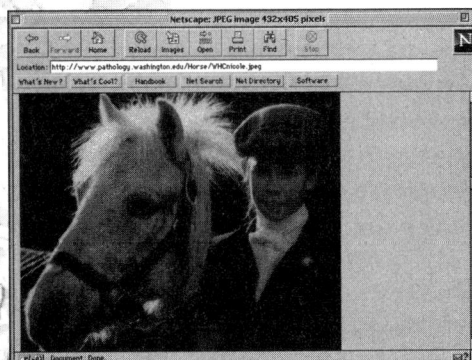

CONTINUED →

http://www.pathology.washington.edu/Horse/Carroll_horse.html

Horse Country is the site to visit if you want to connect with other horse lovers around the world. It offers a complete guide to HOCK (Horse Owners Club for Kids) and recent issues of *Junior Riders Digest*. There's even a link to recipes for unique horse treats provided by *Junior Riders*, and a list of links especially for horse-loving kids. The **pen pal** link is worth looking into, even if you don't want to sign up. There are kids all over the world who either ride regularly or just wish they did and who are eager to communicate with like-minded kids. For the model horse collector, there is a link to the Model Horse Gallery, an **amazing** page of photographs and information about model horse collecting.

There is also an international section with pictures of riding clubs and riding events from Australia to Hong Kong to Ireland. And although the technology hasn't come *quite* far enough yet, there is a joke link to *smell* files for leather, barns, and manure. As if all this weren't enough, Horse Country has a fabulous list of all the features that really *will* be available on this page in the future (they're still working on providing **smell-o-rama**). There are plans for more video and more fiction. Every time you come back to this site you are almost guaranteed something new and interesting to learn about and enjoy.

Linda's Stable on the Internet

http://dsu.edu/~blackl/horse/

Linda is a horse lover without a horse, so she created her own online stable of horse information to fill that **gap**. Look here for links to topics as far apart as the Colorado Horse Rescue organization and the *Hong Kong Horse Racing Journal*. Other personal home pages are listed as well. Specific breeds, such as Arabians or Shetland ponies, get their own links to pictures and information. Horse racing, shopping, and **stud** registries all get equal time. Check out the horse sound files for a real horse stable atmosphere!

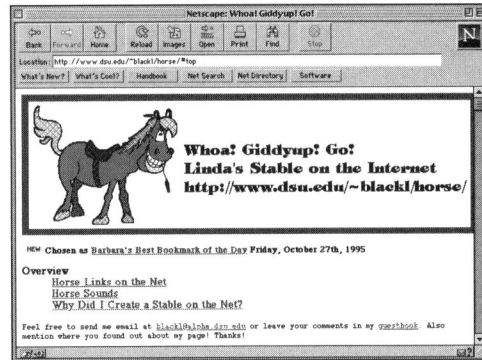

Sandman's Motorsport Page

http://www.li.net/~sandman/msports.html

Sandman pulls together a lot of auto racing information in a page that is easy to use and fun to look at. Racing schedules rub elbows with information on car museums. Different categories of racing — from **drag racing** to **radio-controlled cars** — get special attention. With an eye to **international appeal**, everything from British racing clubs to South East Asian Motorsports is given a listing. This is a great jumping-off point for a racing beginner and a gold mine of information for the racing enthusiast.

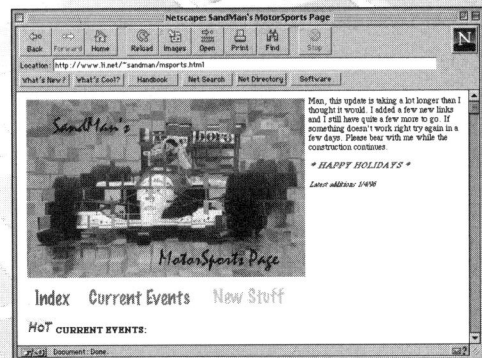

VeloNet – The Global Cycling Network

http://www.cycling.org/

VeloNet is an electronic information desk for cyclists. It provides links to hundreds of pages about cycling, including BMX, bike racing, and personal cycling pages. The site also has a page called CLAIRE (in case you didn't know, CLAIRE stands for **Clean Air and Exercise**) where you can sign up to help collect information on the use of bikes instead of cars. For instance, you enter the number of miles each month you biked, walked, or carpooled instead of just drove, and that information is put together by CLAIRE so it can be compared to people in other cities and other countries. **What have you done to reduce pollution?** Join CLAIRE and have your efforts recognized.

Football

Football Central

http://www.dnai.com/~foley/footballcentral/

Football Central really covers it all: high school, college, Canadian, NFL, World League, you name it. If it has to do with American-style football, this site covers it. From the **turf-textured** backgrounds to the little football icons, this site is fun to look at and easy to get around. Individual team pages and all the major football-related sites are listed. There is so much here, you might want to go first to the sites that feature the Football Central Cool Site Award (a football wearing shades, of course) for a good overview of what's on the whole site.

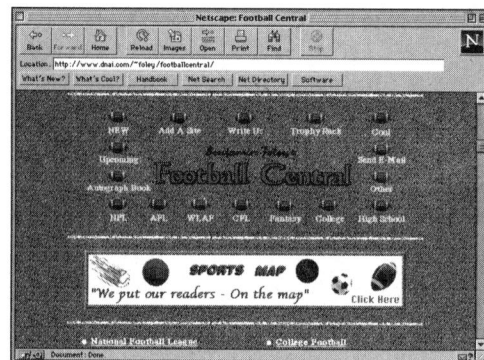

YAHOOLIGANS!

Gymnastics, martial arts, & wrestling

Gymnastics (GYMN Forum)

http://rainbow.rmii.com/~rachele/gymnhome.html

The world of gymnastics is much wider than the little bit most people see on television. For its fans, gymnastics is a year-round obsession. Fans and beginners alike will find plenty of **interesting** gymnastics information on GYMN's page. GYMN has great reviews of men's and women's gymnastics events at every level from all over the world, plus links to other pages of interest to gymnasts. There's news on the latest rules and procedures in gymnastic competition and profiles of up-and-coming gymnastics stars. Check out the picture gallery for some **breathtaking** action.

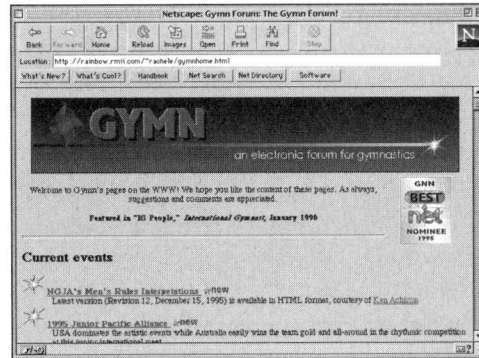

InterMat

http://www.netins.net/showcase/intermat/

A wrestler's ultimate resource, InterMat brings together up-to-date information with **zippy** graphics and lots of links. There's a section on women in wrestling and an extensive list of wrestling sites all over the world. High school and college wrestling teams get equal time, and the list of **tournament** results seems to go on for days. Look up your local team to keep track of how they're doing, or sign up for a wrestling club so you can learn the basics.

Jay Swan's Martial Arts Resource Page

http://www.middlebury.edu/~jswan/martial.arts/ma.html

Interested in learning more about the art of **self-defense**? Then you need to start with this page if you're looking for information on martial arts. It links sites all across the world, from Southeast Asian disciplines to traditional Chinese, Japanese, and Korean martial arts. Even if you don't know the first thing about martial arts, you can go to this page, which covers all the major and minor styles, including Aikido, Kung Fu, Jujitsu, and Tae Kwon Do. Whatever you're into, you can look here for martial arts training centers, teachers, schedules of competitions, and more. If you can't find a link here to your favorite style, you haven't looked hard enough!

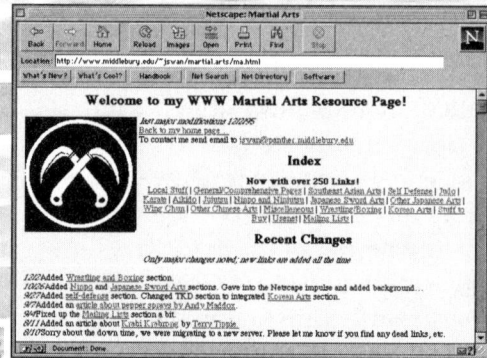

Lisa's Gymnastics Archive

http://humper.student.princeton.edu/~lcozzens/

Lisa claims that this site is under construction, but even unfinished it provides hundreds of archived photos of gymnasts from all over the world. You can look up your favorite star and see **a variety of action shots.** You could spend hours just browsing through the huge collection of photographs! You'll also find a list of links to **gymnastics** articles on the Web and message boards for feedback and suggestions. The site has plans to become a full hypertext guide to gymnastics resources on the Net.

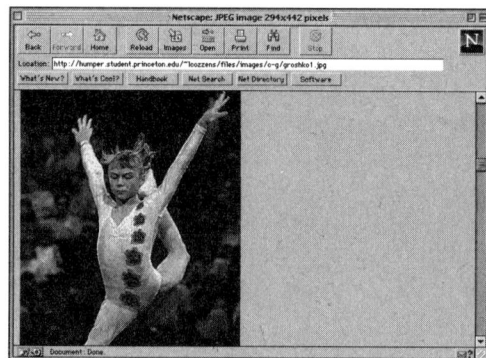

Professional Wrestling Server

http://orion.it.luc.edu/~mlong/wrestling.html

For a different kind of wrestling, check out the Professional Wrestling Server. This site covers the history of professional wrestling in pictures and news stories, but it also offers **up-to-the-minute** information on modern wrestling. There are sound files of your favorite wrestling stars and plenty of links to other interesting wrestling sites. Don't miss the really cool links to the real names of **wrestling's biggest stars**, including those in Japanese wrestling. Did you know that the Midnight Rocker began life as Mike Hickenbottom? Now you do!

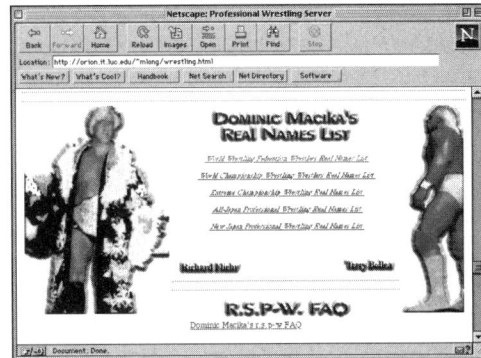

Hockey

NHL Super Open Net

http://pages.prodigy.com/H/O/Y/hockey/home.html

Hockey fans should start here for a good collection of links to everything NHL on the Web. You'll find all the usual stuff — **scores, stats, and schedules** — plus links to information on each and every player in the league. Arguing a point with your hockey buddies? Check out the link to the NHL rulebook and get the official word on what's legal and what's not. The link to team home pages gets you deep into NHL territory, and the site's Hall of Fame link lets you **vote** to induct your favorite players.

The Ultimate Hockey Fan's Page

http://hops.cs.jhu.edu/~zib/hockey.html

Wow! This page takes a while to load, but it's worth the wait. Scott has links to all the useful stuff on the Web that has to do with hockey, but he puts it on the page in a really **cool** way, with small pictures and lots of definitions of hockey words. He also includes bits of hockey history, pictures of hockey greats, and links to every hockey team in the NHL. All this information is on a flame-colored background that **screams** for your attention. It's just a great site!

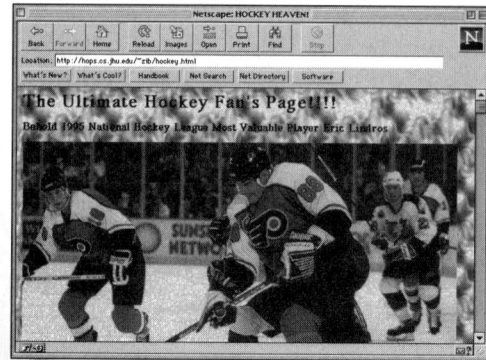

Skating

Are You Ready To Fly?

http://www.ucalgary.ca/~clmcgave/inline.html

Learn to rollerblade without ever leaving your chair! This teaching site takes you step by step through the history of blading, how to get blades on your feet, and how to move once you have the blades on. There's even advanced information on how to do **"everything that looks cool but hurts if you do it wrong."** Of course, you really *do* have to get out of your chair and practice, but this page is a great introduction to the techniques you'll need on the street. For those rainy days when you need a little inspiration, this page also has links to more blade pages.

The Figure Skating Page

http://www.webcom.com/~dnkorte/sk8_0000.html

The Figure Skating Page is *the* resource list for skaters. You can learn about amateur competition requirements, where to buy skates and costumes, or where the nearest skate club is to your home town. There's even a Partners Needed listing, for a pairs skater in search of a partner. Of course there's also a list of skate-related pages elsewhere on the Net. If you're an ice skater, you'll definitely want to see this page. Even if you don't skate, **haven't you always wondered about the difference between a double axle and a double salchow?** Now you can find out.

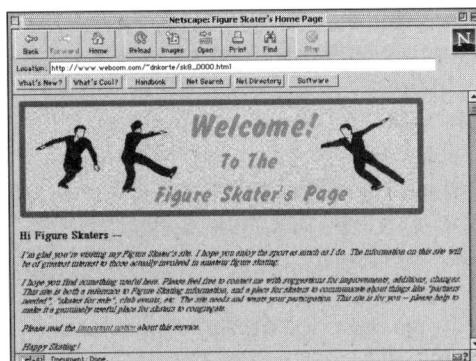

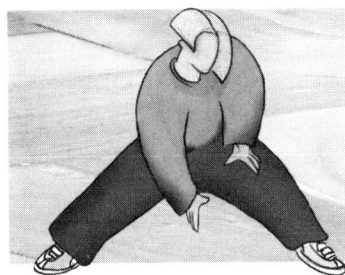

VERy CooL

Take the modem and run!

For best results online, get the fastest modem you can for your computer. You might want to think about getting a faster modem if the one you have is less than 14,400 baud.

Sandra Loosemore's Figure Skating Page

http://www.cs.yale.edu/homes/sjl/skate.html

Sandra's page has been called "the mother of all figure skating pages," and it is easy to see why. She has everything, from great photos to the most complete list of information and sites. Look here for **cartoons of frogs ice skating** and for personal pages on all of your favorite figure skating stars. Other features include a huge list of other people's skating pages, lots of clubs and rinks, and information on ice shows and competitions. Sound files of figure skating commentary round out this packed site. Be sure to go back often — you'll always find something new!

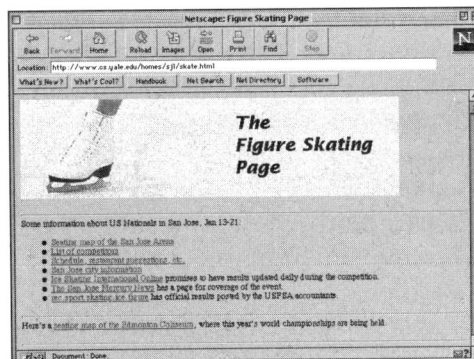

wAY CooL

Soccer & volleyball

Schneid's Volleyball Page

http://www.xnet.com/~schneid/vball.shtml

Volleyball fans will recognize Schneid as a fellow fan. This page has everything a volleyball player or follower could need. Tips on how to improve your game, how to work out and drill for better performance, **tips on strategy** — you name it, this page has it to spare. You don't play? Go look at the links to other pages that have pictures, stories, and books. There's also a lot of useful information on general fitness, sports medicine, and nutrition for the serious athlete.

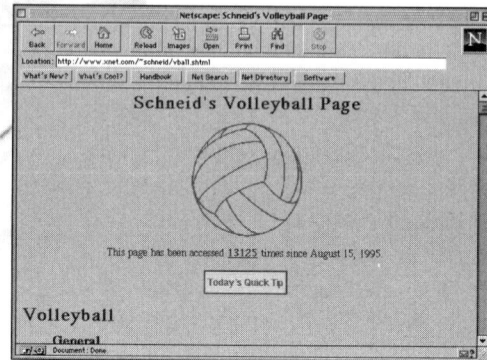

SoccerNews Online

http://www.csn.net/~eid/soccer/sccrindx.html

SoccerNews Online covers the world soccer beat, and it does a good job. You can **check out** any of the major events coming up in the soccer world or click anywhere on the world map for information on that area's soccer happenings. The big World Cup Soccer competition gets special attention. You can also find out how to get tickets for soccer tournaments around the world and read scores of articles on soccer and soccer subjects.

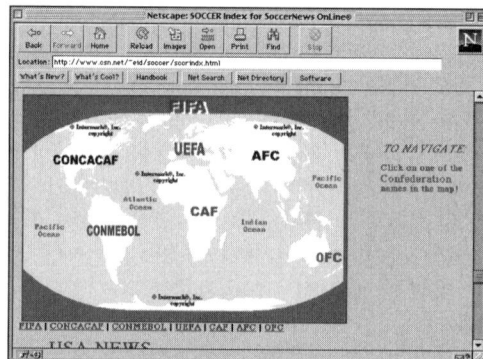

Volleyball WorldWide

http://www.volleyball.org/

You have worldwide volleyball information at your fingertips here, from two-person beach volleyball in California to regulation teams at the Atlanta Olympics to junior volleyball tournaments in Malaysia. You can read up on the rules for men's and women's volleyball and find out when there will be television coverage of a volleyball event. Special links will connect you to sites that have information **specifically** for Youth and Junior volleyball players, ages 7-12 and 12-18. Links, links, and more links — they'll take you everywhere, so **get the ball rolling!**

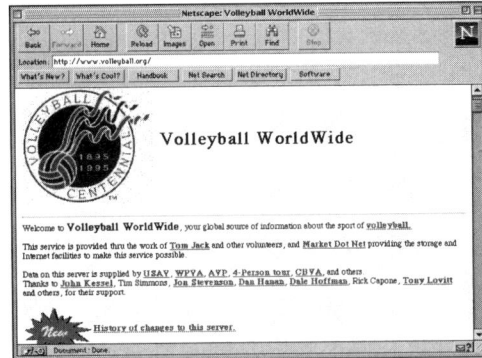

Sports indices

Do It Sports

http://sweb.srmc.com/doit/

Looking for a sports resource that covers your favorite **participatory** sport? Do It Sports (DIS) offers online registration for **sports events** all over the U.S., like mountain bike trail rides, marathons, and other footraces. If you don't find the group you're looking for (is your **spelunking** group having a **Cave-a-thon**?), you can create a page for your group. Calendars of events, games and prizes, and an online community are some of the added attractions of this Web site.

Tennis

Tennis Country

http://www.tenniscountry.com/

Welcome to Tennis Country. **Relax** and stay awhile because you can't do this site quickly. If you really love tennis, or even if you only kind of like it, you'll have fun exploring this huge tennis site.

You have to join the club to get in, but don't worry. This tennis club is free! If you don't want to join right away, you can **explore** the site as a guest. Just click on guest in the opening screen. You might want to read the club rules first; they're mostly the usual stuff about how the Webmasters want you to use the site, but it never hurts to know the rules before you go too far. Next, go to the Tennis Country Store to make sure you've got the right gear for your next match. Just like a good salesperson, the store offers tips and suggestions about gear you might want to buy. If you don't want to buy anything yet or if you want to spend some more time looking, it's OK to just browse!

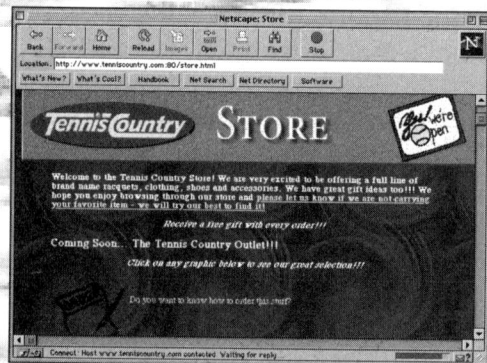

Once you're outfitted, you'll need tennis lessons. In Playing and Fitness Tips, you'll find pointers from **professional** tennis coaches on how to **improve your serve** or hit a better cross-court shot. General fitness tips are here, too, like the importance of warming up before you **play** and how to take your energy level up during a game. If you're not too tired from all this, you're ready to go looking for a game.

Seek and you shall find!

Good indices are everywhere on the Net. Use the search tools in your browser and on the Web for pointers to the topics that interest YOU.

The Junior Club is just the place for you to **drum up** a game. Talk to other tennis kids all over the world in real time. This isn't a place to post your opinions: you can actually **eavesdrop** on a *live* discussion and add your own responses. If you've never tried a chat forum, this is a good time to give it a whirl. Just watch what's happening on the screen, and then type in a response to something you've read. If there are a lot of people online, the conversation can get kind of confusing, but that's part of the fun! It's a great way to find people who have the same interests you do.

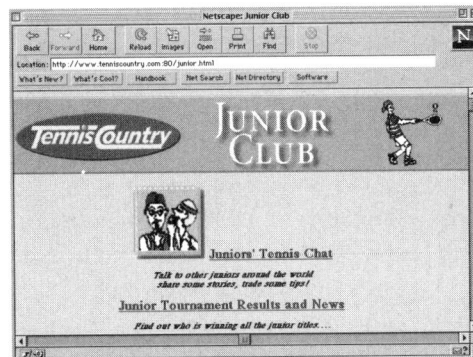

CONTINUED →

http://www.tenniscountry.com/

Now that you've met your fellow tennis fans, go see the other features at this site. If you follow professional tennis, you can find who is playing in which upcoming tournament and who is seeded where. In case you missed your favorite match, there are past tournament results and news coverage of all the major (and not so major) events. Once you've had your fill of all this (and it can take quite a while!), you may want to **plan your next family vacation** around tennis. Tennis Country has dozens of listings of vacation places that have tennis facilities. Or, if you want to get away from the family, go look at the list of tennis camps you can attend. All in all, this site is a tennis extravaganza that you won't want to miss.

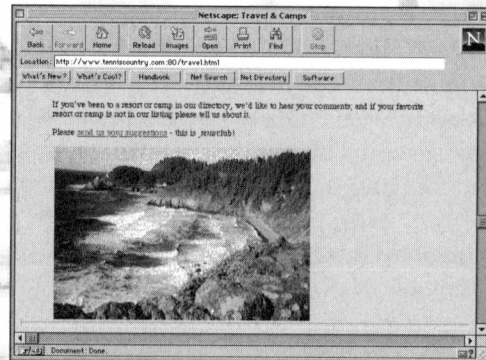

World Wide Web TENNIS SERVER

http://www.tennisserver.com/

The Tennis Server is a useful place to find all things tennis. Subscribe to the **newsletter**, read exclusive commentary about the pros, or vote for the Sport Site of the Year. There are all the usual links, too, like rules and regs, clubs you can join, and pointers to other tennis sites on the Web. If you're a fan but not a player, you'll want to see the latest photos of all your favorite pros and check out the daily tennis news and tournament updates. If you're a player, get tips on equipment and techniques.

Watersports

Drop In! Bodyboarding Info

http//www.sd.monash.edu.au/~jasonl/dropin.html

This site has everything the bodyboard enthusiast could want, and it's laid out really well. There's information on board design, tips on how to ride better, and plenty of links to other bodyboarding and surfing sites. Check out the **totally cool photos** (and add your own). Express an opinion on the relative merits of *lidders* (bodyboarders) and *goat boaters* (traditional stand-up surfers). All you beginners, go straight to the Sponge Speak Dictionary so you can sound like a seasoned pro!

H20 Polo

http://www.h2opolo.com/

If you haven't caught on to water polo, this is a great site to get your feet wet. Of course, if you're already a fan, you'll enjoy all the great information pulled together in one place. One cool link is the Daily Eggbeaters, a daily feature made up of water polo team news, scores, tournaments, stories, and inside info. You're invited to **contribute!** Check out the **great list of links** to other water polo sites and a coach's and player's forum for the exchange of ideas about training and strategy.

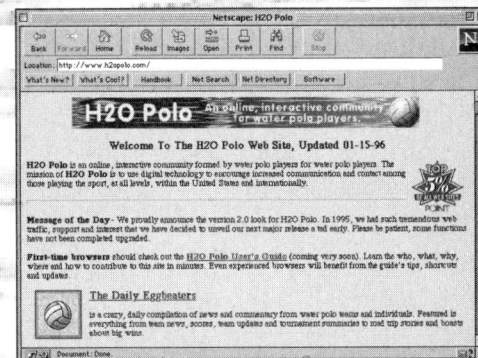

SurfSpot

http://www.surfspot.com/

Whether you're a surfer or a **wanna-be**, SurfSpot has something for you. See Malibu, California, and other spots on the coast at dawn or at any time you choose. SurfSpot has current images from **beaches** in California, updated every thirty minutes, so you can see for yourself whether the surf is up. This page maintains a Surfers Yellow Pages to help you find surfing products, services, and places. Even if you're **landlocked** and under six feet of snow, you can go California dreamin' with the surfing crowd.

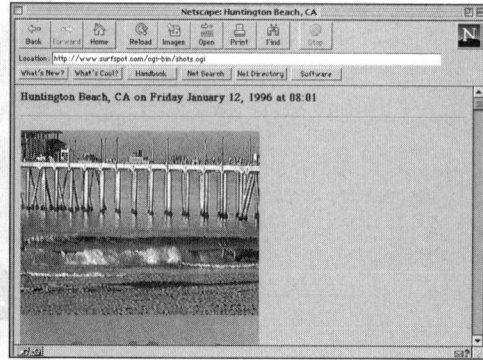

WebSwim

http://alf2.tcd.ie/~smftzger/swim/header.html

Start here for an **introduction** to water-sports on the Web. WebSwim has links to swim-related pages, but also to news about diving, water polo, and general fitness. If you're in training, there's advice on **what to eat**, how to improve your turns, and even different workouts you can try. If you're looking for a swim club to join, or if you follow World Masters Swimming, check here for like-minded people and information. There are even links to international swim pages. WebSwim is **the most swimming you can do without actually getting wet!** Experience it.

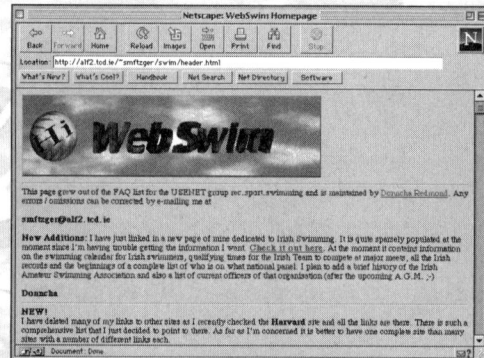

CHAPTER 10

Travel

You have so many places you want to see, and the Web can take you to nearly all of them. Visit exotic foreign countries in South America, Asia, and Africa; travel through the European countryside on a train; or hike the mountain trails of one of many U.S. state parks. All this without packing a bag, buying a ticket, or even leaving your chair! Learn about another culture, investigate a place's history, or just relax and enjoy the scenery. Travel on the Web is as easy as deciding where you want to go.

Travel on the World Wide Web

Around the World in 80 Clicks

http://www.coolsite.com/arworld.html

It'll take more than 80 clicks to go around the world on the World Wide Web, but 80 is a good start. Click on the country or area of your choice, and you'll get a home page for that country or a page from the area. You'd better know your geography because the map doesn't have place-names written in! Since you're going around the world, all you get is a **taste** of each place you visit, but most are good places to start looking for more in-depth information. Some links give you vacation information, while others have population statistics and the country's **national anthem.** It's an adventure!

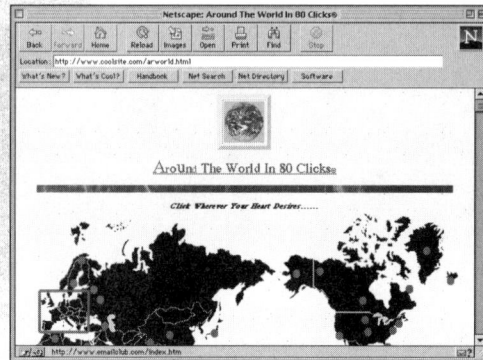

Camera sites are listed by what they look at. For instance, Outdoor Cams offer views of **cityscapes**, complete with familiar landmarks. Airports, restaurants, roads, and schools are just a few of the other outdoor places you can look at. Go right to the type of cam you want or just scroll through all the sites. If you want to look at nature scenes instead of **man-made wonders**, sections on beaches and nature are for you. Be sure to check out the scenery in Mawson, Antarctica!

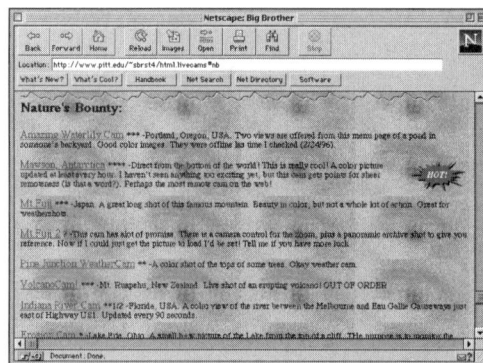

For a different trip, try the Indoor Cams. People have set up video cameras in some **pretty strange places!** Drop in and see people working at their office desks or check out an office building in Croatia. Some camera pages have **zoom features** on their cameras that you can operate from your computer. Look carefully at every page you visit for these and other special features. And remember, **this is live** (or nearly live) video, so sometimes you'll get a picture of nothing much happening, just like in real life!

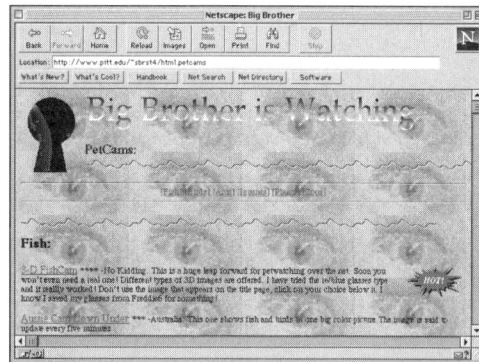

http://www.pitt.edu/~sbrst4/camtitle.html

Web cameras have another advantage: you can check on weather all over the world. Check out the satellite cams, the earthquake update cams, and the outer space cams to get the **inside scoop** about what's happening around the globe. Some of the other features at this site include **links** to some Web camera sites that have different "cool cam of the week" picks and links to information about how the Web cameras work. This site is a great trip all by itself, but it's also a great first stop for exploring the Web in all its weird and wonderful glory.

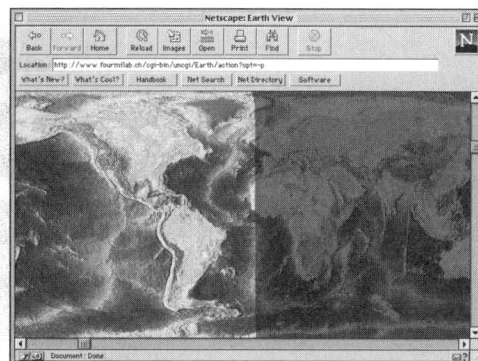

InfoHub WWW Travel Guide

http://www.infohub.com/

Travel the world without leaving your
computer! Just choose a place to go and
the WWW Travel Guide will give you a
list of links that cover that area. More
popular regions have more links, but even
Antarctica has links to penguin information
and pictures of polar bears. Everywhere you
might want to go has a map and a description
of the area. Most of the countries offer special
places to go, neat things you can do, and
places you can stay. Whether you're planning
a trip or not, you can **cruise the world** from here.

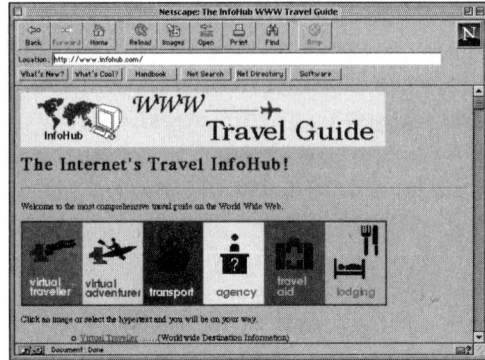

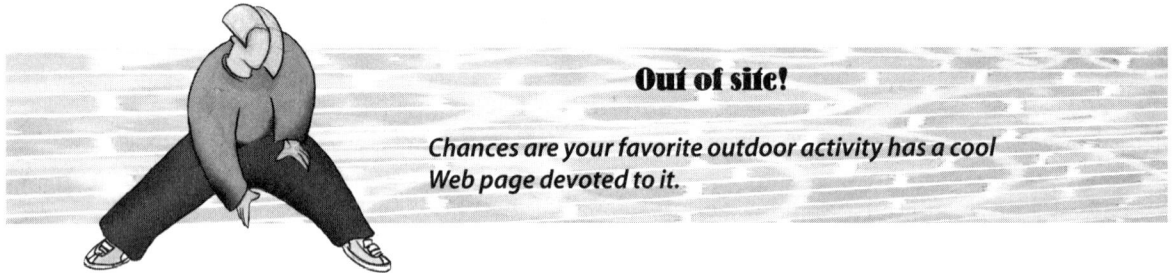

Out of site!

*Chances are your favorite outdoor activity has a cool
Web page devoted to it.*

GORP – Great Outdoor Recreation Pages

http://www.gorp.com/gorp/location/main.htm

GORP is what hikers call trail mix (you
know, like raisins, nuts, sunflower seeds,
and chocolate chips), but it's also the Great
Outdoor Recreation Pages web site. Like
trail mix, GORP is made up of lots of
different little things — when you put them
together, they make a **yummy** treat. You'll
find travel information on places all over
the world that offer outdoor adventures.
Check out the links to national parks and
recreational activities like fishing and
hiking. Other links connect you to videos,
books, and more, all about traveling in the
great outdoors.

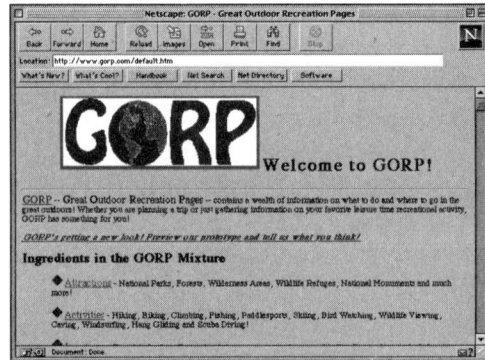

Ultimate World

http//www.ultimatew.com/

Ultimate World is putting together a lot of great info by asking its visitors about their travel experiences. The results? Loads of travel information from across the United States about tons of places, **straight from the horse's mouth** and organized so everyone can take advantage of it. Pretty cool, huh! To find info on a place, just go to the general area, and then to the state, and then to the city. From there you can browse that area's Arts, Dining, Attractions, and lots of other neat things. Listings are rated by the site visitors (remember, that's *you*), so if you've been somewhere, take a minute to **add your own opinions** to the collection.

Virtual Expeditions

http://www.coil.com/~jhegenbe/virtex.htm

Virtual Expeditions is a collection of travel stories and pictures of trips that have been taken, or of trips that are going on right now. You are invited to drop in on a trip that's happening right now and watch the action. Some current trips include a kayak ride down the Nile river, an archeological adventure in Mexico, and a jaunt around the world. Want to **hitch a ride** aboard the Space Shuttle? Hop right on. Some sites include interactive games, and some have Quick-time movies, but all of them are **guaranteed to be exciting** in one way or another.

Windows on the World

http://www.wotw.com/wow/

Press your nose to the glass for a great view of the world. Windows on the World has great graphics and an easy interface that make it simple to see the world from your computer. Click on the world map (or on the country's name) for a look at that country's culture, history, and points of interest. You can also go straight to the kind of **stuff** you're looking for without spending time on the tourist information. Each country has a Table of Contents so you can choose maps, or cities, or history, depending on what you want to know about that country. Check out the news, sports, and weather features to get a real feel for the country you're visiting. Enter the monthly contests for a chance to **win valuable travel prizes!**

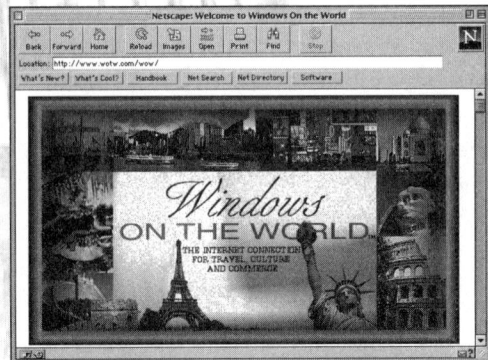

International destinations

Africa: Virtual Africa

http://africa.com/docs/satravel.htm

Virtual Africa's travel and tourism section has tons of information on the kinds of trips you can take in Africa, the places you can stay, and the best ways to get around. Even if you're not planning a **safari**, you'll find everything you need to know about African national parks and about hiking in the African wilderness. This is a real tourist site, so you're encouraged to actually book a trip, but you can read the descriptions, look at the pictures of the wild animals, and save your real safari for another day.

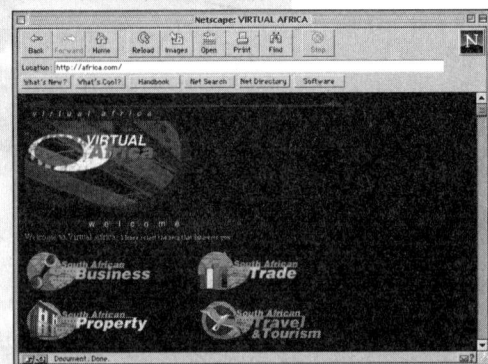

YAHOOLIGANS!

Australia Online

http://australia-online.com/

Go down under online. You'll find travel and tour information, maps and photos of many of the different parts of the country, and history and information on the aborigines of Australia. You may not think Australian is a different language, but just wait until you click on the Diction-aussie, **a dictionary of Australian slang.** Practice out loud with your friends and you'll agree Aussie really might be a foreign language! Download the sound file for a taste of the real thing. See ya round like a donut!

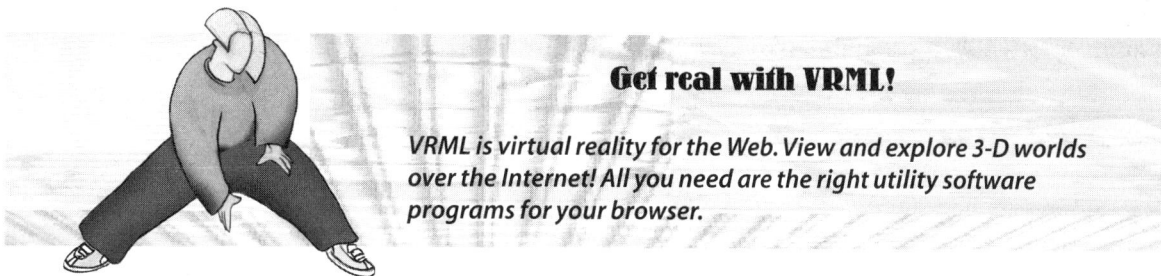

VERy CooL

Get real with VRML!

VRML is virtual reality for the Web. View and explore 3-D worlds over the Internet! All you need are the right utility software programs for your browser.

Brazil: The Wonders of Brazil

http://psg.com/~walter/brasil.html

Brazil has many different faces, and this site does a good job of guiding you through them all. Just choose a region and lose yourself in history and **breath-taking** pictures. From rain forests to major cities, Brazil is a unique blend of cultures from all over the world. This page is mostly in English, but you will find some links in Portuguese, the national language of Brazil. The huge list of links takes you all over the Web to sites about Brazil's economy, Brazilian politics, and travel and tourist information.

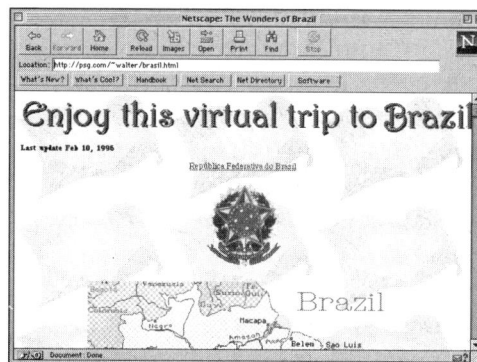

VERy CooL

Canada: Our Home, The Atlas of Canadian Communities

http://www.nais.ccm.emr.ca/ourhome/

Canadian students present their own communities in this digital atlas of Canada. Click on the **interactive** map for the area you want to find out more about, and you'll get a description of the countryside, pictures of some of the points of interest, and a little history of the region, all written by students from the local schools. Other topics include things the students like about their town and things they would like to change. You'll also see some student poetry and artwork. This site is a great way to learn more about what **kids your own age** can do on a Web site, and also to learn more about our neighbors to the north. The whole page is in English and French, so it's also a good place to brush up on your *français*.

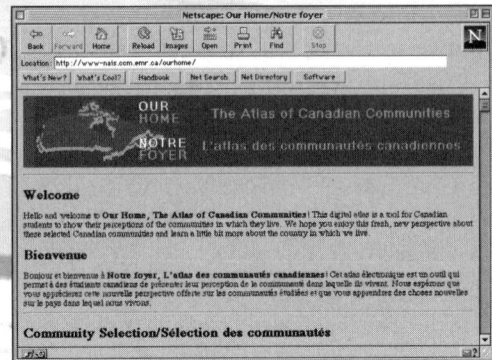

China Windows

http://china-window.com/window.html

China has many different regions and cultures. The China Windows site tries to give you a look at all of the different sides of this complex country through business links and cultural information. Many daily Chinese newspapers are linked here (in Chinese and English), as are tourist and travel information. The links are set up like **Yahooligans!**, by category, so you can go straight to the News links, or the Entertainment links, or the Business stuff. Major cities in China are listed separately. Visit each for a different look at the Chinese countryside, its customs and its people. Because it uses frames and has lots of graphics, this page may load slowly, so be patient.

Germany: Deutschland

http://weber.u.washington.edu/~tuske/Htmls/germany.html

This personal page is a good jumping-off point for finding information on Germany. If you're doing a report on Germany, follow the link to the official Germany site, **complete with details** on the country's politics, its geography, and its people. If you want to do a little virtual travel, click on one of the German cities for a look at a weather research institute in Bremerhaven, or check out the historical city of Wiesbaden. For more travel, other links take you to Virtual Tourist sites.

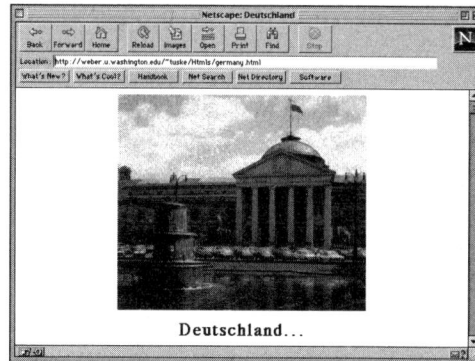

Deutschland...

India: Prakash India Infobase

http://www.webcom.com/~prakash/WELCOME.HTML

Have you ever been curious about India or wondered what it might be like to travel there? The Prakash site has good historical and tourist information, as well as information on India's economy and how the people there live. Check out the articles on **arts and crafts** in India, or read the Women In India section for a sometimes startling look at a different culture. The tourist links are not well organized, but you'll still be able to find some interesting stuff about the Taj Mahal, information about the different regions of India, and some **interesting** articles on tourism in general.

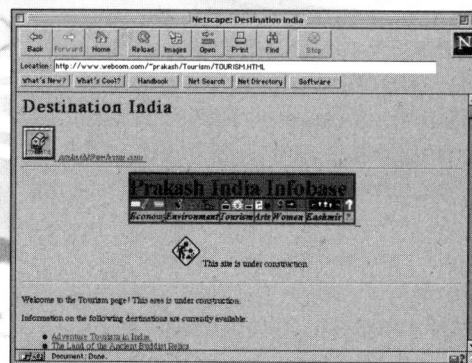

Israel: The (almost) Complete Guide to WWW in Israel

http://gauss.technion.ac.il/~nyh/israel/

It's the Israeli Yahoo! This index is an easy way to get all kinds of information about Israel. Choose a category: Entertainment links you to Israeli TV, music (modern and classical), and radio. **Recreation** has everything from local sports to clubs and collecting pages on the Net. If you're looking for travel and tourist information, you'll find plenty in the Regional and the Society and Culture sections. News and Government sections keep you up to date on the political situation, and Reference has up-to-date event schedules.

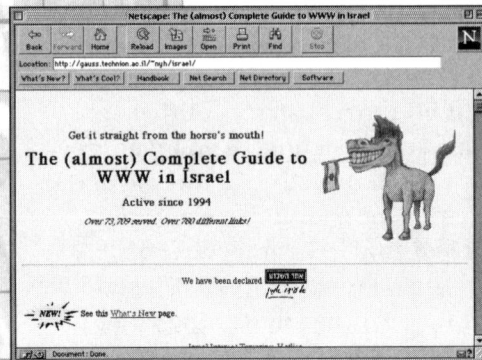

Mexican Tourist Information

http://csg.uwaterloo.ca/~dmg/mexico/turismo.html

You don't have to be a tourist in Mexico to take advantage of all the great stuff on the Mexican Tourist Information site. This site has plenty of history, cultural notes, and lots of interesting bits of information that you'll need if you're going traveling. This site isn't as pretty as others you might find, but it has links to every major region of Mexico and descriptions of many of the best places to go and the **must-see** historical sites.

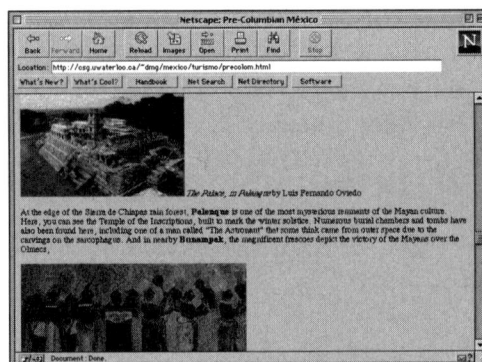

Paris

http://www.paris.org

Welcome to the official site for the City of Light. With over **7,000** pages of information, the Paris Pages may have the most complete online guide to Paris — its **museums**, restaurants, and other tourist attractions. Go first to the How to Navigate page to find what you're looking for and then go lose yourself on the streets of Paris. You'll find plenty of cool pictures of everything, from famous stuff (like the Eiffel Tower and the Arc de Triomphe) to neighborhood life and street artwork. There's a whole section for tourist information, up-to-date events listings, and links to other Paris and France sites. This site is huge, so give yourself plenty of time to find all the **goodies** available here. Note: the whole page is also available in French!

Russia: A Brief Visit to Russia

http://www.hyperion.com/~koreth/russia

For a real taste of Russian life, follow this travelogue through one man's trip to Moscow. The Webmaster stayed with a Russian family in Moscow, and this site wants to share with you all the little details of day-to-day life in Russia's capital. Read about how the whole family had to "shower" with only **a bucket and a teapot** because the apartment had no hot water for a few days. The pictures (there are lots!) are all small thumbnails, so you can read the story without having to wait forever for **big** pictures to load. To skip the story and just see the pictures, a link takes you straight to an index of places and photos.

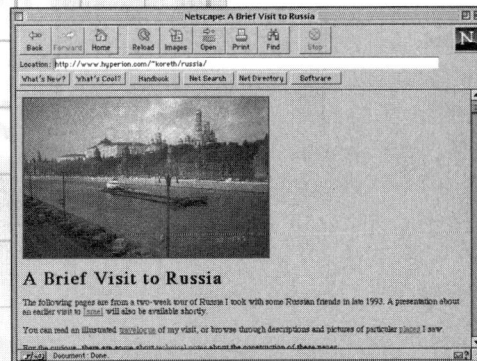

Railroad travel

Liberty's Amtrak Page

http://www.aho.com/amtrak.html

This personal page is one train lover's gift to all the other train lovers out in cyberspace. Liberty's Amtrak Page is a list of links to other U.S. railroad pages, including a link to the official Amtrak Web site, plus a whole lot of reviews of rail travel, both by Liberty and by other visitors to this site. You'll get a little railroad history, a little railroad trivia, and lots of good solid rail info. Links will hook you up to schedules, to lists of books about rail travel, and to plenty of other railroad-related pages. Check out the travelogues for **a taste of life on a train**.

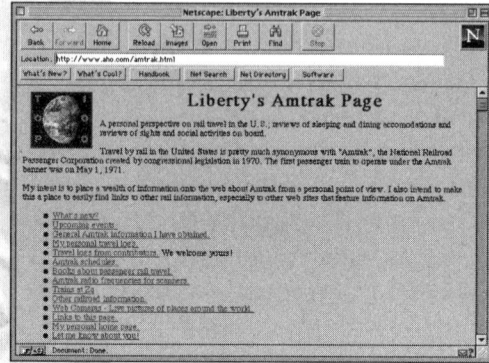

MERCURIO: The European Railway Server

http://mercurio.iet.unipi.it/home.html

Trains, trains, and more trains. The Mercurio Webmaster (with the help of fellow train fans around the world) has put together a huge collection of European train pictures, schedules, and information. If you're looking for train wrecks, you'll find them here! Also train news, train colors and paint schemes, new train products, and links to other train sites. Be sure to check out the Eurostar page for **personal travelogues** and information on the Chunnel, the new train tunnel that goes under the English Channel between England and France.

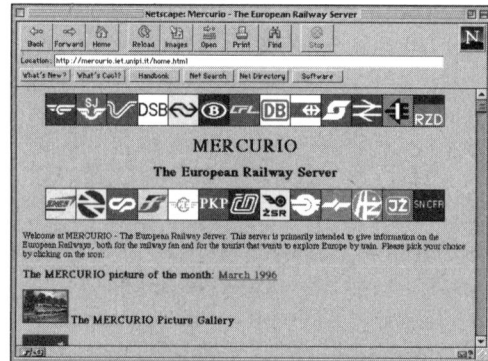

The Railroad Page

http://www.xnet.com/~jamesk/railroad.shtml

The Railroad Page is a **nifty** little index of some U.S. railway sites. You'll find a collection of drawings of nearly every kind of engine ever run by the Santa Fe Railroad (there's pages and pages!) and photographs of Burlington Northern diesel engines in the process of being built. A link will take you to the Illinois Railway Museum for some rail history, a look at current rail topics, and still more terrific pictures of **locomotives**, new and old. When you've gone through everything here, you can move on to the list of railroad-related links. Add your own **favorite** railroad site!

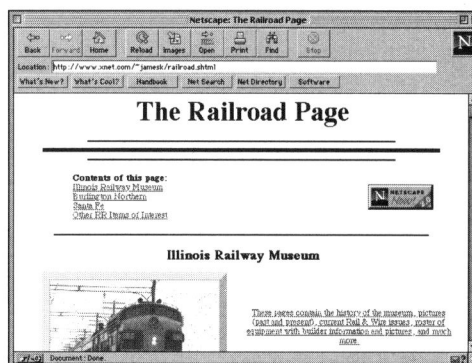

United States destinations

Arizona: Ghost Towns of Arizona

http://www.indirect.com/www/pjcat/ghost.html

Abandoned towns, or "ghost" towns, are the remains of mining towns that were built around the turn of the century and then abandoned. Your Webmaster on this page of ghost town photos and descriptions is a geologist and **abandoned** mine inspector in Phoenix, Arizona, so he makes a good guide through these towns. If you can't get enough about ghost towns, listings at the bottom of the page give you more places to look, and links take you to other ghost town-related sites. Don't miss this eerie little trip into the past!

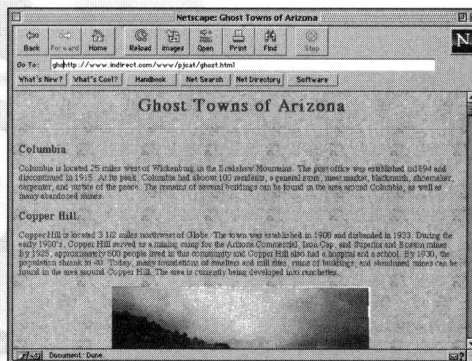

Arizona: Guide to Vacations at Grand Canyon, Flagstaff, and Northern Arizona

http://www.pagehost.com/flagstaff/

Planning a family trip to the Grand Canyon? You'll need to make a stop at this page first. With everything from phone numbers, average monthly temperatures, and mileage from site to site, you can't afford *not* to get as much out of this page as you can. The different places you can go have short descriptions and nice pictures, and throughout this long page you'll find helpful tips from an experienced traveler. Even if you're not planning on going anywhere near Arizona right now, the pictures and descriptions will make you want to go, so **be warned**!

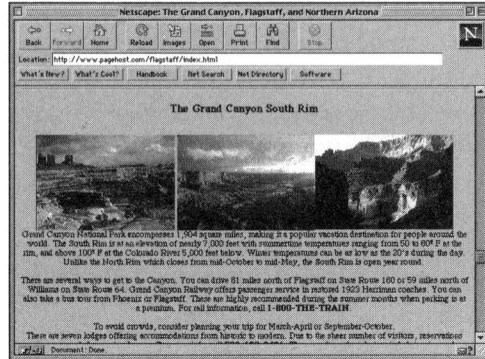

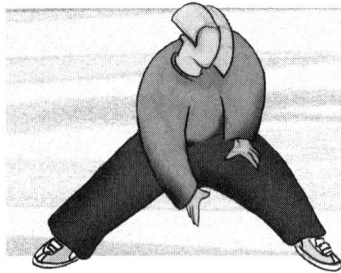

VERy CooL

Java's hot!

What's Java? It's a cool way to run animations and programs right inside a Web page. To take advantage of Java, you need the Windows 95 or the PowerMac version of Netscape 2.0 (or another browser that says it supports Java).

BostonWeb TownNet

http://www.bweb.com/bostonweb/townnet/townnet.htm

Beantown on the Web? BostonWeb TownNet has all the usual visitor info — hotels, events calendar, maps — plus a whole lot more. Check out the BostonWeb Photo Tour for a panoramic view of this historic city by day or by night. The ZoomMap lets you focus only on the part of Boston you want to see and gives you a map and a description of the area of your choice. Be sure to **check out** the links to other Boston-related sites, including government sites, colleges and universities (tons of 'em!), and even a Boston area weather map.

VERy CooL

California: Southern California Explorer

http://www.wdc.net/~sdewan/ca_pictu/index.htm

The Southern California Explorer page
looks small, but don't be fooled: it's packed
with plenty of strange, unusual, and useful
tidbits. One of the niftier links takes you
to a Los Angeles freeway map that gives
you up to the minute reports on highway
conditions. Another link goes to the LA
Current Earthquake Map, so if you're
rocking and rolling you can at least find
out how big an earthquake is happening
under your feet! In California Snapshots,
choose an area and then stroll through
some thumbnail pictures of beautiful countryside, **stunning beaches,**
and unique attractions. Yes, you'll find Disneyland photos here!

Hawaii Visitor's Guide

http://www.maui.net/~leodio/higuide.html

The Hawaii Visitor's Guide may be lighter
on pictures than some of the official sites
about this **beautiful place**, but the
information is the best anywhere. Written
by a long-time visitor and now resident
of the islands, the information is more
personal than an official site, too. Each
island is covered, with tips on where to go
scuba diving, how to plan a trip, and where
to stay. Read up for historical tidbits, budget
suggestions, and pointers to the best
beaches.

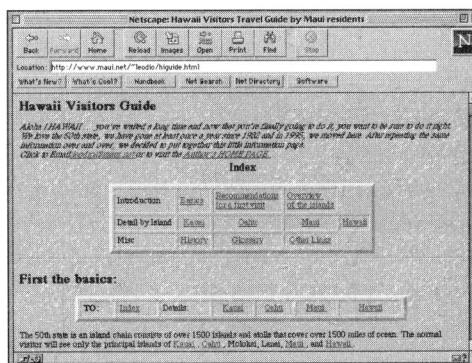

New York City Guide

http://www.mediabridge.com/nyc/

The Big Apple. The City That Never Sleeps. New York City. New York has lots to offer its visitors, and the New York City Guide on the Web covers most of it. The information is listed as **How, Wow, and Now**, for how to get around the city, wow what a lot of neat stuff, and now is when it's happening. For any trip to New York City, first brush up on your street smarts by reading the Survival tips, then check out all the great entertainment and attractions.

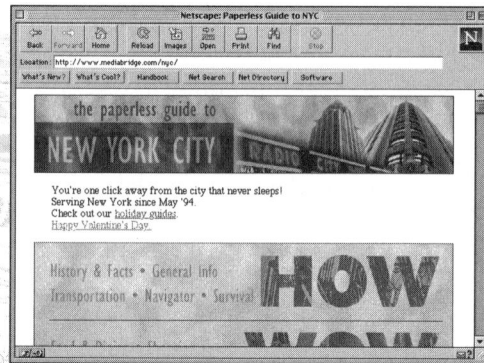

Philadelphia: Historic Philadelphia

http://www.libertynet.org/iha/

Philadelphia oozes history at every turn, so it should come as no surprise that it could have a Web site centered on Historic Philadelphia. Take the wonderful Virtual Tour of Philly's Historic Mile, including Betsy Ross's house, Benjamin Franklin's house, and Independence Hall. If you don't have time for the whole tour, links will take you directly to the places you want to see. Outside of the Tour, you'll find visitor tips, lists of **places to stay**, **places to eat**, and things (other than historic things!) to do while you're in the City of Brotherly Love. The list of links to other Philly-related sites will keep you busy for hours!

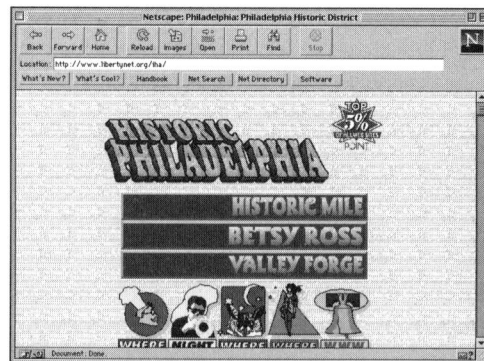

Washington DC Fun and Recreation

http://www.his.com/~matson/

The U.S. capital has some of the best museums, tours, and monuments in the country, and you'll find a complete list of these on the Washington DC Fun and Recreation Page. What you'll also find is a *huge* list of other things you can do in the DC area, like windsurfing, biking, and skating. Local sports teams are linked (in case you want to buy tickets and go to a game while you're in town), along with good basic tourist information, like where to eat, where to stay, and how to get from here to there. To combine history and a visit to a park, **check out the Civil War battlefield links**. You'll have to spend lots of time here to get at everything interesting!

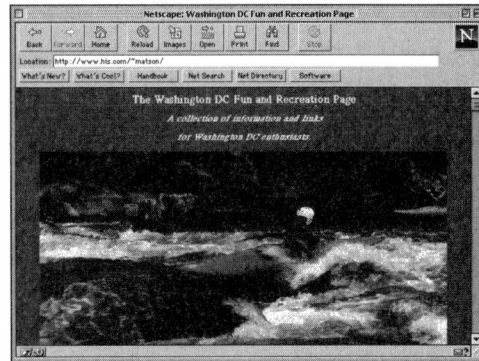

Yellowstone Park: Total Yellowstone Page

http://www.issnet.com/pagemakers/yellowstone/

The Total Yellowstone Page is a tribute to one person's love of Yellowstone National Park. Absolutely everything you need to know about this **popular vacation spot** is listed here somewhere. Just click somewhere and enjoy the scenery.

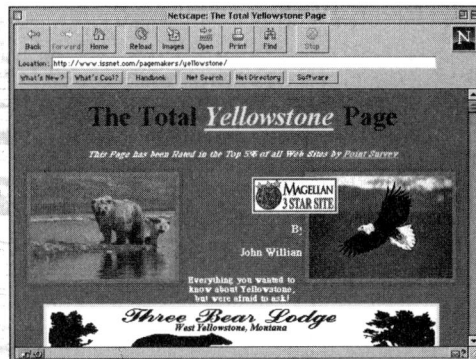

CONTINUED →

http://www.issnet.com/pagemakers/yellowstone/

Check out the Yellowstone History page for a little background on the park. Read the original Act of Congress that made Yellowstone a national park, and find out how the park got its name. Then you're ready to dive in to Yellowstone itself. Follow one of the many trip reports for a first-hand account of a Yellowstone hiking vacation. **Don't miss the true stories of man-meets-bear!**

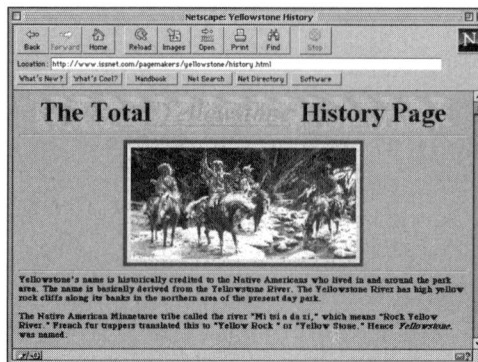

One reason to visit Yellowstone is the variety of wild animals you can see. A trip to Yellowstone can really seem like you're traveling back to a time when there were more animals than people on the continent. You'll find plenty of photographs all over this site that celebrate the wildness of Yellowstone and **the beauty of its creatures.** The page includes tips on how to view the wildlife without disturbing it and some pointers on where to get the best looks. If bears, elk, buffalo, and wolves aren't for you, check out the fishing page instead.

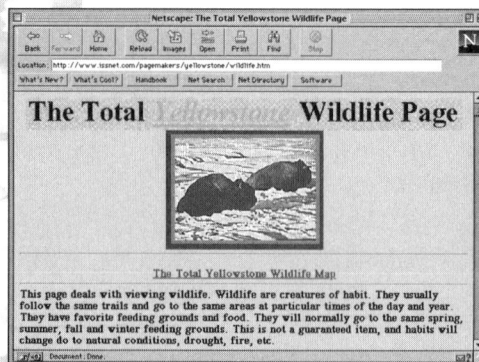

YAHOOLIGANS!

Some of the other useful pages on this site include a large-scale map of the entire park, a campground guide, and a guide to ranger-led tours and other group activities. You'll find one whole page devoted to the famous Yellowstone Geyser, Old Faithful, complete with lots of **nifty geyser-watching tips.** Whether you're planning to visit Yellowstone or you just wish you could, the Total Yellowstone site will get you ready to go!

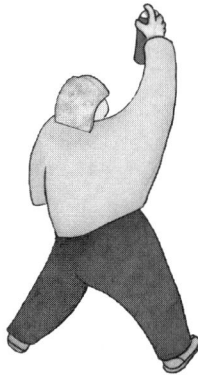

The Total *Yellowstone* Geyser Page

Old Faithful

Appendixes

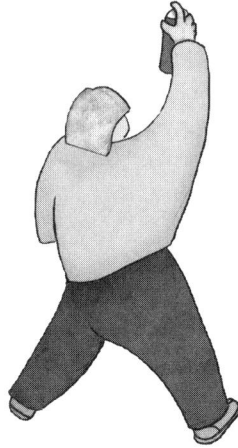

Code Words: Your Yahooligans! Dictionary

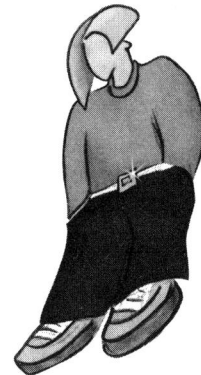

This section contains a list of words and terms that you will find on the Internet.

acronym Handy abbreviations that make your online browsing, surfing and chatting easier. They'll make you sound like you really know your way around the Internet! Look for them in alphabetical order throughout this glossary. They're the strange words in all capital letters (like BTW—by the way).

address The way you get to a place on the World Wide Web. Just enter an address in your browser, and it will look it up for you and get you that page. A Web page address usually looks like this: http://www.foo.com.

AFAIK "As far as I know." This is a polite way to express your opinion.

bandwidth Refers to the speed of your modem and the size of a Web site. If you don't have enough bandwidth (a fast enough modem), information will load more slowly.

browser The software that lets your computer "browse" the information coming to it over your modem. To browse is to look at, to flip through (a book, for example). Some common browsers are: Netscape Navigator, Microsoft's Internet Explorer, and various kinds of Mosaic (NCSA, Quarterdeck, and Spyglass).

BTW "By the way." Believe it, acronyms can save you the time of typing in all the words!

chat, chatroom The way you communicate on the Net. Chatting in a chatroom means typing in your thoughts and responding to what other people write.

cyberspace The whole online enchilada, the big Internet/Web/e-mail package. There's always space for you in cyberspace!

dot, slash The "." and the "/" in the address of a site. You say an address like www.yahooligans.com as "www dot yahooligans dot com." You say special/index as "special slash index."

download, load The process that your browser uses to get words and pictures from the server onto your screen. Pictures and graphics take longer to load than words.

e-mail Short for electronic mail. It's a way to send messages to an e-mail address (like president@whitehouse.gov) across the Internet.

flame When a person online "yells" about something or at someone. There are a couple of ways to spot a flame: lots of exclamation points!!!!! or LOTS OF CAPITALS, LIKE THE PERSON IS SHOUTING. It's considered rude to flame, but it happens all the time anyway.

FYI "For your information." When you're passing along a bit of news or something you think is interesting, you can say it's FYI.

FWIW "For what it's worth." Use it when you're just putting your two cents in.

FAQ "Frequently asked questions." A lot of sites have their own lists of FAQs and their answers. Save yourself some time and read these first!

FTP "File transfer protocol." This is the usual way to get shareware and other software from the Internet. Netscape and most Web browsers can do FTP automatically, so you don't need extra software to get to FTP sites.

host The computer that houses the information you are looking at over the Internet. It's also used in the same way as a Webmaster, meaning the person who put together the site.

HTML "HyperText Markup Language." This is the "language" that Web pages are made up from. It puts the pictures, text, and backgrounds from a Web site into their proper places, so things look right inside your browser.

HTTP "HyperText Transfer Protocol." HTTP is the way that Web pages travel to your browser over the Internet.

IMHO "In my humble opinion." Like FWIW, you're letting people know that you're just trying to be helpful.

Internet Cyberspace, the Web, the Net. They all mean the Internet, a network of computers all over the world that lets you send e-mail messages, chat with your friends, and surf lots of Web pages.

ISP "Internet Service Provider." A service provider gives you an account that you dial into via a modem to connect your computer to the Internet. You have to have some kind of an ISP to browse the World Wide Web.

LOL "Laughing out loud." How else can you laugh on a computer? *tee hee* is also popular.

link, linked, links A way to jump from page to page within a site, or to go to other Web sites. Links are usually words in a different color or pictures that have a colored border, but sometimes they're maps—areas inside a picture you can click on to go to different subjects.

Modem Connects your computer to an ISP (Internet Service Provider), giving you an Internet connection. A modem usually makes a shrieking sound when it connects.

Net Short for Internet. You can be "on the Net," which means you're using your modem to look at stuff on the Internet.

netiquette Manners, or etiquette, that are used on the Net. Netiquette is pretty much the same as the etiquette you already know (basic please-and-thank-you manners) plus rules like no flaming.

newbie Someone new to the Internet. It's OK to be a newbie!

online Where you are when you are using your modem to access the Web. It's kind of like being on the phone line. Offline is where you are now, reading this book.

page Almost the same as "site," but a site can have many different pages to it. Try thinking of the site as a book, and the pages as, well, pages of information. Web pages usually include words, just like a book, but can also have pictures, sound files, animations, and movies.

PMFJI "Pardon me for jumping in." This is a good way to politely get into an on-going conversation.

post, posted, posting To type in a message, either to a live chat room or to a bulletin board. A posting is therefore a message that has been posted.

RTFM "Read the freaky manual." When someone is having trouble with his or her computer and is asking for help, someone might respond "RTFM."

server A computer (one of many!) that holds the information in an Internet site. Some servers host many sites.

site All the Web pages and links together in one spot for a particular school, organization, person, business, or government agency. All the reviews in this book are of sites. A site is an address on the Web.

snail mail The kind of mail that the post office deals with. Think of snail mail as the opposite of the speediness of e-mail. The idea is that the postal service moves at a snail's pace compared to the speed of sending messages over the Internet.

surfing the net Spending time on the Internet. It usually means you're going from site to site, letting the links take you to new and exciting places or to new and boring places!

techie Someone on the Net who knows a lot about the site you're on, or the Internet in general, or both.

thumbnail A way to display pictures over the Net. Thumbnails are small versions of larger pictures. Making the pictures small lets your computer load sites faster, but if you want, you can see the larger pictures by clicking on the small pictures to load a larger version.

URL "Universal Resource Locator." This is the techie name for the site address. If someone tells you about a really neat Web site, you just say, "Great! Send me the URL," so you can go there, too.

Web The World Wide Web, the WWW, the part of the Internet that comes to you through your browser.

Webmaster The person, company, or group who put together or takes care of a Web site. You can usually send e-mail to this person (or persons) with questions about or problems with the site.

WYSIWYG "What you see is what you get." You can say this about almost anything, but it is used a lot in talking about computers that show you on your screen exactly what you're going to see if you print it out.

YMMV "Your mileage may vary." This is another way of saying, "This is what happened to me, but you might have a different experience."

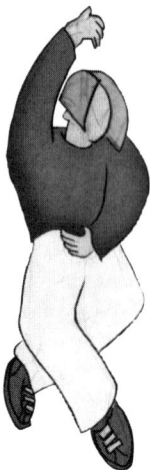

Index by Subject

ARTS

3-D pictures   7, 9

A
architecture   9
arts   4, 5, 11, 12
art school   4-6

C
computer design 6-9

D
dance 11, 12

E
exhibits 5, 6, 10, 11

F
fractals 8

G
galleries 5, 6, 10, 11
gargoyles 2
Gilbert & Sullivan 12
graphics 5,

I
improv 13

L
Louvre 10

M
morphing 40
museums 5, 6, 10-11
musicals 12

P
paints 11
paintings 11
photography 2

S
stereograms 7

T
theater arts 11-14
typography 5

YAHOOLIGANS!

MOVIES & ENTERTAINMENT

YAHOOLIGANS!

SCIENCE AND TECHNOLOGY

YAHOOLIGANS!

YAHOOLIGANS!

Yahooligans!
Be A Surfer Sweepstakes

Statistics on winners

ERIN T.

Favorite Category: school bell

The State I Live in Is: New York

My Age Is: Eleven

My Favorite Hobbies Are: rollerblading, swimming, gymnastics, dance

My Favorite Subject in School Is: English

I Like Yahooligans! Because all the information in it is for kids.

MY 10 FAVORITE SITES ON THE INTERNET ARE:

1) Site Name: React

Site URL: http://www.react.com/

This Is One of My Favorite Sites Because it has amazing graphics and if you sign up React will send you an e-mail for your birthday.

2) Site Name: Disney.com

Site URL: http://www.disney.com

This Is One of My Favorite Sites Because there are a lot of graphics and re-views of movies and many sites about rides and games in Disneyland and Disney World.

3) Site Name: Guide to the 1996 Olympic Games

Site URL: http://www.atlanta.olympic.org

This Is One of My Favorite Sites Because it tells you about the Olympic events and when they'll be held.

4) Site Name: Internet kid's web

Site URL: http://psych.hanover.edu/kidsweb/

This Is One of My Favorite Sites Because you can get a pen pal online so you can talk.

5) Site Name: Discovery Channel Online

Site URL: http://www.discovery.com

This Is One of My Favorite Sites Because it is like you are watching television online.

6) Site Name: Home of the Big Dog

Site URL: http://www.cyber-quest.com/home/big dog/

This Is One of My Favorite Sites Because it has chat links to talk to other kids and a guest book you can sign and also see who else has signed it. It has other links to interesting sites for kids.

7) Site Name:Welcome to the White House

Site URL: http://www.white house.gov~/wh/welcome~

This Is One of My Favorite Sites Because you can learn about the president and vice-president and their families. You can also e-mail them your questions. It has a link for kids and government.

8) Site Name: NASA Homepage

Site URL: http://www.NASA.gov/

This Is One of My Favorite Sites Because you can learn about the space program, and it has a Q & A link to answer all your questions about astronauts and the shuttles.

9) Site Name: Sports Illustrated for Kids Online

Site UR: http://pathfinder.com/SIFK/index.html

This Is One of My Favorite Sites Because it has game scores, stories, and links to the summer Olympics. And it has a link to the Buzz Beamer.

10) Site Name: Kids Web WWW digital library for school kids

Site URL: http://www.npac.oyr.edu~/textbook/kidsweb

This Is One of My Favorite Sites Because it has links on almost any subjects you would need for school projects or just for fun.

JASON H.

Favorite Category: entertainment

The State I Live in Is: Texas

My Age Is: Nine

My Favorite Hobbies Are: reading, computers, baseball

My Favorite Subject in School Is: Science

I Like Yahooligans! Because it's the coolest search engine on the Web.

MY 10 FAVORITE SITES ON THE INTERNET ARE:

1) Site Name: Sierra On-line

Site URL: http://www.sierra.com/

This Is One of My Favorite Sites Because it has lots of games, including Stock Market Challenge and The Realm.

2) Site Name: Joshua Bell's Star Trek Page

Site URL: http://www.dimensionx.com/jsbell/star_trek/

This Is One of My Favorite Sites Because it has lots Star Trek graphics and technical information, plus a cool map of the galaxy.

3) Site Name: Chess Server Game Page

Site URL: http://mlinux.willamette.edu/wdbin/starter.pl

This Is One of My Favorite Sites Because you can watch a chess game in action, pick a player to play against, or start your own chess game.

4) Site Name: The Comic Strip

Site URL: http://www.unitedmedia.com/comics/

This Is One of My Favorite Sites Because it has many good comics, such as Luann, Peanuts, Jump Start, and Dilbert.

5) Site Name: Star Trek Voyager: British Starfleet Confederacy Guide

Site URL: http://www.armory.com/~bsc/voyager/voyager.html

This Is One of My Favorite Sites Because it has an awesome graphic of the original Voyager, plus information about the show and the characters.

6) Site Name: BU's Interactive WWW Games

Site URL: http://www.bu.edu/Games/games.html

This Is One of My Favorite Sites Because you can play Tic-Tac-Toe against the computer and a multi-players' version of Hunt the Wumpus.

7) Site Name: Safe Surf Kid's Wave

Site URL: http://www.safesurf.com/sskwave.html

This Is One of My Favorite Sites Because it has links to so much great stuff. There are links to space stuff like information about the space shuttle and the planets.

8) Site Name: Kool Net Kids

Site URL: http://www.enter.net/~pmorr/koolnet.html

This Is One of My Favorite Sites Because it has nice poems and neat trivia questions.

9) Site Name: Kids' Web

Site URL: http://www.primenet.com/~sburr/index.html

This Is One of My Favorite Sites Because it has links to lots of cool sites and fun things to do. It has links to games and reviews of kids' software and of movies and TV shows, such as the Star Trek Voyager page.

YAHOOLIGANS!

10) Site Name: Jason Project

Site URL: http://www.eds.com/jason/

This Is One of My Favorite Sites Because you can find out about the Jason Project, go on a treasure hunt, and register to win a Jason Project T-shirt.

PATRICK F.

Favorite Category: around the world

The State I Live in Is: Indiana

My Age Is: Nine

My Favorite Hobbies Are:bike riding, crafts, reading, sports computers

My Favorite Subject in School Is: PE gym

I Like Yahooligans! Because there are tons of things to do and places to go.

MY 10 FAVORITE SITES ON THE INTERNET ARE:

1) Site Name: Yahooligans

Site URL: http://www.yahooligans.com/

This Is One of My Favorite Sites Because it has a lot of fun things to do and it is a safe place for kids.

2) Site Name: New labs online

Site URL: http://nyelabs.kcts.org/

This Is One of My Favorite Sites Because it has lots of information and live chats.

3) Site Name: Goosebumps

Site URL: http://www.scholastic.com/public/goosebumps/

This Is One of My Favorite Sites Becauseit has lots of pictures and stuff about the boots.

4) Site Name: Disney

Site URL: http://www.2.disney.com/?GL=H

This Is One of My Favorite Sites Because this place can keep you busy all day and it has games to play.

5) Site Name: Nintendo Home Page

Site URL: http://www.nintendo.com/high/high.html

This Is One of My Favorite Sites Because it has the best information on games. You can get codes, hints, tips, and tricks.

6)Site Name: DoDo land in cyberspace

Site URL: http://swifty.com/azatlan/

This Is One of My Favorite Sites Because I like the wishes for the earth.

7) Site Name: Uncle Bob's kid page

Site URL: http://miso.wwa.com/~boba/kidsi.html

This Is One of My Favorite Sites Because there are a lot of neat places to go. It's a safe spot for kids.

8) Site Name: Where in the world is Carmen Sandiego

Site URL: http://www.boston.com:80/wgbh/pages/carmensandiego/carmenhome.html

This Is One of My Favorite Sites Because there are a lot of fun things to see and information on Carmen and the show.

9) Site Name: electronic zoo

Site URL: http://netvet.wustl.edu/e-zoo.html

This Is One of My Favorite Sites Because it has anything you want to know about animals and lots of pictures.

10) Site Name: NASA information services

Site URL: http://www.qsfc.nasa.gov/NASA_homepage.html

This Is One of My Favorite Sites Because it has all kinds of pictures, videos, sound, and information.

MELISSA M.

Favorite Category: art soup

The State I Live in Is: Pennsylvania

My Age Is: Thirteen

YAHOOLIGANS!

My Favorite Hobbies Are: reading, playing musical instruments, and net surfing

My Favorite Subject in School Is: History

I Like Yahooligans! Because it is a place for yahooligans (kids). Kids can find great stuff here.

MY 10 FAVORITE SITES ON THE INTERNET ARE:

1) Site Name: Classical MIDI Archives

Site URL: http://www.prs.net/midi.html

This Is One of My Favorite Sites Because you can sample really neat music.

2) Site Name: Sol Chat-O-Rama

Site URL: http://www.solscape.com/chat

This Is One of My Favorite Sites Because there is a topic for everyone no matter what your interest is.

3) Site Name: The Spam Cam

Site URL: http://www.fright.com/cgi-bin-spamcam

This Is One of My Favorite Sites Because it is sooo different. Who thought of this, anyway?

4) Site Name: Welcome to Her Online

Site URL: http://www.her-online.com

This Is One of My Favorite Sites Because it's meant for girls only.

5) Site Name: Princeton University

Site URL: http://www.princeton.edu

This Is One of My Favorite Sites Because I hope to attend the Princeton class of 2005.

6) Site Name: Evil little Brother Excuse Generator

Site URL: http://www.dtd.com/excuse

This Is One of My Favorite Sites Because it is just like Mad libs.

7) Site Name: Classical Net HomePage

Site URL: http://www.classical.net/music

This Is One of My Favorite Sites Because it is a very complete guide to classical music.

8) Site Name: New Hope—Solebury School District's HomePage

Site URL: http://www.bciu.k12.pa.us/newhopesole/nhs.html

This Is One of My Favorite Sites Because this is where I go to school and it has some good research links.

9) Site Name: Cool Site of the Day

Site URL: http://cool.infi.net

This Is One of My Favorite Sites Becauseyou never know where you will end up.

10) Site Name: shareware.com

Site URL: http://www.shareware.com

This Is One of My Favorite Sites Becauseyou download till you overload.

SHAD G.

Favorite Category: science & oddities

The State I Live in Is: Texas

My Age Is: Eleven

My Favorite Hobbies Are:collecting cards and computer games

My Favorite Subject in School Is: Science

I Like Yahooligans! Because it is a good web guide for kids.

MY 10 FAVORITE SITES ON THE INTERNET ARE:

1) Site Name: Yahooligans

Site URL: http://www.yahooligans.com

This Is One of My Favorite Sites Because it is a web guide for kids.

2) Site Name: MTV online

Site URL: http://www.mtv.com

This Is One of My Favorite Sites Because I can look at music videos.

3) Site Name: The Cheats page

Site URL: http://www.acsu.buffalo.edu/~cjm2/cheat/cheat.html

This Is One of My Favorite Sites Because I can learn little cheats to help me.

4) Site Name: Yahoo

Site URL: http://www.yahoo.com/text/recreation/games/computer games/cheats and hints

This Is One of My Favorite Sites Because it has a lot of cheats.

5) Site Name: Kids Korner

Site URL: http://www.airmail.net/kids_korner.html

This Is One of My Favorite Sites Because it will connect you to neat places.

6) Site Name: You Can

Site URL: http://www.nbn.com/youcan/

This Is One of My Favorite Sites Becauseyou can look at space stuff.

7) Site Name: Sci Fi Channel

Site URL: http://www.scifi.com/tocl

This Is One of My Favorite Sites Because it helps me keep up with what's on.

8) Site Name: NBA Center Court

Site URL: http://www.nba.com

This Is One of My Favorite Sites Because I am updated in basketball.

9) Site Name: The Sports Server

Site URL: http://www.nando.net/SportServer/

This Is One of My Favorite Sites Because it gives me information on all sports.

10) Site Name: Games Games Games

Site URL: http://www.happypuppy.com

This Is One of My Favorite Sites Because you can download games.

JENNIFER REBEKAH B.

Favorite Category: scoop

The State I Live in Is: Pennsylvania

My Age Is: Twelve

My Favorite Hobbies Are: swimming, reading, watching Hockey, playing with kittens, shopping, making jewelry with Indian beads, going to summer camp, and playing on computers

I Like Yahooligans! Because it is very easy to understand and get around in.

MY 10 FAVORITE SITES ON THE INTERNET ARE:

1) Site Name: Disney.com

Site URL: http://www.disney.com/?GL=H

This Is One of My Favorite Sites Because I love all of the graphics.

2) Site Name: family.com

Site URL: http://www.family.com/index.disney.html

This Is One of My Favorite Sites Because it has things for everyone.

3) Site Name: Penguins-Hockey

Site URL: http://www.penguins-hockey.com/

This Is One of My Favorite Sites Because I like hockey, and the Penguins are the best team.

4) Site Name: Interconnect postcard shop

Site URL: : http://www.icsl.interconnect.net/postcard/+-send.html

This Is One of My Favorite Sites Because sending post cards on the internet is fun.

5) Site Name: Animals of Fate

Site URL: http://the-inter.net/www/future21/fate/index.html

This Is One of My Favorite Sites Because I like pets.

6) Site Name: Prince Edward Island Greeting Card Centre

Site URL: http://www.gov.pe.ca/card/index.html

This Is One of My Favorite Sites Because the postcards are very nice.

7) Site Name: Interactive WWW Games

Site URL: http://www.nauticom.net/www/Server/games.html

This Is One of My Favorite Sites Because a lot of the games are very fun and you do not have to download them.

8) Site Name:The Baby-sitters Club

Site URL: : http://www.scholastic.com/public/Baby-sitters/Baby-sitters.html

This Is One of My Favorite Sites Because I really like the Baby-sitters Club.

9) Site Name: MaKeatie for Dad

Site URL: http://gnn.com/feat/dad/pagel.html

This Is One of My Favorite Sites Because it is a fun site.

10) Site Name: Snoopy's Dog House

Site URL: : http://www.unitedmedia.com/comics/peanuts/

This Is One of My Favorite Sites Because you get to see a lot of the Peanuts comics.

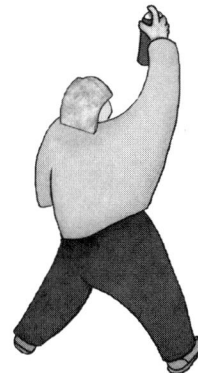

How to Use the CD-ROM and Web Site

In the back of this book, you'll find a CD-ROM. It contains lots of cool software, such as games, demos, and very short movies. It also contains Surfwatch, a program that lets parents screen out the stuff on the Web that only adults should see, plus a version of Netscape Navigator that your parents can use to set up an Internet account.

If you have a Macintosh computer, your instructions start right here. If you have a PC with Windows 3.1 or Windows 95, your instructions begin right after the Mac instructions.

Because of space considerations, we cannot print the full instructions for each game here in this book. For more detailed instructions for each program, go into the program's folder and find its "readme" file, which is almost always called Readme.txt.

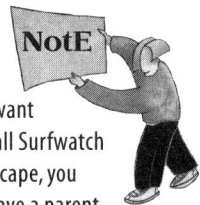

NotE

If you want to install Surfwatch or Netscape, you *must* have a parent do the installation. It's okay for kids to install everything else, like the games and stuff.

Macintosh installation instructions

Mac users: want to try out the games on the CD? Here's what you do:

1. Open up the Software Central folder by double-clicking on it.

2. Open the folder of a game category you want (like Action/Adventure or Puzzles).

3. Open the folder of the game you want to try.

4. Double-click on the game's icon.

That's all there is to it! If you like the game and want to play it a lot, drag its folder over to your hard drive to copy it. This way, it will always be available to play, even if the CD-ROM isn't in the computer. Plus, the game will run faster if it's on your hard drive! But be careful not to fill up your hard drive with millions of games. The amount of space on your hard drive is limited.

Here's a quick rundown of what's on the CD-ROM for Mac users:

Action/Adventure

■ AmoebArena—Play against the computer or watch computer opponents duke it out in this slimy combat over territorial disputes in the galaxies. As a star traveler you will build AmoebArena for resolving such disputes.

■ Icebreaker—Object of the game: Destroy all Pyramids! Choose your own landscape—ice, lava, swamp—and level of difficulty in this demo game. Just remember to ram the blue pyramids, shoot the red ones, trick enemies into walking into the green ones...and don't get caught!

■ Marathon—You have now entered Marathon world, a futuristic action/adventure game with lots of monsters and guns.

■ Scarab of RA 1.4—With only a lantern and some oil, you will enter the Great Pyramid of RA where explorers have gone and never returned. You will travel through mazes looking for keys to unlock doors to continue your search for ancient relics. Along the way you might find piles of gold, water, and food. If you find the Relics of the RA, the most powerful being the Scarab, you will be famous forever. But watch out for the evil Guardian who will seek to destroy you.

Arcade-style games

- Apeiron 1.0.5—As a crystal shard, you must shoot oncoming enemies in the mushroom patch who are trying to zap your energy. Colorful graphics and sound enhance this shoot-em-up arcade-style game. Beware the powerful Pentipede!

- Glider PRO—Fly your paper airplane through a demo house to find a star. Maneuver your plane with arrow keys and catch air from the vents. Be sure to avoid the balloons and watch out for those shelves.

- Poing! 1.0—In this fast-action, colorful arcade game, the goal is to hit targets with the ball. Bounce the ball off of bumpers you set up with the slash and backslash keys. Try to hit all targets before you hear "Uh-oh!" and the clock runs out. Watch out for traps!

Puzzles

- Logical Journey of the Zoombinis—The Bloats have pushed the Zoombinis off their land and taken everything. You will be their guide on a journey to find a new land for these cute and cuddly creatures. Click on the map to enter the Pizza Pass, Mudball, and Mirror Machine where you will solve fun math puzzles and help the Zoombinis build a new home.

- Triazzle—By matching puzzle pieces in a triangle, you can bring colorful frogs to life in the rain forest while listening to jungle sounds.

Stuff you use

- Googool Eyes—These big eyes will follow your mouse around the screen and locate a "lost" cursor. Watch their shifting focus as you move your mouse.

- Holiday Lights 3.0—This entertaining application places fun, colorful Christmas tree lights around your screen and even plays your favorite Christmas carols.

- PageMill—Learn how to make fun and easy web pages through this self-guided tour, complete with demo pages to view the many possibilities.
- PhotoDeluxe—Now you can create art from your own photographs! Put photos on calendars, cards, labels, and more. You can trim and colorize photos and create kaleidoscope effects in minutes.

Stuff you watch

- Launch Pad Kid Safe Desktop—Zoom off with Bingo the dog in his rocket car as he guides you through his world. Explore hidden castles, the land of the dinosaurs, and the creepy haunted house.

For parents only

- Surf Watch—Mom and Dad can use this demo software to guide your surf schedule on the Net.

- EarthLink TotalAccess (with Netscape Navigator)—A Web browser for Mom or Dad to install. Tell them to have a credit card handy!

Windows 3.1 and Windows 95 installation instructions

The cool games and puzzles and stuff are in the folder on the CD called D:\Software. Inside that folder are other folders, one for each game. Usually, each game has a file called Setup.exe or Install.exe. In File Manager (Windows 3.1) or Windows Explorer (Windows 95), double-click on the Setup.exe or Install.exe file for the program you want to install and then follow the instructions.

Most of the programs are for Windows 3.1, which means you can install and run them in Windows 3.1 or Windows 95. Some of the games are DOS games. If you have Windows 3.1, you may or may not be able to run the DOS games from within Windows. It's probably better to quit Windows, start DOS, and run the Setup.exe file for the game. The DOS games seem to run all right in Windows 95, although each computer setup is different. If you have trouble running the DOS games in Windows 95, there may not be much you can do besides quitting Windows 95 and restarting the computer in DOS mode.

Action/Adventure

- Abuse—3-D shooting game where you have to kill the evil things. Double-click D:\Software\Abuse\Setup.exe.

- Icebreaker—Object of the game: *Destroy all Pyramids!* Choose your own landscape—ice, lava, swamp—and level of difficulty in this demo game. Just remember to ram the blue pyramids, shoot the red ones, trick enemies into walking into the green ones…and don't get caught! Double-click D:\Software\Ice\Setup.exe.

Arcade-style games

- Arcade America—Run, jump, and shoot your way through Alcatraz in this demo version of the 7th Level game. Double-click D:\Software\Arcade\Setup.exe.

- Baryon—Enter the arcade world of Baryon for a fast scroll and shoot game. You can even duel with more than one player. Double-click D:\Software\Baryon\Setup.exe.

Puzzles

- Hugo Trilogy—Help Hugo save his girlfriend Penelope from the house she's trapped in. Double-click D:\Software\Hugo\Hwinunr.exe.

- Logical Journey of the Zoombinis—The Bloats have pushed the Zoombinis off their land and taken everything. You will be their guide on a journey to find a new land for these cute and cuddly creatures. Click on the map to enter the Pizza Pass, Mudball, and Mirror Machine where you will solve fun math puzzles and help the Zoombinis build a new home.

- Lynq—Match up the colored shapes on the different pieces so they all match. Matching up a shape forms a "link"—when you link all the shapes, you win! Double-click D:\Software\Lynq\Setup.exe.

- Too Many Geckos!—A tribe of geckos lives along the Nile and new evidence shows that these small lizards actually built the great pyramids. You as the player must reconstruct the pyramids like the insect eating lizards, matching all the geckos inside and out. Double-click D:\Software\Tmg\Setup.exe.

- Triazzle—By matching puzzle pieces in a triangle, you can bring colorful frogs to life in the rain forest while listening to jungle sounds. Double-click D:\Software\Triaz\Setup.exe.

Stuff you watch

- Battle Beast—In this cartoon-style demo, you will see Vermian and Spartacus go head-to-head in a big brawl. Double-click D:\Software\Beastdem\Beast\Demo.exe.

- Cadillacs and Dinosaurs—Watch a fast-action, quick-time movie with Jack steering his cadillac through dinosaur terrain. Will Jack and his caddy escape the big green dinosaur? Watch and you will see.

- Launch Pad Kid Safe Desktop—Zoom off with Bingo the dog in his rocket car as he guides you through his world. Explore hidden castles, the land of the dinosaurs, and the creepy haunted house. Double-click D:\Software\Lp\Lpdemo.exe.

- Loadstar—Ride through a futuristic Star Wars landscape in this space adventure movie demo. Watch as Tully Bodine fires at flying objects along the journey.

- Wing Nuts—Experience the adventure of piloting a biplane as you watch this movie demo. Glide over the Earth as the plane darts through the sky avoiding shots from lethal fighter planes.

For parents only

- Surf Watch—Mom and Dad can use this demo software to guide your surf schedule on the Net.

- EarthLink TotalAccess (with Netscape Navigator)—A Web browser for Mom or Dad to install. Tell them to have a credit card handy!

Checking out this book's Web site

Yes, this book has its own Web site. There you will find a fun assortment of things to read and do. Be sure to send e-mail telling us what you think of the book and Web site. Check it out!

http://www.idgbooks.com/idgbooksonline/YP/kids/

Don't confuse it with the Yahooligans! Web site!

http://www.yahooligans.com

Index

YAHOOLIGANS!

YAHOOLIGANS!

YAHOOLIGANS!

YAHOOLIGANS!

YAHOOLIGANS!

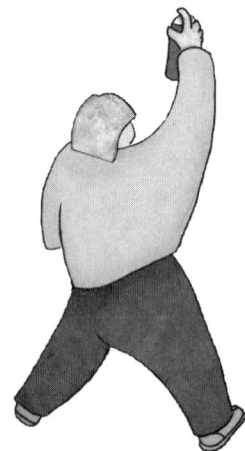

YAHOOLIGANS!

U

V

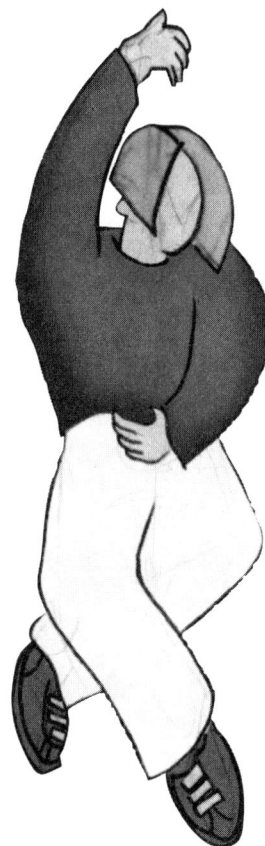

YAHOOLIGANS!

About the Authors

Richard Raucci and Elizabeth Crane live in a beautiful house in San Francisco's Noe Valley with their son, Philip. They became a husband and wife writing team in 1995 to co-write Yahooligans! for IDG Books Online. Both graduated from the English Department of the University of Pennsylvania and have held many jobs.

Richard has published computer- and Web-related books for Springer Verlag (*Mosiac for Windows, Netscape for Macintosh*, and the soon-to-be published *Netscape for WindowsNT*) and for IDG Books (coauthor, *Yahoo! Unplugged*). He also has published articles in various computer magazines, including *Publish, Sunworld, PCWorld/Multimedia World, NeXTWorld, Electronic Entertainment, Mac Computing, UnixWorld, Open Computing*, and *InfoWorld*. He has worked as a Federal Court Clerk, a Psychiatric Technician for the U.S. Navy, and as a computer magazine editor.

Elizabeth has written articles for *Open Computing, InfoWorld, Infosecurity News*, and the *Autodesk Federal Bulletin*, and has been

YAHOOLIGANS!

published in the online magazine *Web Review*. She has managed an international translation agency, worked as a professional caterer, and dabbled in the world of New York high finance.

"We are now (more or less) settled in our careers as writers and as parents. Writing a book together and raising a child together has been interesting. We invented what we call tag-team parenting, where one of us writes and one of us plays with Philip. It's fun. Philip, at age three, is only an honorary Yahooligan, but he'll be on the Web before we know it. Come visit us all on the Web at http://www.well.com/user/raucci/rraucci.html or http://www.well.com/user/ecrane/ecrane.html and drop us a line at rraucci @ well.com or ecrane @ well.com. We love to hear from our readers!"

David Filo, Chief Yahoo Filo, and a native of Moss Bluff, Louisiana, co-created the Yahoo! online guide in April 1994 and took a leave of absence from Stanford University's electrical engineering Ph.D. program in April 1995 to co-found Yahoo! Corporation. Filo received a B.S. in Computer Engineering from Tulane University and an M.S. in electrical engineering from Stanford University. He sleeps every third night.

Jerry Yang, Chief Yahoo Yang, is a Taiwanese native who was raised in San Jose, California. He co-created the Yahoo! online guide in April 1994 and co-founded Yahoo! Corporation in April 1995. Yang is currently on a leave of absence from Stanford University's electrical engineering Ph.D. program and holds B.S. and M.S. degrees in Electrical Engineering from Stanford University. Jerry is a total hack at the game of golf, but likes to play in his spare time anyway.

Colophon

Senior VP & Group Publisher   Brenda McLaughlin

VP & Publisher   David Ushijima

Marketing Manager   Melisa Duffy

Managing Editor   Terry Somerson

Associate Editor   Corbin Collins

Copy Editor   Carolyn Welch

Associate Copy Editor   Suki Gear

Assistant Editor   Mark Morford

Editorial Assistants   Anna Marie Pises, Anne Alvergue

Production Director   Andrew Walker

Production Associate   Christopher Pimentel

Supervisor of Page Layout   Craig Harrison

Media/Archive Coordinator   Leslie Popplewell

Photography   Anwar Collins, Parrish Hughes, Vai Webb

Project Coordinator   Katy German

Production Page Layout   Margery Cantor, Kurt Krames, Stephen Noetzel, Elsie Yim

Proofreader   Christine Langin-Faris

Indexer   Steve Rath

Book Design   Margery Cantor

Cover Illustration   John Ritter

Cover Text Layout   Zaremba Visual Communication

CD-ROM Development   Animated Design

YAHOOLIGANS!

Yahoo! Credits

Senior Producer/Editor   Maury Zeff

Ontologist   Srinija Srinivasan

Graphics Coordinator   Claudia Montijo

Writer   Angela Buenning

Online Kid Consultants

We would like to thank the following volunteer junior editors for their comments and suggestions and sometimes brutal honesty on how to make this a better book for real kids.

Nicole Berger, Adrian Cadoux, Alex Christen, Scott Davis, Cameron Dunn, Victoria Fayer, William Fayer, Cameron Fife, Spencer Gapinski, David Glazer, Natasha Amret Gonzalez, Allison Gore, Antoinette Jonopulos, Jenny Oyallon-Koloski, Jason LeRoy, Christopher Levenduski, Amanda Yvonne Lynn, Anya Marinkovich, Zoe Marinkovich, Jenna Mason, Valerie C. Morgan, Stephanie Ratoff, Jamaica Robinson, Maya Roney, Michele Roney, Jenna Rose, Larry Sandez, Peter Sandez, Benjamin Sumser, Mark Toy, and Zand Ushijima.

How this Book was Produced

This book was produced digitally in Foster City, California. Design and layout were done using Adobe PageMaker on Apple 8500/120 Power Macs. Images were captured using an Apple QuickTake 150 digital camera and were treated using Adobe Photoshop. Typefaces used were Berliner Grotesk for heads and running feet; Multiple Master Jimbo, Lo-Type, and Myriad Multiple Master were used for the text body and Umbra for running heads and folios.

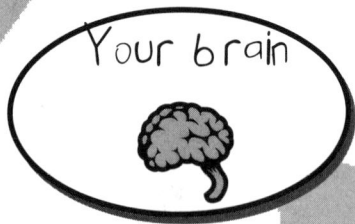

IDG BOOKS WORLDWIDE LICENSE AGREEMENT

Important   Read carefully before opening the software packet(s). This is a legal agreement between you (either an individual or an entity) and IDG Books Worldwide, Inc. (IDG). By opening the accompanying sealed packet containing the software disk(s), you acknowledge that you have read and accept the following IDG License Agreement. If you do not agree and do not want to be bound by the terms of this Agreement, promptly return the book and the unopened software packet(s) to the place you obtained them for a full refund.

1. License.   This License Agreement (Agreement) permits you to use one copy of the enclosed Software program(s) on a single computer. The Software is in "use" on a computer when it is loaded into temporary memory (i.e., RAM) or installed into permanent memory (e.g., hard disk, CD-ROM, or other storage device) of that computer.

2. Copyright.   The entire contents of the disk(s) and the compilation of the Software are copyrighted and protected by both United States copyright laws and international treaty provisions. You may only (a) make one copy of the Software for backup or archival purposes, or (b) transfer the Software to a single hard disk, provided that you keep the original for backup or archival purposes. The individual programs on the disk(s) are copyrighted by the authors of each program respectively. Each program has its own use permissions and limitations. To use each program, you must follow the individual requirements and restrictions detailed for each in the Appendix of this Book. Do not use a program if you do not want to follow its Licensing Agreement. None of the material on the disk(s) or listed in this Book may ever be distributed, in original or modified form, for commercial purposes.

3. Other Restrictions.   You may not rent or lease the Software. You may transfer the Software and user documentation on a permanent basis provided you retain no copies and the recipient agrees to the terms of this Agreement. You may not reverse engineer, decompile, or disassemble the Software except to the extent that the foregoing restriction is expressly prohibited by applicable law. If the Software is an update or has been updated, any transfer must include the most recent update and all prior versions.

4. Limited Warranty.   IDG warrants that the Software and disk(s) are free from defects in materials and workmanship for a period of sixty (60) days from the date of purchase of this Book. If IDG receives notification within the warranty period of defects in material or workmanship, IDG will replace the defective disk(s). IDG's entire liability and your exclusive remedy shall be limited to replacement of the Software, which is returned to IDG with a copy of your receipt. This Limited Warranty is void if failure of the Software has resulted from accident, abuse, or misapplication. Any replacement Software will be warranted for the remainder of the original warranty period or thirty (30) days, whichever is longer.

5. No Other Warranties.   To the maximum extent permitted by applicable law, IDG and the author disclaim all other warranties, express or implied, including but not limited to implied warranties of merchantability and fitness for a particular purpose, with respect to the Software, the programs, the source code contained therein and/or the techniques described in this Book. This limited warranty gives you specific legal rights. You may have others which vary from state/jurisdiction to state/jurisdiction.

6. No Liability For Consequential Damages.   To the extent permitted by applicable law, in no event shall IDG or the authors be liable for any damages whatsoever (including without limitation, damages for loss of business profits, business interruption, loss of business information, or any other pecuniary loss) arising out of the use of or inability to use the Book or the Software, even if IDG has been advised of the possibility of such damages. Because some states/jurisdictions do not allow the exclusion or limitation of liability for consequential or incidental damages, the above limitation may not apply to you.

7. U.S. Government Restricted Rights.   Use, duplication, or disclosure of the Software by the U.S. Government is subject to restrictions stated inparagraph (c) (1) (ii) of the Rights in Technical Data and Computer Software clause of DFARS 252.227-7013, and in subparagraphs (a) through (d) of the Commercial Computer—Restricted Rights clause at FAR 52.227-19, and in similar clauses in the NASA FAR supplement, when applicable.

IDG BOOKS WORLDWIDE REGISTRATION CARD

RETURN THIS REGISTRATION CARD FOR FREE CATALOG

Title of this book: Way Cool Web Sites

My overall rating of this book: ❏ Very good [1] ❏ Good [2] ❏ Satisfactory [3] ❏ Fair [4] ❏ Poor [5]

How I first heard about this book:

❏ Found in bookstore; name: [6] _____

❏ Advertisement: [8] _____

❏ Word of mouth; heard about book from friend, co-worker, etc.: [10]

❏ Book review: [7] _____

❏ Catalog: [9] _____

❏ Other: [11] _____

What I liked most about this book:

_____

_____

What I would change, add, delete, etc., in future editions of this book:

_____

_____

Other comments: _____

Number of computer books I purchase in a year: ❏ 1 [12] ❏ 2-5 [13] ❏ 6-10 [14] ❏ More than 10 [15]

I would characterize my computer skills as: ❏ Beginner [16] ❏ Intermediate [17] ❏ Advanced [18] ❏ Professional [19]

I use ❏ DOS [20] ❏ Windows [21] ❏ OS/2 [22] ❏ Unix [23] ❏ Macintosh [24] ❏ Other: [25] _____
(please specify)

I would be interested in new books on the following subjects:
(please check all that apply, and use the spaces provided to identify specific software)

❏ Word processing: [26] _____

❏ Data bases: [28] _____

❏ File Utilities: [30] _____

❏ Networking: [32] _____

❏ Other: [34] _____

❏ Spreadsheets: [27] _____

❏ Desktop publishing: [29] _____

❏ Money management: [31] _____

❏ Programming languages: [33] _____

I use a PC at (please check all that apply): ❏ home [35] ❏ work [36] ❏ school [37] ❏ other: [38] _____

The disks I prefer to use are ❏ 5.25 [39] ❏ 3.5 [40] ❏ other: [41] _____

I have a CD ROM: ❏ yes [42] ❏ no [43]

I plan to buy or upgrade computer hardware this year: ❏ yes [44] ❏ no [45]

I plan to buy or upgrade computer software this year: ❏ yes [46] ❏ no [47]

Name: _____ Business title: [48] _____ Type of Business: [49] _____

Address (❏ home [50] ❏ work [51]/Company name: _____)

Street/Suite# _____

City [52]/State [53]/Zipcode [54]: _____ Country [55] _____

❏ **I liked this book!** You may quote me by name in future
IDG Books Worldwide promotional materials.

My daytime phone number is _____

IDG BOOKS

®

THE WORLD OF
COMPUTER
KNOWLEDGE

❏ # YES!

Please keep me informed about IDG's World of Computer Knowledge.
Send me the latest IDG Books catalog.

SECRETS™

...FOR DUMMIES™
COMPUTER
BOOK SERIES
FROM IDG

MACWORLD
MW
AUTHORIZED
EDITION

AUTHORIZED
PC WORLD
EDITION
★